Sleeping in the Forest

MIDDLE EAST LITERATURE IN TRANSLATION

Michael Beard and Adnan Haydar, Series Editors

Other titles in the Middle East Literature in Translation series

A Child from the Village
  Sayyid Qutb; John Calvert and William Shepard, trans.

The Committee
  Sonallah Ibrahim; Mary St. Germain and Charlene Constable, trans.

A Cup of Sin: Selected Poems
  Simin Behbahani; Farzaneh Milani and Kaveh Safa, trans.

In Search of Walid Masoud: A Novel
  Jabra Ibrahim Jabra; Roger Allen and Adnan Haydar, trans.

Three Tales of Love and Death
  Out el Kouloub

Women Without Men: A Novella
  Shahrnush Parsipur; Kamran Talattof and Jocelyn Sharlet, trans.

Zanouba: A Novel
  Out el Kouloub; Nayra Atiya, trans.

Sait Faik

Sleeping in the Forest

STORIES AND POEMS

Translated from the Turkish

Editor, Talat S. Halman

Associate Editor, Jayne L. Warner

 SYRACUSE UNIVERSITY PRESS

English translations copyright © 2004 by Syracuse University Press
Syracuse, New York 13244–5290
All Rights Reserved

First Edition 2004
04   05   06   07   08   09   6   5   4   3   2   1

The paper used in this publication meets the minimum requirements of
American National Standard for Information Sciences—Permanence of
Paper for Printed Library Materials, ANSI Z39.48–1984.∞™

Library of Congress Cataloging-in-Publication Data

Sait Faik, 1906–1954.
 [Selections. English]
 Sleeping in the forest : stories and poems / Sait Faik ; translated from the Turkish ; editor, Talat S.
Halman ; associate editor, Jayne L. Warner.— 1st ed.
    p. cm. — (Middle East literature in translation)
 ISBN 0-8156-0804-7 (alk. paper)
 1. Sait Faik, 1906–1954—Translations into English. I. Halman, Talât Sait. II. Warner, Jayne L. III. Title.
IV. Series.
PL248.S288A2 2004
894'.3533—dc22

                              2004022125

Manufactured in the United States of America

Contents

Stories

Poems

Preface

TURKISH LITERATURE REMEMBERS and reveres Sait Faik as its premier master of the short story. In a career that spanned a mere quarter of a century, Sait Faik (1906–1954) turned out some 190 original short stories, two novellas, a few essays, and nearly forty poems. His fame rests squarely on his fiction, which deals mainly with the fishermen, workers, clerks, children, idlers, and mavericks of Istanbul. Many of his principal characters are from non-Muslim communities. The author often speaks in the first person and figures prominently in some of the stories as a persona. With a subtle style that, despite occasional complexities, was attuned to the simple natural rhythms of colloquial Turkish, Sait Faik portrayed the predicaments, maladjustments, and disillusionments of the man in the street, frequently himself, living on the fringes of society.

Among hallmarks of Sait Faik's fiction are narcissistic narration, a style that blends the vernacular with lyric touches, a tender humanistic empathy, and ironic twists in the story line. A romantic at heart, he often approached harsh reality without cynicism and with an underlying sense of optimism.

Sleeping in the Forest contains a representative selection from Sait Faik's work—twenty-five short stories, the first part of a four-part novella, and twelve poems. The translations have been done by a distinguished roster of experts in the field of Turkish literature. The introduction is by one of Turkey's most successful academic critics. The book has benefited immeasurably from Jayne L. Warner's meticulous editing.

Editing the work of Sait Faik is a formidable task. He often wrote in great haste, carelessly. The translators and editors of this volume occasionally struggled with surprising leaps in the story lines, shifting tenses, and stylistic oddities. Numerous critics have dwelt on this type of carelessness. It must be pointed out, however, that there is a counterargument. Melih Cevdet Anday, one of Turkey's eminent literary figures, has defended this lack of meticulousness as a hallmark of Sait Faik's unique style. "As far as I am concerned," Anday said, "Sait Faik was not sloppy in his use of language. Whatever he did stylistically, he did for deliberate effect."

Sait Faik, immensely popular in his native country, has also attracted attention abroad. Books featuring his work have been available in French, English, Russian, and Spanish. Dozens of his short stories have been translated into many languages and published in anthologies and literary magazines around the world. There is one Sait Faik book in English: *A Dot on the Map: Selected Stories and Poems,* published by Indiana University in 1983.

"The Armenian Fisherman and the Lame Seagull" is a shorter and somewhat different version of "An Episode of Two," which appears in my translation in *A Dot on the Map.* The poem "Letter I" originally appeared with the title of "First Letter" in the same book.

"*The Stelyanos Hrisopoulos,*" in a more recent translation by the late Nermin Menemencioğlu (Streater), was in *A Dot on the Map* in Spiro Kostof's translation.

The editors are grateful to Ayşegül Nazik, Beyhan Uygun Aytemiz, and Hivren Demir, graduate students at Bilkent University, who contributed a great deal to the editing and bibliographic work. They are also grateful to Demet Güzelsoy Chafra, who patiently and efficiently typed the entire manuscript many times and made invaluable contributions to the production of this volume.

The present book is a testament to Sait Faik's enduring stature in Turkey and to the growing interest in him in the English-speaking world. I hope readers will derive pleasure from the selected stories of the Turkish master.

Talat S. Halman

Guide to Turkish Spelling and Pronunciation

THROUGHOUT THIS BOOK Turkish proper names and special terms conform to standard modern Turkish spelling. The pronunciation of the vowels and consonants is indicated in the guide below:

a	(like *gun*); var. â (like *are*)	l	(as in English)
b	(as in English)	m	(as in English)
c	(as in *jade*)	n	(as in English)
ç	(*ch* of *chin*)	o	(like *eau* in French)
d	(as in English)	ö	(like *bird* or French *deux*)
e	(like *pen*)	p	(as in English)
f	(as in English)	r	(*r* of *rust*)
g	(*g* of *good*)	s	(*s* of *sun*)
ğ	(makes a preceding vowel longer)	ş	(*sh* of *shine*)
		t	(as in English)
h	(*h* of *half*)	u	(like *pull*); var. û (like *pool*)
ı	(like the second vowel of *portable*)	ü	(like *tu* in French)
		v	(as in English)
i	(like *it*); var. î (like *eat*)	y	(*y* of *you*)
j	(like *measure*)	z	(as in English)
k	(*k* of *king*)		

Of the twenty-nine characters in the Turkish alphabet, six do not exist in English: ç, ğ, ı, ö, ş, ü. The letters q, w, and x are not in the Turkish alphabet, although they may occur in foreign names. The letter ğ has its own capital Ğ but never starts a word. The undotted ı and the dotted i are separate vowels whose distinctions are strictly observed in pronunciation and spelling. These two letters have their individual capitals as well: I and İ respectively.

The few exceptions to authentic Turkish spellings are words that have found their way into the English language and appear in standard English dictionaries, for example, *rakı* or *efendi,* which have their anglicized versions, *raki* and *effendi.* The names of the cities of Istanbul and Izmir, commonly spelled with İ in Turkish, are spelled as they normally are in English, that is, with an I. Names of Muslim Turks and members of ethnic minorities appear in the translations exactly as they are spelled in modern Turkish.

Punctuation and English spelling conform to current standard American use.

Monetary Terms

The stories in this collection cover a period of about twenty years from the mid-1930s to 1954, during which period currency values fluctuated. The changes due to inflation, particularly the rampant increases in later decades, render the monetary references virtually meaningless. All of the monetary references, therefore, have been kept in the original amounts and might at best give the reader some idea about values, prices, salaries, and the like.

Basic Turkish denominations, such as lira and kuruş (100 kuruş = 1 lira), have been retained in the translations. No specific figures for their dollar or pound equivalents have been provided. In a few exceptional cases, common references like "nickels" and "dimes" have been employed for colloquial style. In some stories, the word "para" occurs. Its literal meaning is "one fortieth of a kuruş." Of extremely small value even when it was still in use in the 1930s and 1940s, it became obsolete in the 1950s. Comparable to the British "farthing," para is occasionally used figuratively in the sense of "worth next to nothing."

A Note on Asterisks

For words and names with asterisks, please refer to the glossary at the end of the book.

Chronology | Sait Faik

THIS CHRONOLOGY HAS BEEN COMPILED from several sources, some of which vary appreciably on certain dates. For instance, two of the most reliable sources, Tahir Alangu, *Cumhuriyetten Sonra Hikâye ve Roman* and Behçet Necatigil, *Edebiyatımızda İsimler Sözlüğü*, cite the year of Sait Faik's first trip to Switzerland and France as 1930 and 1931 respectively. Aside from this cautionary word, the editors are satisfied that the dates and other information listed in this chronology are accurate.

1906	Sait Faik born November 23 in Adapazarı* to Makbule and Mehmet Faik (Abasızoğlu), a well-to-do lumber merchant who once served as mayor.
1921	Finishes Rehber-i Terakki, a private elementary school in Adapazarı, and starts intermediate school.
1923	The family moves to Bolu* and later to Istanbul, where Sait Faik studies at the Boys' Lycée until tenth grade, when he is expelled, together with his entire class because of a prank on a teacher.
1925	Enters the Bursa Lycée as a boarding student.
1928	Graduates from the Bursa Lycée and enters the Faculty of Literature at the University of Istanbul.
1929	Publishes his first short story, "Uçurtmalar" (Kites), in the Istanbul daily *Milliyet* on December 9.
1930	Leaves the University of Istanbul without graduating. Goes to Lausanne, Switzerland, to study economics; after two weeks moves on to Grenoble, France, where he studies French at the Lycée Champollion.
1931	After a brief homecoming, Sait Faik returns to France. Attending

the University of Grenoble, irregularly, he visits Paris, Strasbourg, Lyon, Marseilles, and other cities.

1934   Starts publishing his short stories in *Varlık*; starting with the April 15 issue, his stories become frequent entries in this important Turkish literary magazine.

1935   Returns home, teaches Turkish at the Halıcıoğlu School for Armenian Orphans.

1936   First collection of short stories, *Semaver* (Samovar).

1939   His father dies on October 29; Sait Faik publishes second collection of short stories, *Sarnıç* (Reservoir).

1940   Collection of short stories, *Şahmerdan* (Pile Driver); briefly engages in the grain business.

1942   In May becomes a court reporter for the Istanbul daily *Haber*, a job he holds for one month.

1944   First novella, *Medarı Maişet Motoru* (*"The Source of Livelihood"—A Fishing Boat*), is published (republished with revisions in 1952 under the title *Birtakım İnsanlar* [A Certain Kind of People]).

1948   *Lüzumsuz Adam* (The Futile Man), a collection of short stories.

1950   The collection of short stories, *Mahalle Kahvesi* (The Neighborhood Coffeehouse).

1951   Publishes *Havada Bulut* (A Cloud in the Sky), a book of short stories, and *Kumpanya* (Company of Players), one long and two short stories.

        Goes to Paris for treatment of his liver ailment, but returns in five days.

1952   Two books of short stories, *Havuz Başı* (By the Fountain) and *Son Kuşlar* (Last Birds).

1953   His only collection of poems comes out under the title *Şimdi Sevişme Vakti* (Now's the Time for Love), and a novella, *Kayıp Aranıyor* (Search for the Missing Person) is published.

        Elected honorary member of the International Mark Twain Society (USA).

1954   *Alemdağda Var Bir Yılan* (A Snake in Alemdağ) and *Az Şekerli* (Coffee with a Little Sugar), collections of short stories.

Translates Georges Simenon's *L'homme qui regardait passer les trains*. Dies of cirrhosis on May 11.

1955   A collection of short stories, *Tüneldeki Çocuk* (The Child at Tünel*), is published posthumously. His mother establishes the annual Sait Faik Short Story Prize; recipients through the years include some of Turkey's major fiction writers.

1956   *Mahkeme Kapısı* (The Courtroom), a collection of part factual, part fictitious vignettes and interviews, based on court incidents.

1963   His mother, Makbule, dies.

1964   The family home on Burgaz Island* is converted into the Sait Faik Museum and is opened to the public on May 11, the tenth anniversary of his death.

A Note on Sait Faik's Name

Sait Faik's full name was Sait Faik Abasıyanık. His last name, which he took after the Turkish Republic passed its Surname Law in 1934, almost never appeared on his books, presumably because he had already started gaining his literary reputation as Sait Faik. However, many encyclopaedias, reference books, anthologies, and Turkish counterparts of *Who's Who* list him under his surname, and a number of compilations of his stories and critical works on him, published subsequent to his death, have included Abasıyanık.

The present book has followed the practice of referring to the author as Sait Faik. Readers should be aware that Faik is not a last name and that the author should be referred to as Sait Faik, not just as Sait. (His literary friends have often referred to him as Sait in their writing.)

A brief note on the etymology of the name Abasıyanık: It is derived from the traditional name of his family Abasızoğlu. *Aba* means a heavy felt-like fabric worn as an outer garment and sometimes considered a symbol of poverty or abstemious living. The family name Abasızoğlu signified a person who did not have an *aba* to wear, indicating extreme poverty. Sait Faik modified the name to Abasıyanık, meaning a person whose *aba* is scorched. He conceivably had in mind the common expression *"abayı yakmak,"* meaning to "burn or scorch the *aba*" and used figuratively in the sense of "to fall desperately in love." His surname, therefore, literally means "the person whose *aba* is burned" and metaphorically, "the person who is desperately in love."

Introduction | Sait Faik's Utopian Poetics and the Lyrical Turn in Turkish Fiction

Süha Oğuzertem

If works of literature do not carry people into a new, happy, different, good, and beautiful world, what are they good for?—Sait Faik

LITERATURE FULFILLS ITS MISSION if it helps us reflect on the meaning of our lives.[1] Sait Faik (1906–1954) more than met this objective by assisting the readers in this ineluctable task. That is why it has been observed, frequently and correctly, that Sait Faik's works represent a significant turning point in twentieth-century Turkish fiction. His writings have broadened our horizons of sympathy by including people who were earlier excluded from literature. When we read his stories, we learn to appreciate the value of the natural world in which we live. They refresh our sense of place, confirming the emotional significance of our environment. The democratic transformation that Sait Faik induced in the artist's role has made us reevaluate the function of writers in the modern world. When he removed literature from its supercilious heights and placed it within the reach of ordinary mortals, promising everyone lives filled with art, our interest in both life and art was renewed. The phenomenon of Sait Faik thus has a unique place in the literary and cultural history of modern Turkey. However, criticism has yet to fathom the deeper historical and theoretical import of the transformation his work has occasioned. This task will not be complete until twentieth-

1. I am grateful to Jayne L. Warner and Thomas Kenny Fountain for their help in correcting my English and refining the language of this essay. I would like to thank Özge Soylu for helping me gain access to some of the material mentioned in the text.

century Turkish literature is studied in greater depth. Although there appears to be some consensus among critics about the points mentioned, the true legacy of Sait Faik may be brought to light only in the context of a larger, comparative framework whereby his works are compared and contrasted with the multifarious works of his predecessors, contemporaries, and successors. The decades that have elapsed since the author's death are too few for a sound historical perspective to emerge, especially when Sait Faik still has an enthusiastic audience in Turkish society.

Each year, on the second Sunday of May, the devotees of Sait Faik gather on Istanbul's Burgaz Island,* where he lived most of his life, to celebrate his radical humanitarianism and to remember and relearn from his ethics of love and poetics of nature. These memorial gatherings have been organized regularly since 1977, with attendance sometimes exceeding two hundred people. Such was the case on May 16, 1999, when many high school students also accompanied their teachers to the island, and the "meeting," in the words of Perihan Ergun, the devoted organizer of these events, "turned into a rally." These annual gatherings also serve as the setting for the presentation of the most prestigious short story award in Turkey: the Sait Faik Short Story Prize. Given since 1955, it is a cherished possession of its recipients. The significant number of essays that appear each year, usually in May, in literary journals and magazines, many of which are memorial pieces, is another indication of Sait Faik's enduring significance for Turkish literature. The tradition has continued since 1954, when the pages of newspapers and magazines were inundated for several months with memorial essays on Sait Faik by the prominent literary figures of the time. The first collection of essays and poems on Sait Faik was edited by Tahir Alangu, a well-known critic and literary historian, and was published in 1956. Including nearly one hundred pieces that first appeared within a couple of months of Sait Faik's death, the volume effectively memorialized this solemn moment in the history of Turkish literature. Another sign of Sait Faik's ongoing reputation is the number of entries—nearly five hundred—in the bibliography on his works, prepared and published by Muzaffer Uyguner in 1983 (Uyguner, 51–70). Although somewhat dated now, this bibliography of books, theses, reviews, tributes, and poems reads like an impressive procession of distinguished Turkish literati: Nâzım Hikmet, Turkey's foremost poet; Yaşar

Kemal, a leading novelist; Haldun Taner, a prominent playwright; and many other writers and poets, celebrated the writer with their insightful comments and memorable lines. Even Bülent Ecevit, poet, statesman, and several times prime minister, has an essay on Sait Faik. A more recent reference book on Sait Faik cites eighteen books and fourteen theses (Ergun 1996, 33), while a new questionnaire, filled out by Turkey's prominent litterateurs, has named Sait Faik as the leading short story writer of our age and placed him in the top five of all distinguished writers and poets in the Republican period ("Yetmişbeş Yılda").

The tradition of honoring Sait Faik in writing continues today with regularly appearing brief memorial pieces (e.g., Akova) as well as more extended reflections (e.g., Erbil, Fethi Naci, Oktay). The appraisals of these noted poets, fiction writers, and critics strongly suggest that the Turkish readers' generous outpouring of love and respect for Sait Faik is most likely to endure in the near future. It would thus be a mistake to dub Sait Faik a misunderstood artist. It is more sensible to speak of an uncommon but felicitous reciprocation of what the audiences have received from their beloved author. Nevertheless, it would have been impossible for Sait Faik to reach his potential readers if it were not for such dedicated writer-editors as Muzaffer Uyguner and Talat S. Halman. Uyguner is the author of numerous books and articles on Sait Faik, as well as the editor of his extant writings. And under the discerning leadership of Talat S. Halman, generations of translators have been mobilized to give the English-reading world more than one chance to get acquainted with this cherished Turkish author. The gathering of such a large number of readers, writers, critics, and translators on Sait Faik's behalf reminds us of a famous anecdotal story. Sait Faik once wondered skeptically if five or six stories of his would still be of interest in fifty years' time. With his typical modesty, he viewed such contemplation of posterity as an immodest wish (Erbil 1998, 62). He was certainly proven wrong as far as the Turkish readers are concerned. This second collection of his stories in English translation contradicts him even further.

The selections in the present book, which were first published in Turkish between 1936 and 1954, encompass Sait Faik's short but productive writing career almost in its entirety. They are no less representative of the author than are the selections in Halman's previous collection in English, *A Dot on the Map.* All the stories, as well as the courtroom pieces contained in the present volume, may be read as variations on Sait Faik's perpetual theme—longing for love, justice, and utopian harmony on earth. Also ubiquitous in these selections is his distinctive prose style, which combines expressive simplicity and suggestive depth in what has usually been described as "lyrical prose." As a whole, the volume reminds us of Sait Faik's unparalleled talent in portraying single characters rather than in contriving complex dramatic plots. Such concentration of the author's strength also defines the efficacy of the form in which he could be most productive and successful: the short story. The present volume gives us ample occasion to observe the thematic, formal, and stylistic traits of his works. Without studying these aspects of his writings, we cannot interpret properly the Sait Faik revolution in Turkish fiction and its far-reaching literary and cultural implications, some of which I will look at here.

The important (auto)biographical dimension of Sait Faik's writings and his hybridization of literary genres have generally been recognized in Turkish criticism as two significant aspects of the Sait Faik revolution in fiction. Yet, readers of his stories have sometimes been divided over whether or not his stories reflect his actual experiences or are products of his imagination. A related question is whether his first-person narrators, which Sait Faik favored increasingly over the years, represent him in person or are merely distinct personae having little to do with him personally. There are no swift answers to such sweeping questions, for Sait Faik's writings vary considerably in form and content. For one thing, the borderlines between Sait Faik's 197 stories, 63 reportage pieces, and 49 miscellaneous writings (grouped according to Sami N. Özerdim and Muzaffer Uyguner's classification in Sait Faik 1970–89, 15: 157–65) are too fluid to sanction any rigorous definition of a Sait Faik story. Even if we arrived at a reliable definition, we would still be left with radically dissimilar clusters of stories. Especially in the early period, there are stories that may be considered classic in form, although they, too, feature Sait Faik's favorite themes and display his matchless lyrical prose. On the other hand, some of his stories with a first-person narrator do capture the personal voice of the actual author directly, whereas in others we hear the voice rather indirectly. Some stories, obviously documentary in both intent and content, employ vivid profiles in real-life dramas, and they combine wit, irony, and insight in a mood reminiscent of American "new journalism." Other stories with a less obvious documentary intent, such as "Eftalikus's Coffeehouse" in this collection, have proven to have important real-life references and connotations as well (e.g., see Birsel on Eftalapulos's Coffeehouse, the original model for the coffeehouse in the story). Finally, there are the later stories, such as "A Man Created by Loneliness" and "Such a Story," both included in this volume, which feature an "imaginary friend" and narrate in trancelike fashion the extended fantasies of the author. Yet, one cannot quickly deny them the status of "lived experience" just because there is an undeniable element of fantasy in them.

Despite these variations from one piece of writing to the next, the debate is nevertheless pertinent, not for settling once and for all whether or not Sait Faik *always* reported on his actual experiences, but for understanding why he increasingly favored doing so and how he did it when he did. By slightly changing the terms of the debate, we may thus concentrate our attention on a more crucial issue in interpreting Sait Faik's works, namely the problematic relation he had with literature and the act of writing. This issue has not been examined in depth despite numerous instances in his writing that suggest that he repeatedly posed to himself the questions of "why write" and "how to write." Among the translated works, "A Dot on the Map," in Halman's earlier collection, and "The Gramophone and the Typewriter," in the present one, are two significant cases. In previous criticism, this issue has been overshadowed by the emphasis on Sait Faik's stance on "what" or "about whom" to write, the overused yet accurate answer being: the underprivileged, the dispossessed, and the marginalized people of society. Nevertheless, we have a writer who, perturbed especially by the possibility of unwarranted social distinction that writing might procure, poses the question in broader terms, questioning the use and function of writing, and trying to deal with it in ethical and aesthetic terms. The fact that Sait Faik always saw as problematic what ordinary writers usually take for granted must be seen as an important sign of his distinction and originality. But we cannot expect prescriptive formulas about "how to write" from such true originals. Although he made a number of strong statements, such as the one that appears in the epigraph to this essay, that express his views on the mission of literature, his solution to the question of "how to write" in a way consonant with the general mission he proposed for literature is left for the readers' independent investigation.

I will suggest that Sait Faik's novel treatment, or "mistreatment," of time-honored generic divisions (or his genre bending), his apparent shortcomings in novel writing, his opting for open-ended plots, and his gradual abandonment of the third-person narrator in his stories may be interpreted as inevitable outcomes of his search, in the medium of writing, for ethical transparency, that is, for sincerity and authenticity, his chief virtues as a person and a writer. Hence, the radical transformation he induced in the classic story format, namely his intermixture of disparate genres, which we encounter as a problem in classifying his works, may be thought to have resulted from exposing the realistic short story to the kinds of writing that are not (like the novel) "constitutively" but only "conditionally" literary (for the distinction between the two literary regimes, see Genette 1993, 1–29).

No matter how belated the emergence of the novel and the short story in Turkey in the late nineteenth century might be vis-à-vis the West, by the time Sait Faik started producing his works, these genres had already gained the status of "serious literature" in Turkey. Replacing earlier genres based on oral and semi-oral modes of production and reception, these modern forms in a way "guaranteed" literariness within the new system of modern literature, or the literature of the print age. This sweeping change in literary production in Turkey may be thought of as analogous to the preceding transformation in Western letters. As Terry Eagleton notes in *Literary Theory,* "in eighteenth-century England, the concept of literature was not confined as it sometimes is today to 'creative' and 'imaginative' writing. It meant the whole body of valued writing in society: philosophy, history, essays and letters as well as poems" (1996, 15). Eagleton's "valued writing" calls to mind the root of the Turkish word for literature: *edeb,* or manners, and the whole gamut of cultural, ethical, and emotional investments the term historically signifies.

With that background in mind, Sait Faik's literary practice may be considered a resistance to what Eagleton views as a confinement of literature to "creative" and "imaginative" writing, or to "fiction" in the strict sense of the term. Sait Faik's practice not only draws upon but also reminds us of such potentially literary forms as the memoir, the diary, the essay, the character sketch, the journalistic report, the chronicle, and, above all, the letter. Those are forms that do not guarantee literariness automatically, as do modern fictional genres, including drama. Their literariness depends upon the rhetorical qualities of the individual pieces of which they are composed. Since, for Sait Faik, the evocative and communicative functions of literature prevailed over other functions, it is not surprising that the letter, or the idea of it, especially served for him as the quintessential model for literature. Sait Faik adopted this format as a whole or in part, in form or in substance, for several of his stories (e.g., "Waiting for Love" and "Love Letter" in Halman, *A Dot on the Map* 1983, 167–70, 193–95). Hence, what is viewed as Sait Faik's radical innovation in the classical story format may be seen as an attempt to recover the literary potential in those forms that are excluded by an excessively narrow definition of literature in terms of the fictional alone. Therefore, remembering the roots of the short story as a genre may help us better interpret the significance of Sait Faik's practice. As Helmut Bonheim says, "The short story genre itself may be thought of as the result of a confluence of earlier genres: the essay, the sketch and the tale" (1982, 13). Hence, Sait Faik's preferred mode of writing invites a connection with literary history, with earlier notions of literature, which may be viewed by itself as a form of resistance to the ostensibly self-enclosed world of modern fiction. When placed in such a context, Sait Faik's chief trepidation about writing and literature appears to be with impersonal modes of storytelling, including literary realism and certain forms of modernist writing, which have reduced the authors to narrator functions and characters to inauthentic projections of their authors' unfulfilled and, in some cases, vainglorious selves. Sait Faik's literary practice, which may be summarized in terms of an ethics of love and poetics of nature, presents, in contrast, a deep awareness of the existence of everything alive, no matter how the status of natural beings might be marred by the ideology of possessive individualism and widespread prejudice against those who are seemingly unlike us. Therefore, in Sait Faik's reluctance to forego historical forms of literature and in the (auto)biographical disposition of his writings, we may detect the reflection of his desire to be true to himself, and, in his proverbial proclamation, to be "with the readers" (excerpted in Ergun 1996, 60) rather than beyond and above them as certain works of literature insinuate. Hence, whatever one may think of the unity, the completeness, or the realistic probability of Sait Faik's literary works, their personal authenticity, rhetorical persuasiveness, and lyrical quality are beyond doubt.

It is perhaps not so fortuitous that the frequent use of the term "lyrical" in assessments of Sait Faik's work reminds us of one highly relevant employment of it in literary theory. In Käte Hamburger's *The Logic of Literature,* an ambitious and elaborate attempt at circumscribing the literary field in transhistorical fashion, one of the two basic realms of literature is defined as the "lyrical genre," the other being the "fictional or mimetic genre." In Hamburger's rigorous classification, which is also taken seriously by the literary theorist Gérard Genette in his preface to Hamburger's work, the power of "creation" in the strict Aristotelian sense *(poiesis)* is granted to the "fictional or mimetic genre" only, a resolution that entitles the "lyrical genre" to heterogeneous expressions and aesthetic evaluations of all kinds of personal information, opinion, feeling, and the like, including lyric poetry.

This theory proffers interesting help in our venture to define Sait Faik's concept of art. First, it accounts for Sait Faik's increasing predilection for the use of the first-person narrator and the lyric feeling this use communicates. As Hamburger maintains, "we only experience a genuine lyric phenomenon where we experience a genuine lyric I" (1993, 291). Her emphasis is meaningful for alerting us to what Sait Faik, a person always motivated by his concern for ethical transparency, might have felt regarding the use of third-person narration, for in this technique, while the narrator gives the impression of being absent from the story, he or she may also be overly present to the point of knowing what a person cannot normally know, such as other people's thoughts and feelings. In contrast, a person who is overtly present in a narrative cannot possibly engage in such pretense; and, in the absence of a persona's hidden veil, he or she cannot transgress the human limitation regarding the inaccessibility of other people's inner selves. Respecting other beings' privacy is not only a way of maintaining one's integrity, but it is also the very principle on which a deeper awareness of others' independent existence is built. Given Sait Faik's preoccupation with the questions of "why write" and "how to write" without compromising the dignity and the authentic existence of the self and others, his increasing preference for the use of first-person narration in his stories may, therefore, be viewed as an aesthetic solution to a fundamentally ethical dilemma. It is not incidental that a profound awareness of people from all walks of life, especially the humble and the unacknowledged, a sensitive concern for ecology and locality, and a personifying interest in all forms of life, are the typical characteristics of Sait Faik's works. As Halman observes in "Fiction of a Flâneur," his introduction to *A Dot on the Map*, "empathy is the dominant attitude of Sait Faik as narrator and protagonist" (1983, 7). Even in his bleakest moments, his affirmative view of life, his passion for connecting with people and nature do not abate. His capacity for emotional identification with people, with places, and with animate and inanimate objects in nature is in fact so great that it is impossible for readers not to feel the contagion of emotion emanating from his poetic prose. Sait Faik's texts invite readers to make strong evaluations, to avow sympathies and antipathies at all times. In other words, readers are never asked to forget about the dimension of "ought" in human conduct as they are told to do in certain forms of literature carrying the imprint of nineteenth-century literary naturalism and philosophical positivism. Yet, even in its most agitated moments, Sait Faik's prose continues to carry its lyrical touch, never turning aggressive or irate. Therefore, what might initially appear as merely technical choices in Sait Faik's writings may be thought to result from his view of art as a "form of conduct," to use the words of Wayne C. Booth, a well-known theorist of ethical criticism. As Booth puts it, "when art and criticism are viewed as forms of conduct, they lead us into the very battles that we may have hoped to escape by turning to art in the first place" (1988, 137). From what has been stated so far, I hope it is clear that Sait Faik did not view art in escapist terms but as the very field for the ethical battles that humans fight daily throughout their lives.

The fact that we can relate Sait Faik's works more easily to Käte Hamburger's "lyrical genre" than to her "fictional or mimetic genre" is reminiscent, interestingly, of another frequently made observation on Sait Faik's art—that his prose often borders on poetry. What generations of Sait Faik readers have chosen to emphasize in their reflections on the author calls to mind, in turn, the words of the late Cemal Süreya, a prominent Turkish poet, who drew attention to the conjunction between the lyrical I and the almost unavoidable presence of (auto)biographical elements in poetry. Cemal Süreya maintained that "autobiographical elements play a large role in all art. But I think they play a larger role in the art of poetry" (1992, 61). His pithy words to describe the association between life and art in poetry have since become an expression among Turkish readers: "The poet's life is included in poetry" (61). Therefore, it would not be far-fetched to conclude that Sait Faik's life is likewise included in his work, but certainly in a special sense. As Hamburger says, "The lyric I transforms objective reality into a reality of subjective experience, for which reason this still persists as reality" (1993, 286). Hamburger's use of the term "subjective" is again felicitous, for it too has been a widely used term in assessments of Sait Faik's work (e.g., the remarks of Nurullah Ataç in Alangu 1956, 50). Critics have found his works "subjective," especially when contrasted with those of social realists, particularly with the works of Sabahattin Ali (1907–1948), a highly accomplished contemporary of Sait Faik's. The sense of lyrical subjectivity conveyed by the stories of Sait Faik is in fact so famous and so unique that Ayla Kutlu, herself a recipient of the Sait Faik Short Story Prize in 1991, has remarked: "Sait Faik is the only person who started with a central I and was successful throughout. But don't forget that no one has yet captured [the spirit of] his storytelling" (1999, 42).

In addition to elucidating for us the function of the lyric I in Sait Faik's work, Hamburger's theory also helps us appreciate how Sait Faik's idea of storytelling involved more of a sense of the discovery or unearthing of life's stories and reflecting on them than inventing or "originating" them in godlike fashion, acts that are better suited to Hamburger's "fictional or dramatic genre." Sait Faik's celebrated words in "In Search of a Story," translated by Ellen Ervin, effectively epitomizes his general outlook: "Each day hundreds of trains were bringing in thousands of stories and carrying away thousands of stories" (Halman 1983, 100). These words may be taken to summarize not only Sait Faik's view of the relation between art and life but also between his art and his life: stories are not to be made; they are to be discovered, for life never fails to present remarkable stories to the keen perception of the genuine writer. Hence the affinity between Sait Faik's life and work as has been captured in Halman's exquisitely worded observations:

> Sait Faik wrote the way he lived—spontaneously, sensually, impressionistically, experientially, always stressing the authentic touch and the ring of

truth. He probably felt that a story is a microcosm or slice of life and cannot be, should not be, any more perfect than life itself. Above all, he was conscious of human frailty, foibles and follies. In exploring human situations, his stories reflected, not only in substance but in form as well, the flaws of life. (1983, 9–10)

A celebrated passage by the famed playwright Haldun Taner also effectively reflects most readers' impressions:

> Sait Faik was not taking up a subject but a section of life. He was not defending a thesis, but reflecting an experience. His heart was full of love for men and love for nature. Whatever he gazed at reflected the warmth and radiance of this love. Only after he took them as subjects would we learn to appreciate the people and objects that first seemed the least significant.
>
> When Sait glanced at them and told their stories, a screw shell, a watermelon stand, a brazier and a chair, an embowered tomb, a shoeshine box, a searchlight operator, a fisherman, a waiter, a priest . . . all suddenly gained a special appeal. (1983, 138)

These reflections prompt us to take another look at those aspects of Sait Faik's art, which are sometimes characterized as its shortcomings. If his works seem to lack perfection, unity, and dramatic intensity in conventional senses, readers may first ask what is meant by these very words. Likewise, if "literature" has come to connote mainly "dramatic intrigue" and "suspense" at a considerable distance from "ordinary" life, we may as well question the sagacity of such progress in literary production and consumption, as well as forms of writing whose impact derives principally from the titillation of intrigue, secrecy, and revelation. Sait Faik's works demonstrate that such manipulation of audience interest is not a necessary component of literature per se. And if Sait Faik were unwilling to pursue such elevated notions as artistic autonomy, perfection of the work of art, and impermeability of art to life's concerns, conceptions associated at times with literary modernism, it was because he implicitly resisted the separation of art from life in the first place. As Halman emphasizes regarding the connection between the writer's life and art, Sait Faik could not have tried to compensate for life's imperfection with the presumed perfection of art, for art could not be any more or less perfect than life. That is perhaps why, even in his expressions of boredom, loneliness, and despair, there is nothing of the narcissistic disdain for life, or moral cynicism, which is sometimes viewed as the hallmark of "serious" or "high" literature.

Clearly, Sait Faik did not subscribe to a generic notion of literature as defined by others. He did not opt for creating an aesthetically autonomous and socially impermeable fictional universe. Nor did he see literature as an extrinsic tool for achieving immoderate private or public goals. As he conformed to the end to the sublime goal of writing only for his own pleasure and taste, this radically personalizing practice transformed literature into an almost private affair. But this was far from a voluntary confinement in one's private world. What Sait Faik did was to resist gratifying the demands of an increasingly impersonal public, with its endless invitations for writers to sacrifice their integrity. He kept writing as if he were writing for his friends only, for the "company he kept" (cf. Booth), never surrendering his highest ideals and never losing touch with his deeper self.

There is certainly more than a touch of romanticism in all of this, and we should not refrain from using the term "romantic," lest it be understood in a pejorative sense. This term may serve as an important literary point of reference, denoting, at the same time, the cultural framework from which Sait Faik's illustrious work springs. His ideals of bringing down the walls between humans and nature, humans and humans, and humans and their moral selves, strictly echo, across time, the pantheistic, egalitarian, and utopian impulses of such romantic visionaries as Rousseau, Blake, Wordsworth, and Thoreau. The spirit of the discovery of nature, of folklore, of the supernatural, of the child, or of what previously fell behind the borders of "civilization"—or "outside the city walls," as Sait Faik articulated it—before the age of revolution in the West, reverberates, distantly yet equally strong, in his work. Therefore, the term "romanticism" remains meaningful as a literary-cultural designator of values that are still relevant, such as environmentalism. When used in a circumspect manner, it may have the additional benefit of opening doors for meaningful comparisons in literary history among different writers and across diverse literatures. For instance, it would be interesting to compare the work of Sait Faik with that of another "romantic," namely John Steinbeck (1902–1968), who was both a contemporary of Sait Faik and was possibly his closest literary compeer, sharing an inspiring vision of a nonalienated community on earth (see Parini 1995 for a whole array of possible comparisons).

The age of revolution was also the age of nationalism in the nineteenth-century West as it had been in Turkey in the twentieth century. Yet Sait Faik again deserves credit for being more than sensitive to what has been recognized as nationalism's universal blind spots: its class, gender, and ethnocentric biases. As an antibourgeois writer and fierce democrat, Sait Faik always sided with the underdog, as evinced by many of the pieces in this collection that display his distinctive talent in single character portrayals. Therefore, labeling his people "ordinary" or "common" would go against the democratic spirit in which they are conceived, for no characters remain "common" or "ordinary" once they enter Sait Faik's stories; his piercing gaze and thoughtful vision transform them lovingly into unique beings.

A telling anecdote about the original publication history of the sixth story of this collection, *"The Stelyanos Hrisopulos,"* in early 1936, during the heyday of Turkish nationalism, reveals Sait Faik's attitude toward his characters. A letter from him to Yaşar Nabi Nayır, the founding editor of *Varlık,* the longest-lived (since 1933) literary journal in Turkey, and the first publisher of Sait Faik's works, discloses that when Sait Faik first sent his story to the magazine *Yücel,* it was not published for several months. We learn that it was not printed because the publishers of *Yücel* found the story "too cosmopolitan" for their readers' taste. What we have here is an interesting use of the word *kozmopolit* in Turkish, which stands in this context as a euphemism for "non-national" or "non-native." The charge implies that Sait Faik's story fails to cater sufficiently to Turkish national interests and sentiments for the sole reason that it featured Greek nationals as principal characters. Upon hearing this, Sait Faik withdrew his story, asking the publishers to leave the fishermen of a small island (Burgaz) and himself alone. Defending fundamental human equality and emphasizing the humane viewpoint and the local color of his story, he requested, in his letter, to have his story be published in *Varlık.* Yaşar Nabi published the story shortly after he received the letter (Yaşar Nabi 1972, 89–90).

The corpus of writings on Sait Faik is full of such anecdotal stories, which repeatedly reveal his radical humanitarianism as encompassed by his romantic vision. When, for instance, someone he knew asked him, half jokingly perhaps, to get rid of the sea, the fishermen, the unfortunate people, and Greek nationals as subjects of his stories, Sait Faik responded: "I live in Istanbul, which consists of what you have just enumerated" (Alangu 1956, 65). His words in the short-short story "Robinson" have also become proverbial: "I love people more than flags" (trans. Murat Nemet-Nejat, in Halman, *A Dot on the Map* 1983, 155).

I have so far emphasized the uniqueness of Sait Faik as a writer, but it is far from being the case that his utopian-romantic poetics flourished in a historical vacuum. Although it is true that Sait Faik is a true original in the field of the short story in Turkey, the democratic principles of his art are echoed in the poetry and prose of many of his contemporaries, including other such originals as Halikarnas Balıkçısı (1886–1973), Nâzım Hikmet (1902–1963), Orhan Veli (1914–1950), and Yaşar Kemal (b. 1922), to name only a few. Especially in the first part of the twentieth century, they and other writers and poets pioneered and represented the strong paradigm of a rising literary and cultural romanticism in Turkey. These writers and poets emphasized, in their unique ways, the interconnectedness of humans with one another and with nature, resisted the detachment of artists from their audiences, and induced much of today's egalitarian, multicultural, and ecological thinking. No matter how strongly they were resented when they freely associated with fishermen, porters, seamen, peasants, and the like (see, e.g., Ayda 1984, 199), with their efforts, Turkish literature ceased to be the preserve of the aristocratic elite that it mostly was during the previous centuries. Among them, Sait Faik is one whom we still recognize as a pioneer in many ways. He is the one who beckons us to see the universal in the local, all of humanity in one human being, the poetic in the mundane. By limiting his environment almost purposefully, he gave us a literature of depth, the best specimens of what is today called "regional writing." He chose not to look at people but into them, and there he found works of art.

It is best to conclude with Oktay Akbal, a prominent man of letters, and a former winner of the Sait Faik Short Story Prize, whose words remain as fresh today as they were when they were published in 1973:

> For me Sait Faik is in the top three or five of all story writers in world literature. . . . He also has a very firm standing in Turkish literature (both today

and in the future). He leads the company of the few writers we have [in Turkish literature] who will live on in the future. Sait Faik ushered in a new perspective, a new sensitivity in our literature, including such themes as love, compassion, and friendship for and among human beings. He established a new, personal atmosphere for the short story. He had enormous influence on writers succeeding him. He taught us a great deal. That is why his influence still endures. (Alptekin 1976, 213)

Works Cited

Akova, Akgün. "Son Kuşlar ve Son Kuruşlar." *Öküz* (Mayıs 1999): 42.

Alangu, Tahir, ed. *Sait Faik İçin*. Istanbul: Yeditepe Yayınları, 1956.

Alptekin, Mahmut. *Sait Faik Abasıyanık*. Istanbul: Dilek Yayınevi, 1976.

Ayda, Adile. *Böyle İdiler Yaşarken*. Ankara, 1984.

Birsel, Salah. "Sait Adında Bir Balık." Ergun and Kutlu 141–49.

Bonheim, Helmut. *The Narrative Modes: Techniques of the Short Story*. Cambridge: D. S. Brewer, 1982.

Booth, Wayne C. *The Company We Keep: An Ethics of Fiction*. Berkeley: University of California Press, 1988.

Eagleton, Terry. *Literary Theory: An Introduction*. 2nd ed. Oxford: Blackwell, 1996.

Erbil, Leyla. "Sait Faik'te Göz." *Zihin Kuşları*. Istanbul: Yapı Kredi Yayınları, 1998. 51–65.

Ergun, Perihan, and Ayla Kutlu, eds. *Sait Faik Abasıyanık 90 Yaşında*. Ankara: Bilgi Yayınevi, 1996.

Fethi Naci. *Sait Faik'in Hikâyeciliği*. Istanbul: Adam Yayınları, 1998.

Genette, Gérard. *Fiction and Diction*. Trans. Catherine Porter. Ithaca, NY: Cornell University Press, 1993.

Halman, Talat Sait, ed. *A Dot on the Map: Selected Stories and Poems by Sait Faik*. Bloomington: Indiana University Turkish Studies, 1983.

Hamburger, Käte. *The Logic of Literature*. Trans. Marilynn J. Rose. 2nd ed. Bloomington: Indiana University Press, 1993.

Kutlu, Ayla. "Bizim İnsanımızın Hikâyelerini İstiyorum." (Ustaların Seçtikleri) *Varlık* 1099 (Nisan 1999): 38–42.

Oktay, Ahmet. "Kabul ve Red: Yalnızlığın Kutupları (Sait Faik Üzerine Düşünceler)." *Argos* 21 (1990): 59–64.

Parini, Jay. *John Steinbeck: A Biography*. New York: Holt, 1995.

Sait Faik (Abasıyanık). *Bütün Eserleri*. 15 vols. Ankara: Bilgi Yayınevi, 1970–1989.

Süreya, Cemal. "Şairin Hayatı Şiire Dahil." *Folklor Şiire Düşman.* Istanbul: Can Yayınları, 1992. 61–64.

Taner, Haldun. "Sevimli Bir Aylak." *Ölür İse Ten Ölür, Canlar Ölesi Değil.* Istanbul: Cem Yayınevi, 1983. 136–40.

Uyguner, Muzaffer. *Sait Faik Abasıyanık.* Ankara: Bilgi Yayınları, 1983.

Yaşar Nabi (Nayır), ed. *Dost Mektuplar: Mektuplarıyla Edebiyatçılarımız.* Istanbul: Varlık Yayınevi, 1972.

"Yetmişbeş Yılda Yetmişbeş Kitap." *kitap-lık* 34 (1998): insert between 204 and 205.

Stories

World for Sale

Translated by Celia Kerslake

FOR THE FIRST TIME IN HIS LIFE, Emin was going to commit a theft. Emin was a low-ranking official, but he had a position that provided opportunities for thievery.

There had been three times when the vision of suddenly filling his house with that atmosphere of affluence, which he had never known or even imagined, had vaguely impinged on his consciousness: once when he was getting married, once when his wife was dying, and once when his child was born. In different versions of this vision it sometimes happened that an item as necessary as bread and another as unnecessary as a gramophone changed places with each other, so that Emin did not know which he wanted most. On all three occasions the dream that he often used to have as a child, on nights when he went to bed hungry, had come to him when he was wide awake.

And yet, at all of these three critical periods in his life, the desire to steal had been extremely hazy. Perhaps he had experienced even sweeter and more unbearable moments, now that he had finally decided to commit a theft. Even so, the desire itself was quite vague.

Seven years after the birth of his child, when that same child lay dying, he had once again felt the same desire, still not with total clarity but this time with traumatic force—so much so that he had suddenly rushed out into the street and fled to one of the coffeehouses that are strung out along the quayside, all of them hung with mirrors.

It was a golden yellow evening. The streets were swarming with people, among them forlorn but beautiful girls.

As we said, he had fled to a coffeehouse. Two people sitting at a table shouted, "Hey, Emin Effendi, come and play a round of *fitil.**"

3

Emin Effendi forgets absolutely everything else when he's playing *fitil*. He goes almost mad with rage and swears like a street bully, his ears reddening like a child's. The other players help each other in a rather obvious way. Emin is aware of this from the start, but he doesn't abandon the game. When the round is finally over and he is beaten, he blows the cigarette ash off his torn and frayed trousers, expostulating, "F——— the person who pays for the Turkish delight. First you cheat by playing together against me, and then you expect me to pay for it. Well, I'm damned if I will!"

He storms out, and the others, including the proprietor of the coffee-house and the onlookers, roar with laughter. There are always people ready to pay for his coffee: the onlookers, the proprietor, even his fellow cardplayers. The important thing is to get Emin Effendi to play *fitil*. Who cares about the money?

It was during such a round of *fitil* that Emin Effendi, driven by the knowledge that his child was close to death, had forgotten his urge to steal money and had gone straight home. It was four years since his wife had died. His elderly aunt was looking after the little boy, who had a high fever. Serum had been administered, and there should have been some improvement by now.

A thin doctor, with a delicate face and wrinkled skin, sitting at the bedside amid a smell of alcohol, was staring with a melancholy expression at a picture on the wall. He took the child's pulse again. Then he suddenly got up and scribbled a prescription.

"Get this made up at once, and give him a dose every half-hour. It'll calm him down."

The doctor went down the stairs and out of the house so quickly that Emin Effendi didn't have time to get a lira from his aunt and give it to him.

The pharmacist made up the medicine for forty kuruş. With the money that was left over Emin bought a bottle of brandy, which he polished off on the way home. He wasn't at all accustomed to alcohol. His head felt as if it had entered a world that it had long desired. Everything was coming toward him in a warm, rainy nostalgia. Shadows, streetlamps, people, sea, and ships were all motionless in some oily substance, awaiting his command.

In the morning the child was still alive. But his face wore the mask of those who are about to go to another place. "We won't be able to go there with our forlorn, beautiful, everyday faces," Emin said to himself.

He had said this with such an air of indifference. Where were the days when sometimes, as he came home from work, he would find the little one waiting for him on the road, and would feel his heart beat faster the moment he saw him? Where was the clean, loving atmosphere around that child, which would wash his heart and transport these wet Istanbul days up to a high plateau, distant and green, or to pine-clad mountains, deep in snow? It was as if that had been a different child from the one he was now leaving at the point of death.

The desire to steal money crossed his mind again. He smiled. There was no need for it now; the child had died. That day work was so heavy that he didn't even have time for a meal all day. On his way home after work he initially had the sense of being in a murky, airless place. He had an oppressive feeling in his head, and he was thinking about remote, meaningless things. Then suddenly it was as if all the windows had been opened inside him.

Several thoughts rushed through his mind. All at once he thought he had made contact with a world that gave him the sense of living, feeling, and thinking.

This passed as swiftly as a flash of lightning. Everywhere, all the way to the other side of the world and the horizon, had been lit up with a bright blue light. Immediately after that moment he remembered that he had left his child at home on the point of death. He felt an indescribable pain. At that point he turned sentimental. He remembered the little shoes, the thin knees black with dirt, the trousers with patches on their seat. He had never been able to look at the little boy without feeling pity and distress. Now he saw again the child's delicate wrists, his mouth with its rotten teeth, his face which sometimes suddenly looked beautiful and clean. And he remembered the way he would climb up onto his lap.

His mind had cleared. A thousand and one memories, great and small, were flooding in and out. Sometimes he wanted to dwell on one of them, and make himself a story out of it, but it was impossible—so much so that sometimes he forgot what he had been thinking about only a second before, and just as happens when one is falling asleep, he simply couldn't catch the thread of it again.

He arrived home to find the child dead. The neighbors had sent cooked food. He and his aunt sat down and ate it almost peacefully. While they were having their meal the voice of a woman reciting something could be heard from the room where the child lay.

Emin felt a rebellion inside him. "I'm going out, Aunt," he said. "I need to get some air."

But this evening in Istanbul Emin couldn't find the air that he was look-ing for. He was thirty-six years old. He was heavily built, and his face could almost be called handsome. In his loose, disheveled clothes he had the effect of making everyone imagine him to be a sad, strong, and good person.

Emin strolled up and down the bridge. Now this last reason for commit-ting theft had gone. He could get by on his salary now. His only source of en-joyment was playing *fitil* in the evenings. He was not a smoker. If they ordered him a raki, which they usually did, he would drink it. When Emin drank raki he would start to stumble over his words. He would listen heart and soul to anyone who ordered him a drink. There is a certain kind of man who gets himself treated to raki by those who want to talk about things that shouldn't be divulged to anyone. Emin was such a man, and because of this he knew all the taverns of Istanbul.

What had his large brown eyes not listened to in wonder? What acts of heroism, what sufferings, what love stories, what despicable and shameful deeds? He had listened to them all, both the acts of heroism and the shame-ful situations, with the same large, kind eyes, always full of wonder, and he had taken them in, so he could tell one of them to someone else the next day.

Surely such a man would never have any difficulty in finding someone to buy him a drink, would he?

A year later Emin's aunt also died. They lived in a two-room stone build-ing in the upper part of Tophane.* Probably it belonged to his aunt, but Emin had had it registered in his own name. Although Emin had looked after his aunt all her life, he had been made to feel like an orphan in this house. Above all, his wife had suffered untold misery at the hands of this aunt, whom he had feared so much and had now taken to the graveyard.

Emin rented out one of the rooms. In the evenings he would come home and sleep in the other one, and it seemed to him as if he had been living like this for years on end. He had had a dream. He had married, and they had had a child. So where was everyone?

One summer day Emin filled a bag and went off with it. They caught him a few days later, and the money was recovered. He was sent to the Department of Forensic Medicine, where it was discovered that his mental balance was somewhat impaired. Because of this he was released.

Emin did not tell anyone what he had intended to do with the money. The only comment he made was to a doctor at the Department of Forensic Medicine, who approached him in a fatherly manner: "Doctor! Doctor! I was going to buy the world with that money."

So this kind-faced, unkempt man sitting in a corner of the coffeehouse is the man who wanted to buy the world.

"Satılık Dünya"
    Şahmerdan, 1940

A Treasure Hunter

Translated by Celia Kerslake

IN FRONT OF THE DOOR of the house stood a brazier, with a pipe rising up from it. The smell of badly made charcoal burning filled the narrow street. Anyone who was not used to it would immediately feel dizzy.

Fındık* Ali was sitting in front of his house, behind the brazier, with his sleeves rolled up, gutting fish.

It was evening. A fine summer evening. For days Fındık had been waiting for this summer evening, which seemed as if it had come expressly for the eating of fish and the drinking of raki. He had caught four *kırma* fish, each one weighing four kilos, and a few kilos of red sea bream, about three hundred grams apiece. He had sold the big fish to well-to-do people and bought a gallon of wine. There was some vinegar in the house. As for olive oil, because he really hated having to pay for it, he had made all sorts of excuses to İstavro the grocer and had acquired half a kilo, supposedly on credit.

Over time he had run up small debts to the grocer, the baker, the watermelon-seller, and the tobacconist, on the understanding that he would pay them back when he got rich. Only if he got very rich was he going to pay. "I swear to God I'm going to pay," he would say.

Who said he wasn't going to get rich? Well, who? This was the year of the unlucky, they'd soon see!

He was going to make a nice salad. Then he was going to heat up the pan and fry the little sea bream for his own enjoyment. "I won't give the whore a single fish. She can eat pitch, the slut!" he said to himself.

Fındık Ali was a fisherman. One day, fourteen years ago, he had picked up a ramshackle boat for six lira. Up to that time he had worked as a porter, painter, and newspaper vendor, and—shameful to say—had done some

8

thieving. But as soon as he came into possession of a boat he had settled for the trade of fishing, which he was practicing anyway in his free time, partly for pleasure and partly to make money.

Fındık Ali had a wife, a dark-skinned girl who ran a small coffeehouse. But she was rather wily. What most angered Ali was the air she had of not being the wife of Fındık the fisherman. She seemed proud and conceited, not just to her husband but to everyone around her. It was this that really got on her husband's nerves. "Who does she think she is, for God's sake? Whose wife is she? What is this majestic pose of hers?"

Sometimes, on beautiful summer evenings like this, no fish would get caught. If that happened all hell would break loose. Sultana would refuse to give her husband any money. But Fındık Ali could not bear to spend even one perfect, cool summer evening without wine. There were two things he was addicted to: one was wine, the other was old newspapers. And sometimes there was the hookah, which was kept in a corner of the basement. It had not lost any of the blue and red decoration painted on it, but the inside was cloudy, as if the Persian tobacco was still smoking there. But this third indulgence was reserved for days when he was in unusually good spirits. It was a treat to be enjoyed only on days when there had been good fishing, when Sultana had for some reason suddenly seemed like a lovable wife, when he had not quarreled at all with the other fishermen (with whom he never got on well), and when İstavro the grocer, despite having seen him pinch a few onions from his shop, had not said anything about it.

So Fındık Ali did not consider this hookah addiction a problem. But if he didn't get any wine to drink, if he didn't knock back a gallon every couple of evenings at least, the world would change color for him. Everything around him would become hazy, and he would feel a desire to smash things up. Wine was the cause of all his quarrels with his wife. How had he got hooked on this poison? Originally, when he and some friends had been expelled from the second class of the Military Academy, he had gotten into the habit of drowning his sorrows in raki. He would booze about once a week. Then when he began to work for the Unionists[1] he started to have money in his

---

1. The Unionists (Ottoman Society of Union and Progress), often referred to as "The Young Turks,"* were the dominant political force in the empire from the revolution of 1908 until the end of World War I.

pocket. Particularly after the "Incident on the Bridge"[2] he could knock back a three-liter bottle every evening if he felt like it.

On becoming stationmaster at Arifiye* he had picked up the habit of smoking a hookah, sitting in the early evening looking out over the fields of maize and across to the Sapanca* mountains. His passion for reading old newspapers also dated from that time.

Later, in the Armistice[3] period, he had joined the police. "It was that time that I took on this whore," he would say. He would not say where he got her. "You sin for forty years, then one day you repent and mend your ways. She just couldn't help smiling at men. And she would join in the drinking every evening, and get up and dance. I would have gold napoleons jangling in my pocket, my friend—I'm not joking! But I would never go home. Well, once a month or once a year. Not only did I not give the wife a cent, but on the evenings when I came home I would beat her as well."

The woman had a weakness for young, tall, handsome men. "To be honest, I don't think she's been unfaithful to me," he would say, "but she's probably drunk raki and danced in front of other men. I suppose she always turned them out of the house when the time came." And he would continue: "What do I care? No one ever said to me, 'I slept with your wife.' During the Armistice the British locked me up in a place in Galata.* They beat me to a pulp. Then every evening they would give me wine, and I would drown my sorrows. They claimed I helped people get out into Anatolia.[4] And mind you, I'm not saying I didn't! We even smuggled arms, but I didn't do anything without being paid in gold coins. A lot of good they did me—but never mind!"

At that time they were living in Kumkapı.* After getting out of the hands

2. This probably refers to the murder on the Galata Bridge, on April 6, 1909, of the editor of a newspaper that had been attacking the Unionists. The murderer was never found, and the opposition openly blamed the Unionists for the crime.

3. The Armistice of Mudros (October 30, 1918) ended hostilities between the Allied powers and the Ottoman government. It was followed by an Allied occupation of Istanbul, which lasted throughout the nationalists' independence war in Anatolia. It ended with the Treaty of Lausanne, which gave international recognition to the new Turkish state (July 24, 1923).

4. That is, to join the national struggle against foreign occupation.

of the British, Fındık Ali had terrorized Istanbul. If his own claims are to be believed, it seems that Fındık Ali, who was so called because of his rather short height, had been a fearsome tough guy. If only the streets of Galata had tongues and could tell of his exploits . . .

Then we find Fındık Ali suddenly changed. We see him wearing an outfit made of navy blue serge, and yellow ankle boots. On the day that Refet Pasha entered Istanbul,[5] the local Greeks on Burgaz Island,* seeing Ali in a little hut, one of the abandoned properties there, smoking a hookah with his wife Sultana sitting opposite him and his gallon of wine in front of him, said:

"Hello, Ali Bey,* how are you feeling?"

"Just perfect, bully-boys. What about you?"

At that time he was in the service of a gentleman, looking after his garden and in winter keeping watch over the empty house. When speaking of that time, Ali would say, "I was the estate manager," but he would be corrected by others who said, "You were a servant." When he retorted, "Well then, I was a servant—what of it?" No one could say anything back. He would go on: "Is there any trade I haven't turned my hand to? I've cleaned toilets, and I've got rid of people like you. God give me strength!"

But one day Fındık Ali received a sound beating from a fisherman in the middle of the shopping street. After that things suddenly changed for him. Only when he had knocked back a gallon of wine was he able to recover his old form; only then did he start hurling curses at religion, faith, women, and holy books.

Some time later he suddenly disappeared. He was not seen in the village for years.

It was a very cold April. The rain fell endlessly, and great torrents flowed down the little slopes into the sea. In order to be able to be as cheerful as

5. On October 19, 1922, following the Armistice of Mudanya between the Turkish nationalists and the Allied powers, Refet Pasha, appointed military governor of Eastern Thrace with his headquarters in Istanbul, entered the Ottoman capital, to a tumultuous welcome from the Turkish population, to establish the rule of the Ankara government there. The last Ottoman sultan fled the country on November 16.

barefooted people, those who had scarves around their necks and rubber-soled shoes on their feet were rushing to the cinemas of the great city.

One evening, as the northeast wind licked the tops of the wisterias and blew on up toward the pinewoods, I saw the stars. The road was full of a pervasive fragrance of earth and daisies, and the stars were very close. A white cat passed across the darkness between the two houses.

Silence and light seeped out through the oilcloth curtains. People were not asleep; they were still reading, still knitting, still quietly talking.

When I dropped in at the fishermen's coffeehouse, "Madam Sultana" came up to me with an indulgent expression on her face.

"Sage tea?" she asked.

"Yes, sage tea," I said.

The sage tea was like the spring following the winters and autumns, the rains and the snows. Out of the blue- and red-spotted, supple-waisted, slender tea glass, carrying within it a warm climate, rose a steam which, impacting on my memory, conjured up the smell of a *mevlit** night, the fortieth day after a death, or something that might turn out to be inauspicious. The fishermen were talking about the fierceness of the northeast wind, about bread and damaged boats. Sultana was letting her hair, which she bleached with chamomile water, touch my nose. At this point I forgot the smell of the sage tea and asked, "Where's your daughter, Sultana?"

"Where do you expect Sultana's daughter to be? Where would she be? Oh what a skirt chaser you are!"

"No, Sultana . . . come on, tell me! Where's your daughter?"

It's as if I definitely want to say something, something nice. I try again: "Ah . . . I long to see that daughter of yours again; she comes to my mind with a fragrance like sage tea."

"You skirt chaser!"

I know she likes talking about her daughter's beauty.

Then she looks outside, at the wind and the stars, the boats and the shore, and pursues a searchlight that is scanning the sea. "Shall we play cards?" she asks.

What a nice thing it is to be able to talk while playing cards. When a trump is played this should be followed by a long chat. A game is a real game only when it's played in order to change the mood of a conversation.

"Sultana, where's your daughter?"

"She's gone, if you want to know. She's gone to live with that fellow again. He's sure to leave her again before long. Once more she'll land up in a whorehouse. And again I shall have to get her out of there and bring her back here."

"So she loves him then, Sultana?"

"Yes. No, of course she doesn't love him. Why should she? But the money . . . dresses, hats, evening gowns, fine shoes . . ."

"So for your daughter it's not the person."

"Of course it's not the person, what do you think. There are so many guys around her. But she likes glamour and luxury."

"Your daughter is really very lovely, Sultana."

"No more of that, you womanizer! Has that lovely ten gone past?"

"I don't know."

"Come on, you must know. You're going to catch me off my guard."

"Hey, Sultana, your daughter was beautiful, you know."

"Stop it now, I got confused. You moved in for the kill with two twos? Shame on you! I'm beaten. Shall I make you another sage tea? You can have it on me."

"Yes, do, Sultana. What a marvelous smell the sage tea has! Where do you get it from?"

Sultana came back with two tea glasses, and this time she started talking in Greek:

"At that time we used to rent and run the public baths. My husband was a terrible woman chaser. Is there any woman who can't be seduced by a handsome forty-year-old man? On the nights when he made me and Dimitra drunk, he would beat us. 'Whores!' he would say. 'I hear there's nothing you wouldn't do when I'm away. I'm told you receive men in the house.'

"It was true. He was doing it, so why shouldn't I? There was plenty of money then. My daughter was seventeen, and I was doing fine at thirty-four. What wonderful young men used to pass through my hands . . . so tender and fresh . . . I used to choose them in the baths. I still never take a man to bed with me without having seen his body. How much more so then, when a man's body would transport me to another world. It was the same with every Adam, and I was the only Eve. I would really have this sense of being Eve.

"Every Sunday I would get a beating from Fındık Ali. One day—a Sunday—he came back exhausted and depressed. He didn't go out for days. Winter had filled the island with Black Sea trawlermen who had migrated together with the big bonito fish. We had taken in a couple of them as lodgers. One day, Ali caught me with them.

"He looked at me without saying a word. It seems to me now as if he stared me in the face for a day and a night. It was such a long time! Then he went off toward the quay. He loosened the hawser of his boat. Then he came running back to the house, picked up his fish crate, and went off again. That was the last that was seen of him. We later heard that he had gone to the Hayırsız Islands.*

"He didn't come back for a full seven years. He would have his bread brought to him by fishermen who were going out from here. One day, in the late afternoon, remorse got the better of me. Ali was there on the chest of drawers, looking unbearably beautiful. This was a picture we had had taken while we were engaged. His hair had not been combed. His mustache was getting into his mouth. He looked as if he was cursing and swearing.

"The sea was like a millpond. There was no wind. I rushed out of the house in a frenzy. I could feel Ali as if he were inside me. I released the boat from its moorings and rowed for two hours until I was just off Yassıada.* By now it was dark. To the right, in the midst of the English ruins, I saw a faint light. I beached the boat and walked over in that direction. There were ten armed men around a fire. Ali was in the middle of them.

" 'Come on now, tell us,' they were saying. 'Where's the gold? We know you've found the treasure. Out with it!'

"Everyone was aware of the rumors that there was a treasure hidden somewhere on the island. People had assumed that the reason Ali had been living there all alone for years was that he was looking for this treasure. Greek fishermen had secretly spread the word around that Ali had discovered the treasure. To tell you the truth, this was one reason why I had gone to look for him that night. If he had indeed found it, why was he still living there? We could buy a small flat in Beyoğlu.* We could take life easy, and go to the cinema every night.

" 'Honest to God, boys, I don't know, I swear I don't!' Ali was saying.

"They were punching and cuffing him. At every blow he would stagger and fall to the ground. But it was impossible not to sense something in his manner that hinted that he had found the treasure and wasn't telling.

" 'If I found it wouldn't I tell you?'

" 'No, you wouldn't, you son of a bitch.'

"They were pulling his feet close to the fire, and I could hear a sizzling noise. One of them was setting his hair alight with matches, and another was putting out the flames with seawater. This interrogation went on for hours. At first Ali just swore that he didn't know anything. He would say nothing but, 'If I knew do you think I wouldn't tell you?' Then he stopped talking altogether. He just howled. I was frozen with fear and horror and couldn't move from where I was. Toward morning a young man with a beard had had enough. He pressed a piece of red-hot wood to Ali's face twice. The others walked off toward their boats. Now the two of them were left alone. 'You're going to tell me, do you hear?' said the young man. 'You're going to tell me!'

"Ali was groaning. He tried to stand up, but he fell down again. The man helped him up, and they set off toward one of the ruined buildings. Fifteen or twenty minutes later the man emerged from the ruins alone. I didn't see his face. He walked quickly away. Shortly afterward I heard the chugging sound of a motorboat.

"I rushed over to the ruins and found Ali lying dead in a hollow. The knife that had been stuck in his chest had been twisted in another direction before being pulled out, leaving a great gaping wound."

"Define Arayıcıları"
    Vakit, May 4, 1939
"Bir Define Arayıcısı"
    Varlık, XII/193, July 15, 1941
    Şahmerdan, 1940

The Kingdom

Translated by Celia Kerslake

ALİ RIZA BROUGHT THE BOAT TO SHORE on Kaşıkadası* and pulled it up onto the pebbly beach. Then he sat down cross-legged alongside the prow of the boat. For a long time he thought about some rather important things. I say "important," but this is nothing but a preconception on my part. It makes no difference whether it is right or not. How can we know whether a person is thinking about important or stupid things, when even he himself cannot make such a judgment?

He said to himself, "Hey, what the hell am I waiting for? I'll fetch the boys and come and settle here like a watchman. What could anyone say against it?"

He made this observation not in his head but shouting at the top of his voice. Before getting up he thought a bit more. "Well, what could anyone possibly say?"

Pushing the boat out with all his might, he sprang into it with the agility of a rubber ball.

Because he was going to take a customer to catch blue fish that evening, he had come here to collect a supply of bait. The shores of Kaşıkadası are full of needlefish, which are about as thick as a man's wrist, half a meter in length, and have purple bones. He hadn't brought anyone with him, because both his sons were working at other jobs. Needlefish couldn't really be caught single-handed, but Rıza had found a way around this. He had held the fishing line between his teeth as he rowed slowly along, and his rotten

A somewhat different version of this story is part of the novella entitled *"The Source of Livelihood"—A Fishing Boat*, translated by Nilüfer Mizanoğlu Reddy in this volume.

teeth, being even more sensitive than his fingers, had felt when a fish got caught. He had then let go of the oars and, with the fishing line now in his hands, had made the needlefish leap and dance over the sun-sparkling sea as he brought it up to the gunwale of the boat. He had put the little needlefish, which he was going to fry that evening, into a bucket, and the rest he had flung under the floorboards of the boat, to be used as bait for the blue fish. There they had flipped back into life once or twice, and Ali Rıza, as if in imitation of them, had stamped his bare feet on the floorboards saying, "Shut up, you! Drop dead!" Then he had put the line between his teeth and grasped the oars again.

Now, having jumped quickly back into the boat, he rowed as fast as he could to Burgaz* and pulled up alongside the quay which was used for unloading coal. He dropped anchor, and fastened a rope from the boat's seat to the iron ring on the quay. He set off home. Home, for Ali Rıza and his two sons, was the basement of a house. It had a sour smell of food and people. The walls were covered with the elongated ghosts of slaughtered mosquitoes and crushed bedbugs. What's more, there were damp streaks and patches all over the place. There were all sorts of things in that basement: a broken table, two earthenware jugs, a saw, a quilt, a brazier, a glass carafe, a big wine bottle, a hookah tube, a lead pipe, a broken fishing net, and nine or ten sardine boxes. Without wasting any time he swiftly gathered them all up. Then he picked up a piece of brand-new rush matting which had been tucked away in a corner, covered in the remains of a woman's yellow skirt. He heaped all the things he had collected, except for the table, onto this mat, and rolled it up. Then he bound up the two ends with a thick rope, hoisted the package onto his back, and was ready to leave. Just as he was going out through the door he suddenly turned back, saying, "Damn it, I forgot the lamp."

And indeed, a large and elegant lamp, quite out of place in a basement, was standing alone on the broken table, all too conspicuous now that the welter of objects had disappeared. "How blind can you be!" exclaimed Ali Rıza. "When you don't see something you just don't see it."

Having picked up the lamp with one hand and the mat with the other he stopped again. Without putting anything down, he gave the broken table a kick, uttering an obscene curse against the religion of its owner.

He had pulled the door of the basement half-shut with his foot, and was hurrying along. He hadn't gone so much as a hundred meters when he met a bandy-legged fisherman coming toward him with a tray of fish in his hand.

"Hi there, Ali Rıza," he said. "I thought you hadn't got a piece of rush matting in the entire world?"

"Like you not having a table," retorted Ali Rıza.

"I don't know what you mean, mate."

Without bothering to answer, Ali Rıza walked on. He had been badly stung by the fisherman's words, because they reminded him of why he had burnt his old piece of matting.

One evening (last year, probably), when he had had a few too many, his mates had said, "There's going to be a war, Ali Rıza."

He had replied, "What does it matter? After all, I haven't got so much as a piece of rush matting in the entire world—nothing that could get burned. And I'm sixty years old—it doesn't bother me. The whole world can burn to ashes for all I care!"

When he came home the dirty piece of matting, filched from the *gazino** up the hill, which had given him faithful service for so many years, seemed to trip him up at every step. Without further ado he dragged it outside, poured a few drops of paraffin on it, and set it alight just in front of the house. As the night watchmen's whistles called out to one another on that blustery night, the blaze could easily have set the whole neighborhood on fire. When the flames were at their fiercest he had jumped to and fro over them, just as the unbelievers did at the Feast of St. John.* The priest of the neighboring church had been perturbed by the sight of this strange ritual, which he had observed from his window as he lit his last cigarette before retiring for the night. Crossing himself several times, he had hurried to join his wife—that wife who, whenever he took her in his arms, made him wonder what it was about her that had induced him to give up his despotism for her sake.

At last Rıza arrived at Kaşıkadası with his belongings. He found that Hrant, the previous watchman of the island, had left a table, two chairs, and a worn-out rug in the pigsties. These were quite a discovery for Ali Rıza, who took them out carefully. Hrant had also left behind an unframed picture of a spring landscape. Rıza took this, too, cleaned the cobwebs off it, then stood back and looked at it. He liked it.

The floor of one of the two rooms in the little stone building below was completely hidden under a layer of corks, nails, and fishing tackle. He sorted through all these bits and pieces one by one in the hope of finding something useful, but they were all moldy, broken, and of no use. So he tipped them all into the sea. Then he scrubbed the floor of the room for hours, fetching water from the sea nearby. He arranged his furniture, putting everything in its proper place, and hung the picture opposite the window. Then, going outside the door, he stood and looked at this room, which he had created with his own hands, as if he were looking at a painting. He smiled with unalloyed delight, and said to himself, "Now you can light a cigarette, damm it. You deserve it!"

Evening was falling. The seagulls were flocking back to the rocks. The cormorants, perched on the rocks, were gazing into the sunset in a poetic, melancholy fashion, while the heron, proud and imperious in its one-legged stance, was thinking majestic thoughts as if surveying its kingdom.

Ali Rıza flung a stone in the direction of the heron, which rose slightly into the air and flew with some difficulty to another rock. Its wings flopped, and it stayed where it was.

"Damned son of a bitch," said Ali Rıza, "I'm king here now!"

He sprang into his boat like a ball and went to collect his sons from the shops where they were working. He sat them in the boat and brought them to his kingdom. In the spotlessly clean room, smelling only of the sea, and with a beautiful picture of spring on the wall, the boys slept as they had never slept before, and had cool, refreshing dreams.

"Krallık"
Şahmerdan, 1940

The Man with the Bestial Smile

Translated by Celia Kerslake

IN FRONT OF THE WOODEN HOUSE there are a plum tree, a trellised vine, campanulas, and gladioli. Two sisters and two brothers live there. It must be over ten years since their parents died. It's more than ten years since I came to this village, but I haven't got to know them. The girls make cotton print dresses for housemaids and elderly nannies and knit sweaters for them; in the summer they become quite cheerful, and even sing sometimes. One of the brothers works as a cobbler, assisting the master who trained him. He's a quiet, melancholy man who keeps to himself. He lives in the village so unobtrusively that when, one summer, he broke his leg and had to spend two months in the hospital, no one even noticed his absence. In fact, it seemed to me that even his master, the cobbler who comes past in the mornings to collect the shoes that people have put outside their front doors to be mended, was not aware of his disappearance. The other brother is even less noticeable in the village. If he were to be out of sight for two years, rather than two months, I don't think even his own sisters would notice.

This lad intrigues me. He always has a smile on his face. At first this smile, which reveals his strong, white teeth, seems to express innocence and decency, but one look at his eyes tells you that it's actually a sign of stupidity. Indeed, this may be deduced from the very fact that a slight smile is there all the time. The broad grin that displays his perfect teeth is something he generally doesn't let anyone see; indeed, I don't think he tends to look people in the face at all. But for some reason he has a fondness for me. He shows me his teeth, and makes me feel pity for his stupidity. He belongs to the poorest family in the village. I see how youngsters from families such as this work desperately in order to keep the wolf from the door, especially in winter.

The summer is a great thing for them. Houses are rented out, and there's more work to be had. When the terrible winter makes way for gramophones, radios, and scantily clad women, these families, too, join in the general merriment. They don't have much choice but to join in, because if the people who have moved into their rented-out rooms don't have a radio they will certainly have a little gramophone; if they don't, there is bound to be a young woman among them who sings European songs. Merriment seems to be an infection that men catch from young women.

I don't say this lad doesn't work at all. I see him drawing water from the well for the family and the tenants. Because he has his back to me on these occasions I can't see it, but that foolish smile must be on his lips all the time. It's impossible to imagine him any other way. In the mornings he sweeps the little garden in front of the house. For the first ten minutes or so he applies his rough twig broom quite lightly, but then he goes wild and hits the ground with it in a frenzy, enveloping the garden in a cloud of dust. Although our houses are very close to each other I can't see his face through this dust cloud, but I think to myself, "He must have a crazed look on his face." That's how I guess it must be. And I imagine that that stupid smile of his must suddenly have taken on a bestial quality. Since this smile is never absent from his lips I assume that it won't go away even at moments when he is angry, fed up, or on edge. This must be a bestial smile.

I had assumed he never had a job, but neither was he ever to be seen in the places where the unemployed would spend their time. I never saw him at a coffeehouse or encountered him among the jobless men stretched out asleep in the meadows. Nor was he in the habit of strolling along the beach.

There was a time when I was playing truant from the coffeehouses, was tired of boats, the sea, and fishing, and found that playing cards just made me edgy. So I would go up into the pinewoods, doze off, think about the people I loved, and dream about things I was going to do; I would love, be loved, get rich, sink into poverty, read books, and write poems to my beloved. At these times I began to come across him often in the pinewoods. I would be sitting under a pine tree, gazing out to sea, and daydreaming, when suddenly I would hear a rustling sound. I would become all eyes and ears, wondering what it was, and would see a shadow going past in the distance, swaying as it went. He would be walking briskly, as if returning from work.

He would be too far away for me to call out and ask, but I would think to myself, "What is this guy doing here?" These encounters would happen particularly often at weekends.

One day I spotted him under a pine tree. On his face there was still that smile, but also something like anger. "That's it," I said to myself. "This is just what he's like when he sweeps the garden furiously." I looked carefully. No, there was nothing in his foolish smile apart from a certain sadness. I gave him a cigarette and asked if he had been for a swim. In broken Turkish, and showing his white teeth, he said, "Two weeks, then I going to fall into the sea."

We talked a bit more. He laughed as stupid children do. He didn't light the cigarette I had given him.

Saying, "Matches," he thrust a large, pale, thick hand with stubby fingers and turned-in nails into the pocket of his jacket. He put the cigarette into his inside pocket, and stretched himself out under the pine tree.

"Sleeping," he said.

I had been down to the sea for a dip, and my way back would take me under the tree where he had been lying. I saw that he had got up and was walking ahead of me. He's a short man, and it seemed to me that there was a great distance between his shoulders and his head. Was it his head that was big, or was his neck unusually long, or did his shoulders droop particularly low? I think it was a bit of all of these. His head was large and rather flat. His chin was stiff and had no dimple; it gave one the feeling that the head couldn't turn left or right, and in fact I have never seen him turn it. His shoulders were normal, but drooping. He was walking with a forward swaying motion, almost bouncing along, moving his arms very little. There was something about this gait that suggested he was keeping time with a beat, but he was not singing. Perhaps he was humming a song in his head, who can say?

Summer hadn't yet fully arrived, and the influx of outsiders into the village had not grown beyond a trickle. He would lie smiling under the pine trees, looking as if he was waiting for something. I was curious. My curiosity about this man went on for years. I noticed that, when a ferry came in, he would be surveying the quay intently from a distance, through the gaps between buildings. I saw that on Sundays he became what could only be described as happy, with joy seeming to well up inside him. As for that bestial smile that I had imagined, I simply couldn't catch it on his face at any time.

One day in the middle of summer a friend and I were making our way up to the pinewoods in the midday heat. We had brought our lunch and a rug with us, and there was a stray dog following us. We ate our lunch, fed the dog, then lay down and went to sleep. At a point when I was still half asleep I heard a fearsome growling from the dog, which was lying beside me. Wondering what was going on, I woke up fully. The dog was looking in a particular direction as it growled, and was making movements as if preparing to attack.

"Catch it, Sarı!" I said.

The dog and I walked over toward a grove of quivering strawberry trees. Suddenly someone sprang up from the undergrowth. When he saw me, fear flashed across the man's face. His lips parted. I saw a man smiling like an animal, whose teeth reminded me of those of a hyena, which I have never seen. It was he. He was smiling, but this was a hideous, bestial smile. He approached to within three paces of me, and then took one further step. I moved back. His mouth had gone dry. The area around the edges of his large, now pursed lips was covered with extended strands of dried spittle. As he could not breathe through his mouth, his nostrils were pulsating, and one of his cheeks kept twitching just below the eye.

"Hey, what's going on?" I asked.

He moved off, muttering something or other. As he did so he gave the dog such a smile that it backed away.

Completely mystified, and full of misgivings, I stepped back and sat down where I had been before. A strange distress, or perhaps fear, had taken hold of me. Had he killed someone? This was the face of a man who had killed, or who wanted to kill. Or was he going to set a house or a village on fire? Or to attack anyone he encountered in the streets, biting women and children? Or was he the sleepless maniac who wanted to kill people who were asleep?

After only about ten minutes he appeared again. I was lost in thought, speculating about him. He didn't stop in front me, but continued on his way. When he looked in my direction I saw that his face had returned to normal. He must have wiped his lips, which were no longer white around the edges.

The saliva had returned to his mouth. His pursed black lips had relaxed and regained their pink color. He smiled naively, stupidly.

Making a twisting motion with my index finger and pointing to his head, I said, "Are you a bit crazy?"

"No, no," he replied, shaking his head violently from side to side. He came up to me in a friendly manner, and grasped my arm. We went to the thicket where he had been before.

"Look," he said.

I looked, and saw a couple lying under a pine tree. The girl had gone to sleep on the man's arm. The man was gazing up at the clouds flitting across the sky, and smoking a cigarette. We looked at them for a while. Then we started walking back to where we had come from. He was scrutinizing me in a way that I could almost call intelligent, trying to find out whether or not I thought he was right.

"I haven't got a wife. That one's beautiful," he said.

Almost imperceptibly, a white tongue darted around his lips. Then, apparently, he heard something; he raised his long head and stopped as though listening. His eyes had taken on that bestial look again. He must have seen another couple in the distance. With furtive steps and head held down, he walked off in that direction.

"Hayvanca Gülen Adam"
    Varlık, XIV/312, July 1946
    Lüzumsuz Adam, 1948

Life Outside the City Walls

Translated by Celia Kerslake

GETTING OUT OF THE CITY is like escaping from yourself. Our memories, our passions, our friendships, our infidelities, the good and the bad things in us, our wretchedness, and our shame are all left behind in the city. Here we're surrounded by trees, fruit, vegetables, and animals. Look, there are walnut, fig, mulberry, plum, and terebinth trees . . . and squash, cucumbers, maize, and sunflowers . . . and dark, yellow, red, fat, thin, rich soil.

Lie down in the shade of the walnut trees, and tell your troubles to get lost! Go to sleep. Sleep as long as the flies crawling round the edges of your mouth will let you. Even outside the city the heat is scorching. What an inferno it must be back there, with only the treeless blocks of flats for company.

Escaping from the city doesn't mean escaping from history. In the walls of Istanbul,[1] which stretch away to your right, history, in the form of crumbled ruins, is visible at every step. The towers have long since collapsed into each other, the battlements have disintegrated, the palaces collapsed, and the roads along the walls are overgrown with thistles and hemlock. The asphalt highway speeds us from one gate to another, but it's so treeless, and the sun burns down so fiercely.

Is everything outside the walls good, or is it that I have changed? Every person, every animal, every object here seems to have come straight out of a fairy tale.

---

1. The city walls that figure in this story are the land walls on the western edge of the old city, running from the Golden Horn in the north to the Sea of Marmara* in the south. The Byzantine Emperor Theodosius II built them in the fifth century. In this story the narrator is traveling northward along the middle section of the walls.

I saw an old witch herding the fairies' sheep. She was looking at me, displaying two horrible gray teeth. I tried to take a photo of her.

"I won't have my picture taken unless you pay me twenty-five kuruş."

"Well, that's not bad! You might have asked for even more. They don't even pull teeth out for twenty-five kuruş. But come now, don't be difficult; let's agree on five kuruş for me to take a picture of you. Everyone else offers me money to take pictures of them, and I refuse."

"No way."

"But I'll snap you anyway."

She turned her back on me.

"Look, even the sheep know they're being photographed, and they're looking at the camera."

"Why do you take any notice of the sheep? They're animals; they don't understand about money.

"So you do, do you?"

"At Mevlanakapısı* the *simit*s* are twenty-five kuruş."

A man had come and joined me, and was sharing my amusement. He had slanting eyes and a sparse beard, and he spoke with a Tatar accent. As soon as we had left the delightful shepherd-witch alone with her sheep, I turned round to see whether they had disappeared. They had.

Now, as I walked on with Şehreminli[2] Mehmet Ali, the leather-scraper, he was saying, "Women? God preserve us from them! Mine pushed off and left me. I earn twenty lira a week. She said it wasn't enough for her. What does anyone want with a young wife, anyway? Now I've found an old witch like the one that was here just now, and we live together."

"Without getting married?"

"Well, I haven't divorced the other one, have I? I've no idea where she is. Anyway, even if I was divorced I still wouldn't have married this one. I'd be afraid that when we got married she too would push off. As long as we don't marry she lives every day in the hope of getting married, doesn't she? That hope keeps women's minds off other things."

"Is it much further to Topkapı*?"

"No, it'll take about half an hour. This is Silivrikapısı,* then comes

2. The epithet indicates that the man is from Şehremini, a district just inside the city walls, near Topkapı.

Mevlanakapısı, and then Topkapı. As soon as you go through the wall there, you'll find the tram."

To our right the walls were pressing down on each other. If you want to watch the lizards playing hide-and-seek among the cracks, there's no need to go right up to them. The lizards have grown so big that, believe it or not, I've seen ones that are a meter long. If you don't believe me, ask Mehmet Reis,* who is sitting here in the shade, keeping watch over the fig trees between Silivrikapısı and Yedikule.*

Mehmet Reis seemed to have sprung like a live character from the pages of one of those two wonderful novels by dear Osman Cemal, *The Gypsies* and *Big Fatma*.[3]

"This is Elekçi Baba,* and this one is Bağdadi Baba.* The story goes that the Conqueror of Baghdad was very upset that Baghdad just wouldn't fall. He would roam about in disguise outside the walls of Istanbul.[4] One day, while he was wandering like this, he came across an old man sitting in the shade of a terebinth tree. The old man said, 'Don't worry, Your Majesty, Baghdad has just fallen!'

"The sultan, annoyed at having been recognized, and also by the old man's talking as if he had received a wireless message, said, 'How should you know, old fellow?'

"Bağdadi Baba replied, 'Mount on my back, Your Majesty, and arrange for a grave to be dug here by the time we return.'

"The sultan sprang on to Bağdadi Baba's back, and in the twinkling of an eye they were at the gates of Baghdad. When the sultan saw his own troops pouring through the gates of Baghdad he was greatly relieved. In a twinkling they were back at Silivrikapısı, where the old man sat down in the shade of the terebinth tree and gave up his spirit."

"What about Elekçi Baba?"

---

3. Osman Cemal Kaygılı (1890–1945), a popular Turkish novelist and short story writer who wrote about the urban poor and fringe communities like the Gypsies.

4. This does not conform to the historical facts. On each of the two occasions when Baghdad was captured by the Ottomans (Süleyman the Magnificent in 1534 and Murad IV in 1638), the sultan had led the campaign in person and was present at the successful conclusion of the siege. Roaming about the capital incognito was a well-known habit of Murad IV in the 1630s.

"I don't know the story about him. But there used to be a *türbe*[5] here. It was destroyed in a fire. When you went inside there were two sieves hanging there. You would recite the *fatiha*,* and say what your problem was. If it was something that was going to come right, the sieves would start to whirl round."

The mulberry-sellers on their way from the Şehit Nizam orchards and the Kozluk mulberry groves stop for a rest at the coffeehouse beside Bağdadi Baba's grave, before taking their trays piled high with mulberries into the city districts inside the walls. One of them, a young man, said, "Help yourself, brother! Eat as many as you like! Don't worry—it's not taking food out of the mouths of orphans. And take a picture of us too, so you'll have something to remember us by."

Another one said, "These mulberries are from the Şehit Nizam orchards. This year the sea breeze blew a lot, and the fruit didn't ripen. It was ruined! This fruit needs an offshore breeze, a northeasterly. If the sea breeze blows you can say good-bye to any profit. As you see, these mulberries haven't got any taste."

Şehreminli Mehmet Ali had vanished without a sound, as if able to transport himself miraculously from one place to another. Old Mehmet Reis, who had once been the leader of a brigade of firefighters, showed us the huge mace at Silivrikapısı, which had belonged to İdris, a soldier in the army of Mehmed the Conqueror. He said it was so heavy that even three people together couldn't move it from where it lay. But when İdris the Janissary grasped it, he would rush with it into the midst of hundreds of men, and use it with devastating effect.

Next he showed us the gigantic fishbone suspended from hooks on the wall of Silivrikapısı, which had been there since Byzantine times. And then he took us to the Seven Martyrs—seven graves side by side.

"Who are the people buried here, Mehmet Reis?"

"They're said to have been Albanian chieftains who rebelled against the sultan."

---

5. A *türbe* is a small, usually polygonal, building erected over the tomb of an important person. The *türbe* at Silivrikapısı of the person more commonly known as "Elekçi Dede," and thought to have been the standard-bearer of Mehmed II, did indeed burn down in 1925. The word *elek* means "sieve."

I saw that on one of the tombstones there was the inscription: "Here lies the severed head of the famous Tepedelenli Ali Pasha, former Governor of Janina, who for more than thirty years ruled unchallenged in Albania." [6]

Beside him lies his son, Veli Pasha, and beyond him his grandsons. The severed heads of all of them are there.

But we'll turn back to the men of our own day, and listen to Mehmet Reis telling his life story.

"You ask what I did for a living? It's a long story. What I was actually trained in was quiltmaking. But I was young and wild, and soon began to live the life of a tough guy."

"How old are you, Mehmet Reis?"

"Over sixty-five."

"*Maşallah!** No one would think it."

"I joined a fire brigade, and also did upholstery and quiltmaking jobs. One day I suddenly found I'd got involved in tobacco smuggling. Of course, you mustn't imagine me like I am now, a wheezing old cart horse. My hands and feet were good for something then. We would just head off for İzmit,* or İznik,* or Karamürsel.* We would go into some Greek village and spend days just eating, drinking, and sleeping. Then we would pack what was left of the tobacco into our saddlebags. It was lovely stuff, that tobacco—all zigzagged, and silky as a girl's hair. We would go from one village to another. There was a fellow from Herzegovina, called Arab Muhittin, may God rest his soul. My, there was a daring smuggler for you, a lad who didn't know what fear was! We would load the stuff into boats, and take it to Anaçıpay,* or Ayastefanos,* or Bakırköy.* At night we would send word to our friends, and they would immediately come to meet us. Then we would transfer the stuff, and as soon as we got to Silivrikapısı we would chuck the saddlebags into the ditch beside the city wall. We would take up our positions and start

6. Tepedelenli Ali Pasha (1744–1822) became famous in Europe as Ali Pasha of Janina. Although nominally an Ottoman-appointed governor, he took advantage of the weakness of Ottoman central authority at that period to carve out for himself a virtually independent principality in the western Balkans. When the government eventually took steps to subjugate him he reacted defiantly, making an alliance with the Greek rebels and seeking to provoke revolts elsewhere. He was killed in a final confrontation with Ottoman troops, and his head was sent back to the capital.

fighting with the guards, with guns or knives. It always ended up with them running away. Oh, those were the days! You could get a flagon of raki for four kuruş. We used to drink the devilish stuff by the tankful!"

Mehmet Reis was so absorbed in his memories that he let the Villager* cigarette he was holding burn his trousers.

"God sees anything that burns,[7] but I've seen it first!" he said.

With his gnarled fingers he smothered the burning spot on his trousers, and went on: "Then the Balkan War[8] broke out. After that I went to Çanakkale,* and all around Baghdad and Basra.[9] I came back to find I'd become a wheezing old cart horse. You should have seen the grand houses I furnished, my son! There was İbrahim Pasha's, and Ethem Pasha's and Enver Pasha's.[10] They've all burned down and gone, of course. In later years I became an offal-seller. But anyway, God gave me a good son, and thanks to him I get enough to eat, and to smoke as well, without having to beg from anyone."

"Where are you from, Mehmet Reis?"

"I was born and grew up in Silivrikapısı."

When we left Mehmet Reis under the terebinth tree beside Bağdadi Baba's grave, he, too, vanished.

Now we were in the space within the walls themselves, neither inside nor outside them. We were standing between the two gates, in front of a cartmaker's shop. One cart was being repaired, another had been painted and was being left to dry. Such beautiful pictures had been painted on the side of the cart—a stall piled high with watermelons, a village in the distance, a rising moon, the setting sun, fields of crops, two sunflowers swaying in the wind, a lamb, a donkey foal, ducks bathing in a stream, a bunch of roses. Carters and greengrocers both share this passion for pictures.

7. In Turkish, the verb "to burn" is also used to express human pain or distress. The normal meaning of the proverb on which Mehmet Reis is punning would thus be "God has pity on anyone in distress."

8. The Balkan War of 1912–1913 was the penultimate disaster for the Ottoman Empire. Initiated by Montenegro, Serbia, Bulgaria, and Greece, it resulted in the loss of almost all of the remaining Ottoman possessions in Europe.

9. This sentence presumably refers to Mehmet Reis's service in campaigns of World War I.

10. The three men mentioned were all Ottoman generals.

"How much do they ask for painting these pictures on a cart?" I asked the cart-repairer.

"Forty lira. But that's not the important thing, sir. What you should be asking is 'Who does these?' "

"These what?"

"These pictures!"

Without waiting for me to ask, he started explaining: "The person who does them is a twelve-year-old boy. He does them out of his head, sir. If you think it's a matter of looking at something and copying it—no way! I swear it all comes out of his head. They say he was apprenticed to a cart-painter at the age of eight. Four years later his master packed up his bags and headed off back to his hometown, saying 'I'm leaving behind me here a painter worthy of Istanbul. I can't work in a place where there's someone I can't compete with.' "

"Wow, I've got to see this painter!" I said.

"I'm afraid you're out of luck. Every carter in town wants to get hold of him to do the pictures on his cart. If he's here one day he's in Zeyrek* the next, and Edirnekapı* the day after that. He paints a cart a day, sir, a whole cart."

"How much does he get for it?"

"Forty lira!"

I feel I have a duty to pass on this message to those of our artists who work with paint: If any of them are gifted enough to compete with twelve-year-old Hasan, forty lira can be earned in one day by painting a cart. If they think decorating carts is beneath them, and prefer to go on holding exhibitions, that's up to them. I've said my piece, and I can't be blamed if they don't listen!

"This kid amazes me," said the cartmaker. "He's really incredible. He only has to narrow his eyes a bit and think for a moment, and he produces a beautiful scene for you, the likes of which you can't find anywhere in our mulberry villages."

As we were making our way from Silivrikapısı to Mevlanakapısı, an offshore breeze came up, and with it Şehreminli Mehmet Ali, who had earlier vanished, reappeared. He comes and goes like the wind, this fellow! He took us up on to the broad top of the walls, and we walked over to a group of three or four tents.

We could see people sitting in and around the tents, working bellows, tinning saucepans, hammering copper trays, or making tambourines. Others were dancing or singing. Others still were stretched out full length on the ground, gazing up at the sky, daydreaming. Overhead sparrow hawks and falcons hovered and aircraft droned. Gramophone music was blaring from one of the tents. A girl walked past, her plump hips swaying. Her lips were wet, soft, thick, and fleshy, her skin was the color of ripe wheat, and the look in her eyes was that of a woman full of sexuality and full of passion.

Yes, now we were with the gypsies. Two newlyweds were lying in a tent of their own, daydreaming. Gold-dipped copper bangles jingled on the girl's wrists.

"We're tinkers," said a tall young lad. "We go from house to house, collecting copper pots and pans to be retinned. When harvest time comes we work in the threshing grounds. At the first sign of cold weather we move off to Edirne and round there."

They didn't say much, or laugh much, either. Nor did the young kids follow us around saying, "Five kuruş, five kuruş! Please, mister, forty para!" Because they were all busy working—men, women, and children. The bath-bowls, frying pans, and saucepans gleamed as sand and tin were poured onto their heated surfaces. The only people not working were the couple who had obviously just got married in the last few days. The boy was very young, and the girl was wearing a silver belt around her waist. They were playing a gramophone and gazing into each other's eyes. There were also some tiny children belly dancing in the open air. And a woman was trying to breast-feed her child. She kept pushing her nipple, which was the size of a black mulberry, into the baby's mouth and taking it out again. The child itself was as dark as a black mulberry.

"Sur Dışında Hayat"
    Yedigün, 755, August 24, 1947
    Havuz Başı, 1952

The Stelyanos Hrisopulos

Translated by Nermin Menemencioğlu

WINTER CAME TO THE SHORES of the island with the southwesterly winds. There are no houses to the southwest, where the arbutus and pine trees meet. There are huge, savage rocks, strange birds, and deep precipices. When the southwest wind blew beyond Kalpazanlar* Rocks, the houses to the northeast came quietly to life. The summer residents were gone. The bathhouses had been taken down, and the mansions stood sulking, deserted. Here and there small boats had been pulled ashore. This was the time for fishing. The big motorboats were snorting up to the shore, and all day long the tuna and the bonito swam round and round the island. Endlessly the big boats carried fish to the big city, and then a little money, a couple of sacks of flour, a few kilos of meat back to the island.

That year the fish had been scarce, as the winter had been severe. Even the priest, intent upon confessions, was forced to reflect on the matter of a few fish and harsh winter.

Since early morning Stelyanos had been preparing his *çapari.** The nets he had repaired were long since ruined, the lines he had prepared during the summer were tangled up, the boat's paint had flaked off, the house was in complete disorder. There were no fish this year. The summer residents had not spent money as freely as in previous years. Even their fish had been bought from other fishermen. They had been of no use to him. And Trifon got sick as the winter began. Medication was expensive on the island. To go to the city was a big problem. Trifon wasn't going to school. Since he taught himself at home, his books and notebooks cost a bit of money.

Stelyanos is going fishing tomorrow. He makes sure the turkey feathers of the *çapari* are pointing right, ties up the traces where they have snapped, changes hooks that have gone rusty. Plenty of fish tomorrow, and he could buy a little paraffin, a little sugar, a pair of trousers and a sweater for Trifon, maybe a cap for himself. If only he could buy something for the house, bring a little gift to Trifon, say, a book of stories about fishermen or a large picture of a ship that he could hang up in the small room where Trifon slept.

Stelyanos goes fishing in the evening. Heaven knows when he will be back. Trifon falls asleep waiting for his grandfather. He is dreaming: there is a ship in front of a rock. Is Trifon on board the ship, or is he standing on the rock? A tremendous wave that looks as though it might at any moment hurl the ship against the rock is approaching. Then, it is not clear how this happens, it does hit against the ship. The distance, a meter or so, between the ship and the rock always seems about to grow less but it doesn't, nor does it grow greater.

While this dream was in progress, Stelyanos returned. The wind, as he came in, played havoc with the room. A photograph or two fell from their places. The lace fluttered.

"Were you asleep, Trifon?"

"Yes, I was. Any fish, Grandpa?"

"No. It's as if the whole big sea was empty."

"Why, I wonder?"

"There must be some monster about, Trifon. Why else would there be no fish at this time of year?"

"Grandpa, did you ever see a monster?"

Stelyanos, whenever he asked himself that question, was not so sure. But when he was asked about it by others, he was so full of monster stories, had seen so many times, at midnight, enormous creatures flash angrily across the phosphorescent surface of the dark waters. The stories and realities got mixed up a little, then, the creatures that peopled his imagination and memory became like the ones that lived in the sea.

What, at any rate, was so mysterious as the sea? Who knows what lovely, beautiful fish, what violent, unimaginable monsters there were in the depths that lines and nets could not reach.

"I did, Trifon. One winter, we were out for tuna, and we'd heard there was a monster prowling about our sea mark—a so-called cotton fish. They say the young of this kind weigh twenty, twenty-five kilos. The big ones swallow their young at the sign of danger, they vomit them afterward. Think of the size, Trifon! Rüstem Çavuş* caught one that evening. Those of us in the other boats lined up around him. It was stark white, just like cotton. But the mouth, you should have seen it! Maybe as big as this door, it was. And no teeth. When Rüstem Çavuş stuck his knife into its belly, we found four live young fish inside. They say if you catch only the young, the sea becomes turbulent, and all the cotton fish attack the boats and capsize them. That evening we didn't wait for that to happen, we fled. Then another evening ..."

The stories followed one another. Feeling a vague terror, Trifon fell asleep again.

The winter can be as hard and long as it takes, the fish may be few, still summer will rear its head above all privations and come to those who wait for it.

Stelyanos Hrisopulos was the owner of a small house covered with earthen plaster. Summer vacationers rented the two upstairs rooms. Stelyanos was busy in the basement room, three steps below street level, repairing his nets. The ceiling was higher than a man's height, but the darkness in the little room seemed to force one to bend, and gave a blurred, dreamlike quality to the yellowing snapshots taken in front of churches, along sea shores, among fishnets, and on board fishing boats. Looking at them, Stelyanos saw the eldest daughter of the Hrisopulos family pulling at the oars with the air of an empress, little Trifon laughing, his bright teeth gleaming; and he loved the friendly twilight, which swept away all ugliness. All in all, with its many dead, and its two live members, the Hrisopulos family was a handsome family.

On a lace tablecloth fine enough to ruin the eyes of the young girl who made it, beside a miniature raki decanter whose red had flaked here and there, stood a small ship that Trifon had taken many days to build. Next to the ship there was a photograph of Yovana, Stelyanos's younger daughter and Trifon's mother. It had been four years since Yovana died. Trifon was now twelve. His photograph at eight, like the ship and the small fishnets on the table, dated from that year. It hung where a ten-year old might not reach it.

Stelyanos Hrisopulos's most remarkable feature was his neck. No other man's neck can be like that of a fisherman, a strange, dark column rising between his body and his head, bulging with nerves and sinews. Great was the effect of the wind and the sun on the wrinkled skin. This column, which gave a young fisherman's face its energy, life, and color, appears indestructible in all fishermen, so that no matter how old a fisherman and how wrinkled his skin, his head seems young and vigorous, his neck is straight and strong.

Stelyanos Hrisopulos knotted his nets and at the same time he sang a little song. His elder daughter had eloped nine years ago. His younger daughter had turned out more sensible, and she married and established a household. One winter, a wind cutting across the broad shoulders of his son-in-law had sunk his boat. He was rescued with difficulty, but pneumonia had turned this man, who was tall and sturdy like a plane tree, into a likeness of the thin summer lodgers who sometimes rented part of the house. Stavro had gone outdoors on the sixteenth day, and had died of the same disease on the twenty-fifth day. Stelyanos's younger daughter had not forgotten this young man with the huge arms and the stern look. She had died of tuberculosis. His elder son was in Greece; heaven knows what he was doing there. For four years now there had been no news of him. After Stelyanos's younger daughter died, he had no one left but Trifon.

The stern look, the neck of steel, the careless, unruly curls, Trifon got from his father. From his mother he got only her temperament. He had quick sudden bursts of joy. He had the laugh of robust people who have a way of bursting into laughter all of a sudden and taking people by surprise. Then his long Greek face turned almost round, the eyes grew tiny, the mouth with the pointed white teeth drew open like some sort of strange box. In the same way, sadness came to him suddenly. A word that might only make other children smirk would hurt him, bring tears. Stelyanos was knotting his net and singing a song, and at the same time he was thinking of little Trifon.

Thinking of Trifon, what could the grandfather do but smile? No gesture was as faint and imperceptible as this smile. No one could say of him that he was a man who had lost three dear ones. This smiling face was the face of the happiest of men. Perhaps a crook, thinking up some deal, would laugh like that. Perhaps fishermen, having rented their boats for forty kuruş an hour, might seem as thoroughly good-humored. Let no one disturb Stelyanos when he is thinking of Trifon. He was always thinking of Trifon, but more especially when making a net, spindle in hand, the boy's mischievous acts and sweet little jokes came to his mind. At other times, Trifon must not unfurl a sail, must not catch a cold, must not go out to sea in such weather. Trifon must not fall asleep under the pines. Trifon must not get into a fight with street children—these interdictions kept the old man patrolling the streets. Trifon was therefore very near now, somewhere. Not out sailing, or fishing, or swimming. Where then was Trifon?

Trifon was at the foot of the plane tree by the house, beside the chair with its straw seat. He was busy building a second ship. This was to be a ship that no twelve-year-old child had built before. It was to be the ship of a young man who, quite obviously, is going to be a sea captain. The ship of a man who is free and belongs to no country and is full of the desire to set sail, to go away. The ship of all that a man could remember or imagine—waves and storms and calm seas, or strange fish, or men that were like us and men that were altogether different. With this ship one could go down to the shore, one could tie a string to the flagmast at the stern, and the sails of the ship could fill with wind, and the owner of this ship, standing there as she sailed with the wind, might think of other lands and other seas.

"Are you there, Trifon?"

"I'm here!"

"Don't get lost now."

"I'm building a ship."

"What, again!"

"This one's not like the other. It's going to be very big. It will go fast, like the currents."

"And what's its name going to be, Trifon?"

"Its name?"

The boy plunged into thought. First his mother's name had come to mind. With Yovana on the tip of his tongue, he remained silent. If he uttered this name, phantoms would flit across his grandfather's eyes again, memories would swell like waves. The old man would wait, like a calm sea, then would keep quiet. Trifon does not like this stagnant and heavy atmosphere. He repeats: "Its name? Uh . . . I'm going to call it *The Stelyanos Hrisopulos.*"

The old man puts his spindle down on the lace tablecloth, bends with laughter and repeats his name, the name of the ship: "*The Stelyanos Hrisopulos!*"

He goes on laughing and repeats: "*The Stelyanos Hrisopulos!*"

Living creatures, flowers, streams, blue-eyed friends, these things held no meaning for Trifon. Only the sea, stretching right up to his eyes, which, when he lay on his back, made him think of schooners with great empty decks, of freighters with their paint flaking, their metal rusting in the sun, gave substance to the air he drew into his lungs, made living a pleasant thing. The rest was empty, meaningless, nothing. Perhaps the earth was of some use because it provided timber, hammer, and a saw to build his ship with. Trifon did not love the earth; he felt respect for it. Many of those he loved lived there, under it, where the mind could not follow them. But how odd were the people on the surface, running here and there in circles, hoping to make a few kuruş. How insipid, when they said that they had not a moment to stop and look at the sea. And the children at school—not for one day, one evening, would they forget their school and look at the sea, full of thought. Were lessons as beautiful as the sea, did they hold as much knowledge? Trifon did not even want to be acquainted with children who couldn't swim. When he was not within sight of the sea, he endlessly made little schooners, with his adze, strange little boats. Each day he made a new boat or took one apart that he had made before, started building a new one. He watched the boats sailing past the island and wondered whether all the other seas were like this one that spread out before him. If only he had a boat of his own, a big boat of his own, a boat with a crane! To sail on, never stopping for more than three hours, passing the city lights at top speed, from a distance of seven kilometers. Never stopping for more than five hours, from city to city, from sea to sea, people to people, country to country.

This one is going to be a beautiful ship. It will have no passengers, but still, it will not at all be like the others he has made.

Now the ship is ready. For Trifon this ship is a world. Trifon feels something fluttering inside him because of this ship. When he looks at it he feels a softness, a kind of shock, a giddiness, as when he walks past the little girls on the island. For him this ship is a blue-eyed girl. And the strangest thing is that Trifon himself has created her. This blue-eyed girl loves Trifon, unlike the real blue-eyed girls.

It was noon when he launched *The Stelyanos Hrisopulos* from the breakwater to the northeast of the landing. The ship was a meter long. It was painted white. Its bowsprit was decorated with a gilded flower, like the one big yachts have. Just below there was a hole for the anchor. In the hole was a small piece of lead polished with quicksilver. And written right next to it, in gold letters, was the name of the ship, *The Stelyanos Hrisopulos*. There were three small sails in front of the mainsail, one of them square-rigged. The mainsail was very clean and strong, and white as snow. Trifon had worked on it for days, bleaching it again and again with sulfuric acid, drying it carefully. Everything on deck was held together with thin brass wires, with skillfully tied lines of yellow thread.

The sails were movable. Every detail on a yacht's deck had been reproduced faithfully. Portholes had been pierced in the sides of the ship. The portholes were covered with bits of glass and their frames were painted yellow to simulate metal.

You could imagine a miniature crew inside this ship as though you were reading of a Gulliver voyage.

The ship's flag was red, with a question mark in the center. Someone had told Trifon that a ship that crossed the ocean bore this mark. Trifon had tied the flag to the flagmast with a piece of the English twine his grandfather used on his own foresails and fishing lines.

After it was launched the ship seemed to hesitate a little, like a living thing. It did not feel the wind, which was cut off by the landing. It remained this way until it came on a level with the landing. At exactly that point it slanted to one side and all its sails swelled. As Trifon let out the English twine, it flew like a kite.

Trifon played this game for days on end. His grandfather never worried, now; he knew, weaving his nets, that the boy was stretched out on the pebbles letting out or pulling in his ship in the summer breeze.

The village children, including those who owned motor launches and green and white sailboats from the Japanese toyshop on the mainland, held a conference under a large pine tree. The necessary arrangements were made for the sinking of *The Stelyanos Hrisopulos*. Engineers appeared among the children, guns were built, rifles were prepared, big stones piled to one side.

As usual, Trifon came down to the seaside with his ship, almost as big as he was, in his arms. There was not a sound, not a sign of the motley enemies the ship had attracted from the first.

The shipway, which Trifon found destroyed every morning, was intact as he had left it. He installed his ship on it. As soon as he had pulled out the stopper, the ship slid along the well-oiled shipway and plunged into the sea. A slight breeze was blowing. The twine kept unwinding and the ship sailed before the wind, lying a little to one side.

At just the right moment the gun, made of a stovepipe, went off behind the pine trees. The stone fell to one side of the ship and seemed to speed it on its course. A second gun and a third went off, but there was no direct hit. Trifon was so startled that he did not even have a chance to pull the ship back. After the third gun went off, he let go of the twine.

The Stelyanos Hrisopulos was sailing as fast as she could go. The sixteen children, some of them owners of yachts with gilded decks manned by imitation sailors, came out with stones in their hands and in their pockets.

They sank *The Stelyanos Hrisopulos.*

"Stelyanos Hrisopulos Gemisi"
    Varlık, III/61, January 15, 1936
    Semaver, 1936

A Tale of 1,476 Nickel Kuruş

Translated by Geoffrey Lewis

ONCE UPON A TIME I worked as a commission agent.

In front of me there is a garden. A little way beyond lies the sea. A seashore with no quay. Oared boats laden with barrels of olive oil, powered boats laden with walnuts, beans, hazelnuts, potatoes.

In the garden, children. Some have baskets on their backs, some have ropes round their waists, most are barefoot, some have on their feet torn boots, not their own. The season is winter.

It so happened that the winter in the city that year was not particularly severe. The place I call a garden was in fact a rubbish dump.

What comes to mind when we hear the word "garden": flowers, birds, trees, children or childlike people, wouldn't you say? Here there were neither flowers nor birds nor trees. And yet this rubbish dump did resemble a garden. A garden without birds or trees or flowers; in the holes here and there where rainwater had collected, boats of wood or paper. And a host of children. And porters as well. Sturdy, robust porters, illiterate to a man, swearing under their breath at their heavily mustachioed teamleaders and clerks wearing neckties.

The children were gambling beside the garden pools or, if you prefer, the puddles amid the rubbish. Life gleamed on the milled edge of a nickel kuruş. On the coin passing from one filthy little hand to another, something smiled: life. To be made happy by one kuruş! One kuruş won at gambling brings another. With one kuruş they were being instantly transformed into the happiest creatures in the world. In the garden, flowers were blooming, birds were singing, the foul-smelling shore was filled with the scent of iodine from faraway beaches. A commission agent, reduced to despair by being swindled over the sale of seventy sacks of beans, was scolding the happy children gambling for the nickel kuruş.

"Hey you! Aren't you ashamed of yourselves?"

They're not ashamed, old man, they're not ashamed. And why should they be? One nickel kuruş is forty para. One para marks the time when life begins. From then on, forty para means forty somethings. The amount of happiness one person may lose when a para is transferred from his pocket to someone else's has no importance for us. Let us consider the other person, the happy one. The despairing and the sorrowful see the rubbish dump as worse than a rubbish dump. Those are the ones you should be sorry for, Mr. Commission Agent, those are the ones you should fear. The others are such nice people! The happy ones are those who sense Paradise in this rubbish dump. From now on this place is a garden. Roses can be gathered here, carnations, violets. Here finches sing. There may even be exotic birds, and date palms and baobabs. These children are on your side, Mr. Commission Agent! These are people who know the value of a kuruş.

All of a sudden the children were moving away. One of them was putting his basket on his back and simultaneously having another try at winning twenty-five kuruş. The friend he was gambling with was preparing to add to the twenty-five he had earned by the sweat of his back the fifty he had won for fun, to relieve himself against the huge wall of the vacant lot and then perhaps to leave his basket at the coffeehouse and go to the cinema. Maybe he was also meaning to light a fire alongside the wooden Customs shed and wait for his friend to return to the rubbish dump after earning another twenty-five kuruş.

These children do not feel shame, old man! You had better go back to your beans, your receipts, your checks!

Your intelligence does not encompass this business. You are incapable of feeling this happiness.

The children would come into the garden that lay before me. On Sundays I was never at my window; I used to wonder whether they were there and I waited impatiently for Monday. If I wasn't unwell, by half past ten I'd be at my window.

That day there was no one to be seen in my garden. When I say no one, I mean no gamblers. But there were porters, elderly Muslims leaning on their walking sticks coming back from the market, rich fat Christians returning by boat, beautiful Gypsy women setting down on a punctured olive oil barrel the tin mugs they held in their hands while begging, skinny women gazing intently at a torn potato sack and the area around the sacks. The rubbish dump had been washed clean by the southwest wind. The smell of seaweed and garbage, mixed with an odor of rotten fish, was flooding in through the open panes of my window. All right, so where were the gamblers? They're bound to come soon. For the moment, let me turn to my drawer. It was full of kuruş. I had sold a box of eggs and got paid with ten kilos of nickel. It was rather as though we had done a deal by barter. Something like what savage tribes do: nickel for eggs, eggs for nickel. Money didn't enter into it. What am I supposed to do with all this nickel?

The youngest gambler is the first to arrive. He is a seller of peppermints. He wears a white linen jacket. He's the one with the newest trousers. Between his trousers and boots there is a gap the width of a hand. Who knows; perhaps this child yearns to wear shorts. Yes, he does, but fancy a peppermint-seller wearing shorts in this kind of milieu! But then gambling isn't right either. Soon after, a group of spectators in very short pants arrive, playing hooky. They, too, come every day to this garden. They never gamble, they just watch. They go into partnership with someone who's run out of money. Last of all there appears that huge, swarthy creature, that unspeakably foulmouthed fellow, the fearsome hustler. A man standing in front of the shop bawled them out, and one of them shouted back at him, the thick-necked one with flowing black curls, whose cheeks had never seen a razor and were covered in raven-dark down: "What's up with you then? If you've got a complaint to make, go to the police! Every day you drive us crazy with your noise!"

The man replied, "Dog!" and withdrew inside the shop.

I counted the kuruş. There were one thousand, four hundred and seventy-six of them. I scattered them out of the window. First bewilderment, then pandemonium.

When they had done what needed to be done, they looked up at the crazy man in the window. I closed my shop, never to open it again. Now I roam the streets in a happy madness, bought for ten kilos of nickel.

"1,476 Nikel Kuruşun Hikâyesidir"
  Büyük Doğu, II/42, August 16, 1946
  Tüneldeki Çocuk, 1955

The Gramophone and the Typewriter

Translated by Joseph S. Jacobson

I LOVE THESE TWO LITTLE MACHINES, produced by the human brain after many days of thinking, that make life so easy for us. Whoever it was (Edison?), who thought of not letting the beautiful voices of the living and the dead disappear, might have died without ever recording his own voice. He must have said, "I have a cracked voice, what's the use of preserving it? Let the good voices remain in the world." I don't know who invented the other. He must have been a clever seal maker. Doesn't the typewriter look basically the same as a seal? Like the seal that disappeared since the signature came into being. The typewriter is something like the imprint of the letters of the alphabet. You just punch the keyboard and the letters make their imprint without producing any meaningful words in any language.

The radio and the gramophone are not related at all. The gramophone is a sui generis idea. I never needed a radio. As to the gramophone, not everybody has a need for it, but I can say that I have. I don't even like the radio. Pardon me, but the voice of a man in Paris talking in my room seems fake to me. He's not really talking in my room. Anyway, would I let that chatterbox babble in my room? Also, the radio stations make me listen to what they themselves want to listen to. Maybe, I don't want what the other people make me listen to, what they choose; just as I choose the book I read myself, I should also choose the woman with a lovely voice that I would want to listen to. Are we still in school? I should at least have the right to choose what I want in my own room. I simply don't love the radio. It has so many annoyances: To begin with, it is a source of disturbance to the neighbors. Then what about its influence in stirring up ambitions to become a member of the bourgeoisie? The man is a butcher; his wife pesters him to buy a radio, but he

44

cannot buy it. Then one day he makes a few hundred lira by selling buffalo meat as veal and comes home with a radio that has one green eye. In the evening, heavens, so many sounds from so many places! But the wife couldn't even hear them because of her bragging. The radio is used in innumerable vile doings. That shameless instrument is a spy! You can't take one step in the world, without its knowledge, even if you are a great state. It has made inroads into the police cars. In America, they say, even the thieves have two-way radios in their cars.

Moreover, that machine ruins the human imagination. For example, I used to think that in India there was a music suitable for India—the starry Indian nights, the Ganges, the crocodiles, the temples, the elephants, the large-eyed and large-breasted passionate women, pariahs, a thousand hymns of a thousand religions, the hissing of the snakes, the poison, the jewels, the pearls, millions of enlightened and educated men, the silks, the Lahore shawls, and the tropical jungles. But the first time in my life I heard over the radio the slight, sluggish, and lifeless music of that country of complexity, exoticism, and poetry, my imagination was ruined.

The gramophone is an altogether different thing. The gramophone is a friend, a companion—a modest machine. One evening, I sat on the grass near an Edirnekapı* neighborhood, overlooking the cemeteries, where they still use gas lamps in their little houses, and they have never seen a radio and I listened to the sorrowful tunes of country music. I said to myself, "It must be a beautiful girl who's playing these tunes." A blond, bubbly, naughty girl with shiny blue eyes, a nose covered with freckles and hair shimmering with the morning sun, stuck her head out of the window and said, "Uncle, did you like my records, shall I play more?"

I was embarrassed and walked away. Then I saw another gramophone (a relic of the old days) with a red horn on the lap of a beautiful Gypsy girl. Seven workers from the tannery had bought one. They played it by the walls in Yedikule* and danced. There was a slightly hunchbacked, quiet young man who sells newspapers on the bridge. His gramophone and his records were something to be seen and heard. On Sunday mornings he used to come to the island of Burgaz* with his curious machine. He always had a smiling expression on his face. He was utterly lonely. He used to put his gramophone under his arm. One of his shoulders was narrower than the span of a hand,

and the other shoulder had a bone sticking out as if it were broken. His neck was bent.

I always wondered where this poor fellow went all by himself with his gramophone. One day I followed him. He went to a deserted beach and got undressed. I thought, when this man was naked he would have a body like Quasimodo's—hairy and full of fat and folds in the most unexpected places. But this man whose face looked like a cute monkey's face had a crooked body when he was naked. Yet this was still a humanlike body: white, slim, and without any fat, with the ribs sticking out; an ordinary body.

He used to set his gramophone on a stone ledge. He turned a brown record around trying to read its label and put it down gently; he cleaned the needle with his thumb and index finger and played a ridiculous old fox-trot with a screechy sound. I can now imagine him sitting on a rock farther away from the gramophone. The cigarette in his mouth has gone out. His white hunchback is sticking out. When the record is finished he would light his cigarette again and play the other side: a tango that ends up with *C'est votre main, Madame*!

Well, what I am trying to say is this: the gramophone is nonpareil as an instrument of pleasure for the civilized man. It heeds the small and pure pleasures of people and contributes to their enjoyment. It doesn't harm anybody. I used to adore the gramophone horns. In the old days they made such a racket in the coffeehouses; they had the right to, after all they were important. Then, they all shut up; the poor ones didn't even have a chance to say, "Hey, we're special, you people, you're snobbish, but tomorrow you'll come back to us. You unfaithful people, you'll appreciate us later. There won't be any more loud singing in the coffeehouses. Those green and red horns will be gone. There will be an attempt to modernize me. Perhaps I won't enter into the large salons anymore. It doesn't matter. I will find my proper place. I will belong to the countryside and to the poor. No matter what, I will be the gramophone of the single man, of the working girl, and of the woman of a poor neighborhood."

However, the gramophone went away without being able to say any of these things. It was quite obvious that it was different from the radio; this was so well understood that even the radio stations couldn't manage without it.

Although the typewriter doesn't always claim superiority over hand-writing, it has become a friend, or a kind of older brother of handwriting, while declaring its animosity to another thing: printing. What's printing? The instrument of lies, falsehoods, blackmail, stealing, malice, and vulgarities. It may say that it prints thousands, or tens of thousands of copies in an hour, it may boast, and it may think itself big, but it is nothing more than a hysterical woman ready to jump into the arms and the laps of the evil and vulgar people.

It is possible to write something bad with the typewriter too, but only to be sent to the printer. Besides that, the worst thing the typewriter can do is to write business letters. However, in business letters one doesn't write about matters that one feels guilty about afterward. At worst what one would write would be trite phrases. Since the typewriter has broken the rim of the circular mold called the seal and has thrown it away, it has no enmity against the molds; it only remembers them without paying much attention.

When one talks with the typewriter he is tempted to ask, "How about the anonymous letters?" But, fortunately, the typewriter is a chatterbox, it doesn't hear and keeps praising itself. It talks about love letters, memoirs, good novels, poems that are not going to be published, short stories, and the meaningless words like ABCD, or AGHTCZ, of young children that express their joys and their games. Then it proceeds to the subject of anonymous letters: it is for sure that the anonymous letters can be base, vulgar, dishonest, and sly. Deceiving people is not considered an intelligent act. However, I think intelligent people are the ones who are gullible. Because of this, there is a need for these letters to open the eyes of a citizen. The letters make the people who don't feel unhappy feel unhappy. And save a person of honor, who was called dishonorable behind his back, from the clutches of a woman. The typewriter allows the anonymous letters to be written, only for the sake of this.

While we were in my friend's room listening to a Bach concerto, one of us was copying his poem on the typewriter, and praising the gramophone; I made the typewriter chatter. We had a great time. My friend was a good poet. You don't know his name. His poems were published here and there, and many people liked them. But, now, he doesn't have his old fame. His name isn't well known. Yet, when his name is mentioned among us, with the exception of a few ambitious and jealous ones, each one of us can recite a couple of lines from his poems. We would become sad and pensive. Our sweetheart may pass by on the street with a stranger and won't even look at us. A working girl may smile at us from a window. A snobbish college girl may make fun of us. All we can do is to stick our hand into a pot of basil and caress its leaves as we would the head of a young child. We then smell the aroma of our palms, and go away.

My friend, the poet, has a minor job. He has a little room in Beyoğlu* on Kâtipçelebi Street, twenty-eight books, newspapers, a prayer rug he inherited from his mother, a photograph of his father wearing a captain's uniform with epaulettes . . . and a gramophone and a typewriter. He has a good collection of records. Some nights we invited two educated young women (one of them liked his poems and the other one liked my short stories); we played records as one of the young women talked to me and the other one typed my friend's poems. One day, one of the young women had a pretty good idea. My friend couldn't possibly have his poems printed as a book. No publisher existed on the Babıali Avenue* who would do this. No way! There wasn't a single publisher who loved poetry.

The young woman's idea was great. We were going to produce a poetry book of sixteen pages. Using carbon paper, we could make five copies of each page. We bought some paper. The young women started to work alternately. It was really hard work. We played Tchaikovsky and Mozart for them. We lighted our cigarettes and watched their bright heads with a defiant sense of gloom, wondering in which rich man's bosom those heads would end up. In fact, before we had come to the fiftieth copy, the young woman, who had this original idea, got engaged. When we went to her engagement party, in a carefree voice, she told us: "We couldn't finish your book."

"Well, it wasn't fated!"

"Come on let's dance. Don't worry."

She and my friend danced and at the end of the dance the young woman kissed my friend. The family of her fiancé was shocked, but they didn't break the engagement. After all, the rich girl was marrying the rich boy. The other young woman, too, stopped coming. She preferred the places where there was dancing.

Later we men friends got together: We stomped our feet, we drank raki, we beat each other up, we listened to the symphonies, to saxophones, and clarinets. Sometimes, we sang the songs of Kâğıthane* and the tunes of belly dances. If we had money we invited the girls who expected to be paid. I didn't know much about music, but when people who knew a lot about music came, I stuck myself into a corner and waited there until the discussion about poetry began.

One evening we invited a friend who was familiar with classical Western music. My friend, too, in his own way, appreciated and loved the great works. We sat around and played a symphony. This fellow explained to us and we learned what a symphony was and wasn't. We tried to learn the difference between a symphony and other forms of music—almost, anyway. Our friend, the music aficionado, talked endlessly and enlightened us.

At some point my friend said, "I am going to play Mozart's *Turkish March* for you; now listen!"

Then there was some talking, and as I was trying to understand a comparative analysis of the difference between Beethoven and Bach, my friend had already wound the gramophone and was playing the record.

The young music aficionado told me this: "Listen, mister! Do you hear the sounds of the horses of the Turkish raiders?" I listened; yes, I did hear the sounds of bells, rustling, and the violins that sounded like crystal-clear sounds in snowy weather.

The record was finished. My friend smiled: "I played the wrong record, this isn't Mozart's *Turkish March*, it is something by Tchaikovsky."

We burst with laughter. We beat up our music expert as though it were a joke and poured a whole gallon of wine over his head.

On a winter day, as a heavy snow fell, my friend and I carried the gramophone and the typewriter that had such important places in the life of my friend to our dear old Yüksekkaldırım.* My friend needed money urgently. His beloved girlfriend was coming out of the sanatorium. She had neither a coat nor a shirt . . . and both her shoes and my friend's shoes were too flimsy to keep the water out.

"Gramofon ve Yazı Makinesi"
Varlık, XIV/313, August 1946
Mahalle Kahvesi, 1950

The Story That Dropped in My Lap

Translated by Geoffrey Lewis

I HAD COME OUT OF THE OFFICE with our secretary and we were walking down the hill. The secretary of *Seven Days* magazine has slanting eyes, is of medium height, will still be toddling along briskly in old age, and takes a lot of getting used to, but once you do, that's an indispensable friend. The secretary loves to think and I believe loves to elicit other people's ideas by appearing to oppose them, even if their ideas are identical.

We had begun a conversation about the world, about making a living, about the human race. We are living at a time when one thinks of nothing else. If we were to talk about love, that would immediately be shameful. Talking about flowers doesn't do; the conversation soon dies.

The secretary was saying, "My friend, God provides for everyone. If he didn't, you wouldn't get through the street for starving people."

I was saying, "God doesn't involve himself in this business," and as I was trying to continue the secretary asked, "First of all, are you or are you not a believer?"

I think I hadn't the strength that day to give an immediate answer to this question.

I said, "That's a different problem. I can only say this. He doesn't get up every morning and share things out: this is for Hasan, this is for Ahmed, this is for Christo, this is for Moiz, that's for Kirkor."

"Then what does he do?"

"I don't know what he does. But people get up in the morning, even people who've filled their larders, they get up and think what they're going to do that day and how they can keep the wheels turning. Some run around and sweat, some lay their heads on the line, some their muscles, some their legs, some their backs, some their shoulders."

"Still, God provides them with their sustenance."

"God doesn't send them their sustenance. People earn it by sweat, fatigue, toil."

"Certainly. He's not going to send it to them while they sit around doing nothing, you know."

"Very well, then how do you think he sends it to the black marketeers?"

"In a truck!" is the repartee, and we laugh together.

We had descended the Babıali* hill and reached the door of the New Post Office without either of us really accepting that God was likely to send mankind presents down from heaven in a basket.

The secretary pointed to the scene around us. "They're all running, these humans, do you see? For bread money. This scurrying, this chasing around (pointing to a porter who had just stuffed a hefty loaf under the harness supporting his load), is for that."

A white-jacketed waiter holding a tray was hastening to deliver lunch to an office. Behind him, a young man, with his sleeves rolled up and no jacket, was walking, almost running, waving a paper. Behind him was a porter, barefooted, with three-quarters of a loaf in one hand and waving a rope in the other. All of a sudden I think the jacketless young man with the rolled-up sleeves, who couldn't be anything but a merchant's clerk, had collided almost imperceptibly with the restaurant waiter—the tray the latter was holding plummeted to the ground. The plates broke. A brain, green salads, and three stuffed peppers were strewn on the road.

The waiter picked up the tray. Without a glance at the faces of the crowd that had quickly gathered, with the tray on his hip, totally disheartened, he stood stock-still, staring at the stuffed peppers.

He stayed like that for a moment. It wasn't hard to divine what was passing through his mind. All of us thought he would pick them up and replace them on his tray. That was the first thing that occurred to him. He looked at the stuffed peppers. He turned to the dust-covered brain. He looked at it as if to say, "You! You! It's all your fault!" His face turned bright red. Bewildered. At the same time he was thinking about his boss. He looked as though he would burst into tears if you touched him. Then he submitted to a statement, a decision, that was passing through his mind. He seemed to be saying, "I couldn't help it, boss. It was an accident." Just to be doing something, he collected some of the broken pieces of plate. He glanced once more at the peppers, but this time he did not look at the brain. Then he walked away. Brooding over the stuffed peppers and the brain were two children, an immaculately dressed gentleman, and an old lady. We were standing on the opposite pavement. All of us were gazing at the fallen objects. We hadn't even looked very closely at the waiter. Today I cannot properly remember his face. What age did he seem to be? What sort of man? Tall? Short? Thin? Fat? We were all looking at the stuffed peppers and the brain, and the finely cut green salad that had fallen beside them. We were looking at the peppers as if we were saying to children who had done something awful, "Disgraceful, isn't it, you naughty little things! Is this conduct worthy of you?"

It was just at that point that the porter who had been walking ten or fifteen paces behind, the one who had stuffed the large loaf under his harness, approached the peppers. Perhaps as I tell you what happened I cannot convey the speed of it all; this whole incident was over in some twenty seconds. The porter came swinging along, not slackening his pace but not hurrying either. He did not look at the things on the ground as though he was walking to them, as we did; he simply bent down and selected the biggest of the fragments of plate, half of which the waiter had collected. He picked it up, he put the brain on it, and then a long, dry, bony wrist reached for the salad a little further on. He put the green salad stuff on top of the brain. He picked up and examined a small yellow object, which at that distance we could not quite make out. It was a slice of lemon. Then he straightened up, tucked his rope into his waistband, and bent down again. He kissed his bread, which he placed on the ground, then put the hand that held the broken plate beneath his harness. With his now empty hand he grabbed the stuffed peppers. He said to the old lady, "It's a sin, Auntie, a shame. At least it ought to go into somebody's gut." Then off he went.

The secretary looked at me and I looked back.

"You see," the secretary said, "how God sends everyone his sustenance?"

We both knew perfectly well that this was no more than coincidence. It really was just an odd coincidence. Yet it was a coincidence that came neatly on top of our thoughts of a moment or two before. The world was still turning and people were still struggling and scurrying to get their daily bread. They still had to work and wear themselves out more and more with every passing day. There was no power regulating this from on high. Only people could find a remedy for this, and that by cheating others of their due. All over the world, people were thinking about this business. Wars were happening because of it. This business of bread and something to put on it could be solved only if people thought of and loved one another, refrained from wronging one another, realized that every human being was an entity like themselves. It was not every day that plates were broken and stuffed peppers fell to the ground.

And yet . . . one could not resist the sweet smile that this beautiful heaven-sent coincidence had brought to the unshaven face of a lowly porter. But there was another side to it. Maybe the proprietor of the restaurant had fired the waiter. Maybe he would dock a portion of his week's wages.

The secretary had thoughts exactly like mine, yet still tried to provoke me: "God rose up in the morning. He got the chef of the Nefaset Lokantası,* Mehmet Effendi of Bolu,* to prepare for Hasan or Hüseyin the porter's brain salad and stuffed peppers!"

Then came another glance. I understood.

"That's how it is," I said. "And at the cost of a brain salad and three stuffed peppers, it has fallen to his servant Sait to sit down and write it up."

"Ayağıma Dolaşan Röportaj"
Yedigün, 772, December 2, 1947
Tüneldeki Çocuk, 1955

The Lower Cabin

Translated by Geoffrey Lewis

IN THE TIME OF THE BEST WEATHER, on those days when the gulls fly contentedly over the water, distances vibrate, and the blowing of the winds is no more than the breath of a sleeping child, there is no one in the lower cabin of the steamer.

He went all the way down, tossed his jacket across several seats, took his cigarettes out of his pocket and put them on the seat, carefully placed his matches on top of the packet, and thought about the things that his imagination created: mansions, apartment buildings, cafés, women and winter days, children he was very fond of, birds, ants, frogs setting summer nights to music, sunfish caught on the point of the hook.

For the moment there was no one on the stairs leading down to the lower cabin. A little later, one or two people would come halfway down and, resting their hands on the upholstery of first class, peer down at the faded linen seat covers and go back up, preferring the wind the steamer made as it sliced through the hot summer day. Or someone else would come, quiet, not speaking, tired, and worried; he would take off his shoes and stretch out full length on a side bench.

The wind and the surface of the sea would come into the lower cabin with their violet lights and go away, turning like the shadow of a fan on the white ceiling.

Flies came and settled on his nose, his bare arms, and his mouth, which was open and watering with a strange contentment. Having no inclination to move his hands about, he drove the flies off by moving the muscles of his face and nose. He thought about flies. He had read somewhere that they flapped their wings 350 times a second. Didn't he try to love life, to caress someone 350 times a second, to settle 350 times a second on something like honey?

Suddenly a man appeared on the stairs leading down to the lower cabin—a man in his sixties, clean shaven, holding some packets. He looked quite extraordinarily tired, but he did not have the pallid and suffering face that accompanies tiredness. Though tired, he was smiling and happy. He came and sat directly opposite the man who was looking pensively at the shadows of the sea, the sun, and the world of ocean on the ceiling. The old man heaved a deep sigh. But this sigh was something different from the sigh of those who cannot carry the burden of life. It was the sound uttered by people tired of looking for inexpensive things on this hot summer day in the filthy and beautiful streets of this miraculous city called Istanbul.

"Tiredness, young sir, fatigue! I'm sixty-five years old; what can I do? I get tired very quickly now. Not like I used to be."

"You have to be a child not to get tired in this weather, Pop."

"The temperature is in the mid-thirties. I don't know, that's what the paper says."

"It feels like it. In this weather no birds fly."

"But these flies don't get tired."

"I read somewhere that flies flap their wings 350 times a second. It seems that the muscular strength of insects is a miracle, Pop. Some insect or other—I don't know what—weighing a gram can lift a steel ruler weighing two hundred grams, they say."

"It's the truth. What about ants? The loads they carry! More than their own weight! What strength!"

They fell silent for a moment.

"Where do you live, sir?"

"Burgaz.*"

"Not a bad island, that."

"For the views, yes."

"You're right. I know what you mean. It's hard to find anyone to talk to. They say there's a lot of Greek spoken there. My son lived there for one summer. For a whole month he didn't come into town, he was trying to put on some weight. He was a quiet lad; you couldn't get him to open his mouth. When he finally came home, how he talked to us! We said, 'What's this all about, Nurettin?' and he said, 'Daddy, I haven't spoken Turkish for a whole month; what do you expect?' "

Sleep was overcoming the young man. The old man was talking, jumping from his last civil post to the Gallipoli* campaign and from that to Ankara. He said he had come into town today to collect his pension and had gone all round the market to buy some odds and ends. The young man wasn't so much listening to the time, the events, the incidents, and the old man's day, with its filmlike, dreamlike quality; he was lost in watching it. He did not feel the steamer coming alongside a quay, the lights on the ceiling going out with a soapsuds rustle, the lower cabin suddenly becoming dark and cool.

The old man said good-bye and disappeared.

To the man lying down—the man now alone—he had left his son Nurettin, his daughter Kevser, the trench warfare on Gallipoli, the medal, his civil service job in Ankara, Mahmutpaşa,* and his sons-in-law. The man lying down was seeing a house with a tower, on Kınalı Island,* burning in the evening sun.

As soon as the old man appeared at the foot of the hill, little children came running. In one of the packets he was holding there were chocolates, in the other a pair of sunglasses, a present for Nurettin. In the same packet there was—you'll never guess.

"A swimsuit! Oh how lovely! What a neat thing!"

He puts on his slippers. The water has been drawn from the cistern. He washes his feet. At the window overlooking the lights of the Bosphorus, the old man, in a dream condensing his sixty-five years into sixty-five seconds, waits for them to call him to supper. The presents were forgotten. Loneliness and old age set out on a journey as fast as a ship, for a land unknown.

"Father!" They are calling, "Father! Come on, supper!"

Father has flown through the open window and away.

"Alt Kamara"
   Şahmerdan, 1940

From A Cloud in the Sky

Translated by Geoffrey Lewis

IF I TELL YOU that my knowledge of the life of this long-legged, flat-stomached, malevolent-looking, fair-haired man is not limited to what I have learned from various third parties, don't believe me. And it would be as well if I didn't write down the things people say about him. Not that it's right to declare that gossip is worthless; at least there's some pleasure in the damned thing. It's rather like those while-you-wait photographs. If need be, we can speak of the aura of gossip that broods over this man. We're not afraid.

With his dog beside him, he was sitting on the low wall of a vacant lot overlooking the sea. The dog was squatting on its haunches, its front paws straight up, like a statue. Nose cold and wet. Every now and then it made little squealing noises and looked at its master as if to say, "Let's go!"

The man lit a cigarette and said, "Sit! Stay where you are!"

The dog stretched its front paws, put its nose between them, and closed its eyes. A light breeze stirred its yellow fur and the man's stiff yellow and white hair.

The lines of the man's face told a story. They expressed what you see in the faces of those who have never been loved, who are worn out, who drink too much, who, having previously been good-looking, have suddenly lost their looks, and those who have had an education; in short, those who are inwardly sick. From this man's face, too, if you had nothing better to do, you could search out and extract much information. You must believe me when I tell you that the seven or eight lines round his eyes indicated not that he had laughed a great deal in his time but that he habitually turned his face to the sun and squinted. When he looked into the mirror, he told his dog that these were not laugh-lines but the result of gazing at the sun. Can one assert that a remark made to a dog has not been overheard by a neighbor? All right, not a neighbor but the postman? Maybe the letters he daily distributes, forever titillating his curiosity, have brought him to the state where he will say to anyone who offers him a cigarette, "You know that fellow who chats with his dog? I tell you, friend, I took him some letters yesterday. The front door was ajar and I could hear some conversation coming from inside. Naturally I pricked up my ears. I said to myself, 'There's no one in this house besides the man and the dog. Lord! What's going on here? What the hell is he doing? Who's he talking to?' I stuck my head round the door and had a look. Would you believe it, he was talking to his dog! The man's a Turk, comes from Rumelia. He was talking to his dog in Greek!"

The man who'd given him a cigarette says, "For goodness sake, what was he saying to the dog? Or don't you know Greek?"

"Me not know Greek? For fifteen years I've been a postman in this village, where there's no shortage of Greeks. Of course I know Greek! Only . . . my throat's parched. Would you be kind enough to get me one of those bottles of soda from the man over there? It's not easy, you know, tramping all round the neighborhood. Honestly, sir, some evenings when I take my boots off it's as if my feet weren't the ones I started with that morning; they're almost twice the size. Ah! The swine's soda's cold. That's unusual. Where was I? Yes, I had a look, there was talking inside and I listened. He says, 'Do you think I'm old? No, I know you don't. When we wander over hill and dale, do I get tired? You'll say I've laughed a lot in my time and that's where I get these lines at the corners of my eyes. And my mouth. Not a bit of it, my dear fellow. I don't say I've never laughed; I have, but not with all my heart and soul. In fact, whenever I want to laugh like that, something my mother used to say comes to mind: "Laugh a lot and you'll weep a lot." That's what she used to say. I just can't laugh the way I'd like to. You know there's a minimal sort of smile you've got to give people, like when you meet someone. That's the most I've ever been able to achieve in my moments of greatest happiness. But when I actually meet somebody, I never manage a smile; I'm scared I'll weep for it later. Old chum, I've talked too much. You see what I mean: these lines are not the result of laughing, they're from the sun. Yes, plain ordinary sun. You know me, I walk a lot in the sun. And look, I want you to notice this. There are more lines by my left eye. It's because I screw that eye up as I walk.

It's been weak ever since the day I was born. Thank goodness the other one's fine and I manage. If it weren't, I'd have had to wear a monocle. Think about that, chum! Me, a dandy with a monocle!' "

If we suppose that the postman told his story just as I have written it, what follows? He didn't, but if to what he said you add his voice like the hissing of a serpent, his spiteful attitude, and his yellow snakelike gaze, you will concede that when the man to whom he'd spoken passed the story on to someone else he could have reported no other conversation, could not have added to or subtracted from the postman's squirming, his way of looking at you, or his hissing voice.

And now, revealing my writer's secrets, because I'm about ready to write what else there is to the story besides the bits that have cost me the price of a soda or a cigarette, I shall offer a small introductory note. For the rest, I shall continue to write in such a way as to make the reader ask, "How on earth did he learn this?" As to how I did it, that I'm not telling. I'm not telling, but I cannot refrain from adding this: it may be that I lived in the same house as this man. Maybe I am this man—I shall not say. For example, if I were to write, "In the privacy of his room he scratched his head," you might inquire how I knew; did I see him? Or if I were to say, "When he woke up in the morning he felt an inner weariness," what a ridiculous sentence that would be! The reader could well ask, "Are you that man? Come on! How do you know what was going on inside him?" As my story continues I am preparing to commit the same errors; forgive me. I wonder, did I mention at the beginning my close kinship to this man? Before I come to the real topic, there is another point I must make and that is the extreme closeness to me of the man in this story. If I write down what other people know of the man, such as the postman's chatter, that means that I am writing at the same time, that there is no connection between the man and me. Let this henceforth be known.

I don't think the postman is correct when he says that he avoids people. There is certainly a reason for his roaming about on his own, which he may not know himself. He thinks it's because he doesn't belong to this tiny island. He's a big-city man, from one of those cities with a population of over a million. But in a little place like this no one gets on familiar terms with him, no one has a drink with him, no one talks to him. They may chum up with him at first in order to find out something about him, but afterward they can all withdraw and leave him alone with his dog. Nobody concerns himself with him. The one who says the last word about him doesn't have to be a postman; it can be a barber who says it: "It is love that has brought him to this condition."

What's the matter with the man? You can't say he's a man like us; there's no need to state the obvious. Friend, I tell you the man talks to his dog! On the other hand, we hear tell and we know that a lot of people talk to inanimate objects, to walls, to figments of their imagination, to beds, to mirrors. Some even talk to their neckties. Girls talk lovingly to the trousseau in their bottom drawers, boys to their own bodies.

It is a fact that poets talk to the stars and the winds, to women they don't know, to lakes, to far-off lands, clouds over two thousand meters up, migrating birds. Fishermen talk to their boats and their hooks and to fish. Yet the fact that this man talks to his dog has given rise to a tremendous wave of gossip in the neighborhood. For my part, I don't believe it is love that has brought him to this condition. And, if you ask me, there is nothing unnatural about the man. But no one shares my opinion; what can I do? Indeed, the poor fellow himself is convinced he's slightly crazy. My notion about why he talks to his dog is that although he likes people he doesn't talk to them. How shall I put it? It is because in his psychological relationship with people, while he is greatly addicted to them and curious about them, he is quite incapable of learning about them.

We'd better revert to our items of gossip about the man. They say he has two shops in town, from which he collects rent. He is also said to work as a merchant's clerk; where, or in what line of business, nobody knows. The merchant, they say, is a man like him: unmarried, not talking, showing no affection to anyone. When they are together, they say no more than hello and good-bye.

There is the following fact, too. At one time, they used to say, he talked to a young person on the ferry. It is even said that there are people who heard the middle-aged man deep in conversation in the bow of the boat with this eighteen-year-old girl, and even heard him sing. The eighteen-year-old's father got wind of it, and after a stern warning she stopped talking to him. Sometimes they would come face to face on the last boat, but she would go and sit with two girlfriends, while the man with the dog would wander around for a bit and then go into the bow and whistle quietly and hum a tune. Though he never greeted anyone, he used to greet this girl, and the odd thing is that she would acknowledge his greeting. It is even said that they would exchange a few words, along the lines of "How are you? Are you all right? How are things?"

That's it; that's the sum total of the gossip about the man. Everyone knows that much. What reveals to us the man's real secret is—I have to say it—a small dog. A yellow dog with intelligent eyes, an ice-cold nose, and fur rippling in the breeze. This is his dog all right, but I am using it here as a means to an end. I mean to say, the dog is somewhat if not wholly fictitious. The reason is that a dog can never make us understand a pitiable man's life, his illusions, his disappointments, the fact of his being alone in the world. Dogs do not show their love as we do, in speech or in writing. A dog runs, wags his tail, licks his master's hand. Listen to my fictitious dog:

"This morning he woke up early. At his subdued whistle, I ran to his side."

If I let the dog tell the story, I think any pleasure there is in it will be lost. So I approach the man myself, with the intention of making friends with him, this man who sits on a low wall in the evenings, puffing a cigarette, this man whom nobody loves and nobody talks to, from whom everyone recoils.

"Sir, with your permission . . ."

I light a cigarette and sit beside him. He must have felt that it was up to him to open the conversation, for as I was petting the dog he murmured, "Do you like these creatures?"

"Sir, I'm mad about them!"

"To tell you the truth, I never did like them much, but now I'm really used to them. This one's mother belonged to the landlady at the boarding-house where I once lived. That was before this one was born. The poor woman died and I couldn't get the dog to leave me. I liked the landlady a lot. After a while, the dog died—the mother of this one, I mean; this one is male. Someone asked me for the puppy around that time and I was on the point of giving it to him, but when the mother died I decided to keep it, to remind me of her."

That evening we talked of nothing more important than those few sentences. Neither of us understood anything about political events, or didn't want to understand them, or we each presented every idea we had about political matters in a manner calculated to be acceptable to the other. What I'm saying is that we talked politics.

When I got home that evening, I simply couldn't understand what the postman saw in him. He was an ordinary man, a totally commonplace man. That rich grocer across the road from us leads an infinitely more interesting life. Don't you agree, my friend? The grocer's thoughts are completely involved with olive oil, beans, flour, and chickpeas. His worldly affairs are nicely organized, his children go to good schools, they dance, they dress at the height of fashion. What beautiful English his daughter speaks! A graduate of the American College, which is really something. How happy that makes her father! How proud he is of her! You should hear him tell the story of how he came from the island of Chios, became apprenticed to a grocer, eventually took over the entire running of the business, with the owner looking in from time to time, then how one day the owner brought his daughter along and offered her to him in marriage. From then on was the busiest period of his life. How he advanced step by step, filled his cup drop by drop. Everyone could see the tiny shop in the Fish Market, but how could those with no notion of the tiny shop's huge warehouse possibly know what lay beneath the Fish Market? The Kurd at the door was implacable. The iron hatches of these fearsome Byzantine warehouses were not visible to every eye. Everything was there, to right and left of those greasy black pavements in the medieval labyrinth, resounding to oriental music, where porters shouted and carts collided. The grocer himself was light-skinned, while his wife was dark. Was the boy with eyes the color of lavender honey his own child? His nose was Greek, his shoulders broad. He reminded his father of Alexander the Great. So the grocer was not devoid of culture. He was crazy about his son. He was fond of his daughter and proud of her English. That apart, people in Greece were reported to be dying of hunger. In the coffeehouse he was downcast, at home with his wife he seemed on the verge of tears. He would say to her as he drank his coffee, "Let's get five or ten kilos more and put it on one side, my Elenitsa. You never know what tomorrow will bring."

Beyond that, Yani Effendi's life story came to a dead stop and I could carry it no further. It was my fault; couldn't I have taken a little trouble and written a mammoth novel by entering Yani Effendi's house and describing a number of parts of it that were unknown to me, just as Balzac did when he traced step by step the life of a perfumer?

At the time when I was involved with Yani Effendi, I was unable to see the man with the dog, who aroused everyone's curiosity, including, at first, mine, though later I lost interest in him. Had I chosen to do so, I could have caught him every evening as he sat there on the low wall and, by slow degrees, learned a great many things about him. But no, I don't want to become involved with strange people. No good comes to me from them; what I need is loving, laughing, shouting folk. This man isn't alive enough to qualify. He has no one but his dog. He talks only to his dog, he doesn't love humankind. Let us move on again to the postman's observations.

"Sir, no one has ever seen this man buying anybody a cup of coffee. Please, let's go into this café and have some coffee. Just see what news I have for you about him!"

"Some other time."

I don't want to listen. I am engrossed in Yani Effendi. At the moment I am making friends with his son.

My friendship with Yani Effendi's son lasted five days at the most. In his own way this young man had some attractive sides to him, but I found it excessively wearisome to converse with him. I, too, talk about women's thighs, about poker, dancing, movies; who doesn't from time to time? But the same conversation night after night gets on my nerves. True, there was no harm in it, but one evening I realized he was giving a bad imitation of some film star or other. Let us concede that in America one may converse with Mr. John Payne,[1] but I ask you, what is there to converse with him about in Istanbul? At the moment, all that the young man and I do is laugh together, but in a few days we won't be laughing. I began to give up writing the life of Yani Effendi and to return to the trail of the man with the dog. It was a good thing I had made a long break. The first time he had been very shy, but when he saw me now he offered me a cigarette. Because of me, he berated his dog.

1. John Payne (1912–1989), an actor who appeared in dozens of films from the 1930s to the 1980s (not to be confused with John Wayne).

"My friend, I'd really begun to worry. There was no sign of you. Where have you been?"

"A bit of a cold. It kept me in bed all week."

"Better now, I hope?"

He told me how he'd once caught a cold and didn't manage to get rid of it because at that time he couldn't do without swimming in the sea, so he had spent virtually all summer sniffling. As he told me that, this man, who told his dog that he never laughed, was chuckling away like anything. No doubt because of a long friendship with the postman, I had the impression that the dog was giving him a funny look.

I think the time has come to talk about the postman at a little greater length. As I mentioned earlier, I found no fault in him apart from his habit of ferreting out small secrets: a person's few bad habits, something confidential between two people, some incident that should not have gone beyond the four walls of the house.   ·

Is the postman a good man or a bad man? Whichever he is, what does it matter to me? The one thing about him that does matter to me is that I like him a lot, although sometimes he drives me mad. He sits on the ground three paces behind you, so that you can't utter a single sentence to anyone else. There's nothing much that I'm not prepared to talk about at the top of my voice in front of everybody, yet once the postman gets behind me and pricks up his dreadful ears, I fly into a rage. I lose track of what I mean to say. I want to speak quietly. Then I tell myself, "He can take two words of your sentence, add twenty, and dream up a whole story. Be careful."

Something of this sort did in fact occur. I have a friend, name of Ahmet, who has taken a room for the summer in old Mademoiselle Katina's house. He went swimming the other night. Two other friends were talking together in a place where the postman happened to be; he was three paces behind them. This is what was said: "Katina's lodger Ahmet went for a swim last night, in that wind! He asked me to join him, but . . ."

The postman caught the words "Katina," "Ahmet," "last night." This is what he made of them.

"Come on, barber! Give my beard a bit of a scrape, eh? Just look at the story I've got to tell you! You know Ahmet, who's living in one of those houses up there? Well, last night he threw Katinaki into a boat—you know, her father's the famous chocolate manufacturer—and they went across to Heybeli Island.* They jumped into a carriage and went straight to Pine Harbor. I'd been watching them from that headland over there as they went by in the boat. A bit later I saw a lighted carriage going along the circular road on the island. Honest, I saw it with my own eyes. The driver waited for them at Abbaspaşa. Ooh! Tasty, isn't it, old fellow? There'd been rain the day before. Imagine the scent of the pines! And the perfume in Katinaki's hair! Enough to drive a man mad, eh, old fellow? Ahmet Bey's* a naughty boy, isn't he? Those eyes! He's a wiry young chap; I only hope he didn't hurt Katinaki, soft little creature that she is."

That was the postman's story, just like that. He has a narrative and inventive ability that bears witness to a power of imagination denied to a first-rate writer like me.

Here is my analysis of the reason why he picks up all these trifles. Although outwardly it appears he divulges great secrets in exchange for such minor favors as coffee, tea, soda, a shave at the barber's, a shot of raki, a bunch of grapes, and so on, if you ask me it is not for these insignificant rewards that he unearths people's hidden aspects. I realized it from seeing that if there's no one else to listen to his stories he tells them to Zafiri, who is quiet and doesn't enjoy gossip, who, far from buying anyone a drink or anything, isn't lucky enough to have a cup of coffee for himself in the course of a day and doesn't even know Turkish properly. Or to Zeynel Effendi, the retired ticket collector, who is quiet and doesn't enjoy gossip any more than Zafiri does. The postman's passion for finding out secrets and telling what he finds is a manifestation of his wish to understand in his own way the world in which he lives and to shape it nearer to his heart's desire.

Often have I grown angry at this trait of his. Besides exposing a lot of dirty linen, there are times when he dirties a lot of clean linen. The things he has to tell about a man are never innocent facts. But there is nothing one can do about it; it is he who bears the responsibility for them. So it is he who has to live in the houses he builds out of lies on a foundation of truth. I confuse what the postman says about one man with what he says about another, and I forget it all. And in the end everyone has done the same. We keep wavering between belief and disbelief.

I have not concealed the fact that I am a writer. It's no disgrace, you know, being a writer. Yet I have never liked proclaiming the fact to the world. If now I write in the mornings in a corner of the coffeehouse, in full view of everyone, it's because of him. In the old days I used to go and write in the pinewoods. Now—what joy!—I have a table. Coffee is brought to me. Girls pass in front of me. I can write openly and freely.

What I am trying to say is that the postman has been useful to me. "He sits in the pinewoods, writing letters. I wonder whom he's writing to? What is he writing?" From things I've written and then torn up, he has extracted such significance that I have been ashamed. On one such occasion I came within an ace of being beaten up. They advanced on me, saying, "He's got the cheek to write down the way we live! Who the hell does he think he is?"

I have devoted a lot of space to the postman. Let me accept him as he is. Let me leave to public opinion the question of whether he's a good man or a bad man. He has been useful to me, so let me not defame him.

He caught me one morning as I was going for a swim. "Look," he said, "the man with the dog! He's sending letters to his paper!"

I looked. An envelope addressed to the assistant editor of a certain newspaper. "Could be," I said, not looking at him. Then my eyes met his. So odd was the look we exchanged that the same evil, brazen wish might have been passing simultaneously through both our minds. Again I looked away. "Could be," I repeated; "perhaps it's a letter of complaint or a letter to the editor."

Again our eyes met. No judge could ever have decided which of us at that moment was the guilty party and which the accomplice; who was egging on whom.

We tore the letter open. We did not hurry to read it. First we went and got an envelope, which we addressed like the original envelope. Then we squatted down at the foot of a lone boulder on the beach. On a sheet of paper folded into four were written these lines:

"*Sir,*

I am sending you this modest story as my entry to your short story competition. I do hope you will publish it if you like it."

On some more sheets, folded in half, was the following sentimental story with a very poetic title:

Moonlight

Once I was madly in love. You must admit I was justified. How could one fail to be in love with her? (Then came a highly romantic description of his beloved, which we rapidly skipped.) I was living in a village across the Sea of Marmara.* We used to come back together every evening. I shall not lie to you; my love is strange, though it ought not be so. Falling in love ought to be like being struck by a thunderbolt, after which you should devise some way or other of attaining your goal. I like this kind of love, but it's not for me. Certainly at first I have to have a bit of encouragement from the one I'm going to love. The rest is easy. With the second piece of encouragement I get, I feel I'm being caught and I try to escape. With the third piece, I'm done for and I am madly in love.

Once again it had happened. The second time I saw her, I felt that the boat was heading for an unfamiliar, unknown country, that I was going to a place where I would never again see my native land, my homeland, the land I loved. A melancholy feeling swept over me—I was about to say "an indescribable melancholy feeling," but describe it I shall.

All other loved ones were far behind: my language, my homeland, my parents, my house, my field, my friends. They all surrounded me—it brought tears to my eyes—and they spoke. "You're leaving us! How can you? Shame on you! Is this really happening? Is this what you meant to do to us? We would never have expected it of you! Are you really going? Will you never come back? Is it for her, is it really for her that you are leaving us? Take a close look! You won't regret it! You won't be sorry!"

The boat cleaves the calm sea, the stars follow us. On the boat the familiar faces are erased. We go on. I want the journey to be prolonged. I cannot even hear what my loved ones are saying.

Who it was who introduced me to her, how, on what occasion, I have totally forgotten, for everyone and everything except her is forgettable. Beyond her are there stars in the sky? Is there a ship on the seas? Even the sun does not exist, because it does not rise at night. And the moon, this strange, pale-looking thing, not fifteen days old, very rare in the daytime, does it exist? There were long minutes when I forgot even these. How beautiful was the face of the world! What fictions can be invented! Even such facts as the moon, the sun, the stars, birds, whistles, violins, and ships may all be lies! Oh the face of the world, oh that person! What might be done if one had both!

The third time, I sought her and I found her. She half recognized me, half didn't. I was upset. The fourth time, I gave her a casual greeting, as if I knew her slightly, and went on past her. My whole being flowed toward her as rivers flow toward the sea. "Well, let it flow!" I said to myself. "Don't get involved, my boy!" On our fifth encounter I did not greet her.

I went into the bow and sat down. There was a beautiful moon. Was it the full moon, or what? Lover and moonlight. Two words, so banal, but rooted so deep in the past. It may have been on a moonlit night that Adam realized he was in love with Eve. And especially after that, after Adam and Eve! Neither the lover in the heat of noonday nor the unhappy fellow puffing a cigarette at the window on the longest night of the year is more unhappy than one in this moonlight. Well, I won't say unhappy, but there's no need to look for another word. The man on the line between happy and unhappy is the lover in the moonlight. In the moonlight, you know, feelings about love are tinged with both good and bad. Think of a lover committing suicide in the moonlight! A joyful lover. Unhappy enough to find joy in death, but as happy as the joy that will come with death. ("That bit's awful!" I said to the postman.) I was thinking almost exactly along these lines. An ice-cold lip touches my mind. Roaming around within me was a woman with warm lips and a body of marble. She spoke: "Hello!" She came and sat beside me. "How are you?"

"Terrible," I answered.

"What's the matter with you?"

"Nothing, nothing at all, but . . . oh, I don't know." We fell silent.

A little later she seemed to be coming closer. "What's on the moon?"

"On the moon?" I thought awhile, then told her all I remembered from school. "There's nothing on the moon. Empty, meaningless, dead. No air, so there are no living creatures. Dead stones, darkness, chasms, rocks. This very moonlight is false. It has no light of its own. What you see is the reflection of the light thrown on it by the sun. There's nothing there. Nothing at all. Cold; perhaps not even that. I wonder whether the concept of heat and cold can exist where there's no air?"

"One cannot live on the moon?"

"I told you, there's no air."

"All right, what if one brought air, with oxygen?"

"Well, I can't really make a guess about that. Maybe for a few hours or days. Just enough to stroll about, to satisfy one's curiosity. Possibly."

She looked up at the moon. She seemed to put her head on my shoulder. Or it was the moon that made me think so. Suddenly I was ready to give my life for this moonlight. "Darling!" I said, "Are you mad? Is it thinkable that there are no people on the moon? Only people who love each other live there. Early one evening, two people become one and decide to leave here and they go together. Most who go together go there. If I were to take hold of you now and we were to go to the bottom of the sea and never come up again, a host of creatures different from ourselves would pick us up from the bottom of the sea and take us straight there."

She laughed, such a beautiful laugh. I had turned all the geography books upside down and with my new theory I was able to hold my beloved's hand.

I suppressed my laughter. The postman laughed a great deal. His face had undergone an odd change. His curiosity about people had vanished. He made it clear to me that he had no wish to find out the secret aspects of anyone's life. This is how he put it.

"They're all alike. I used to think this man with the dog was a strange person, different from us in a lot of ways. The tragedies I used to dream up, the guesses I used to make! It really puzzled me, how a man who kept clear of people and talked to his dog could be a man like me or you. Now, to know what's in all the letters I carry, I don't have to open them. I know it all by heart."

He walked away, up the hill.

"Havada Bulut"
   Serialized in *Büyük Doğu* in 1946
   Havada Bulut, 1951

From *The Courtroom* | The Tea Thieves

Translated by Geoffrey Lewis

THERE WERE THREE MEN in the dock, middle-aged, avuncular, unassuming in dress and manner, weather-beaten, and unshaven.

The judge said, "Very well, you, Hasan, let's hear what you have to say."

Hasan Özer's nervousness was apparent from his voice, and as he told his story he kept twisting and turning the sailor's hat which he held in his hands:

"Twenty-five years I've been working on the motor-barges. Nothing like this has ever happened to me. It was a Wednesday. I moored the rowboat at the quay. Before I started off home, I rolled up and folded the tarpaulins on the boat. Then I left for home. When I came 'to my duty' in the morning (that's what he said, not 'to work' but 'to my duty') I saw that the tarpaulins I'd rolled up were spread out over the gunwale. 'Oh my God,' I said to myself, 'what's all this?' I picked them up, and what do you think I saw? Two boxes. 'What's this, then?' I asked myself. It turned out to be tea."

"How did you know it was tea?"

"Hüseyin Yazıcı told me, sir."

"And then?"

"Well, sir, I ran off to the coffeehouse and shouted for Hüseyin. 'Hüseyin!' I shouted. 'Come here! What's all this, so early in the morning?' "

"What time was it?"

"Six."

"I see, and what were you doing on the quay at five in the morning?"

"It was my time for work, sir. And it wasn't five, it was six."

"Go on."

"Well, sir, Hüseyin and I came along to the boat. As soon as he saw the boxes, he said, 'They're tea chests.' He jumped up on the boat and put the boxes on shore. Then he carried them away."

"Did the tea belong to Hüseyin?"

"No, sir."

"In that case, what was the idea of letting him carry them away?"

"It was silly of me to do it, sir."

"It's going to be difficult for me to believe it was just silliness. Very well, what did Hüseyin do with them?"

"He took them away and sold them."

By now, the hat Hasan was holding was all crumpled up. When he obeyed the judge's order to sit down, he put the poor thing between his thighs and squeezed it tight.

Now it was the turn of Abdurrahman Yirmibeş.[1] As we were shortly to learn, if Abdurrahman had been gifted with foreknowledge he would have made it Onbeş instead.[2]

Abdurrahman Yirmibeş was older than the others, a married man with children, calm, easygoing, steady of nerve. This was his story:

"Sir, I was sitting in the coffeehouse with Hüseyin there. This Hasan the boatman came in and said something or other and Hüseyin said, 'Right, coming.' Then he said to me, 'Come on! You too! You can help.' So I went. First we went to Petro's wife's place, and there I saw some tea chests."

"How did you know they were tea chests?"

"You can easily tell a tea chest, sir."

"Were the chests open?"

"One of them was, and we put the tea in a sack."

I thought that it may have been that Abdurrahman Yirmibeş put a handful into his pocket and brewed it that evening. A heavenly scent filled the room, which was heated by a charcoal brazier. I imagine that Abdurrahman took a puff of his cigarette and a sip of his tea and said, "That's what they call real tea!" with no thought for the consequences which were going to spoil the pleasure of a handful of tea and his fifteen-lira fee. If such a thought had entered his mind he would have cheered himself up by saying, "What's that got anything to do with me, friend? I never stole it; all I did was carry the loot."

But he was continuing his story. "We took it to Asaf the oil dealer on the olive oil wharf, and handed it over to him."

1. This surname, Yirmibeş, literally means "twenty-five."
2. Onbeş means "fifteen."

"Didn't you know it was stolen goods?"

"No, sir."

"Did you think these men were tea merchants or commission agents?"

"No, sir, they're both fishermen, boatmen."

"And so?"

"They said take it there and I took it there, sir."

"And how much money did you receive?"

"Fifteen lira."

"That's not bad for a porter's fee in this day and age. For fifteen lira one could bring two chests from Baghdad, my son."

Abdurrahman grimaced as though the tea he had drunk had gone down the wrong way. It was impossible to tell whether it was his lamentable greed for a handful of tea that brought that sour look to his face, or whether he was wondering if he would have to pay through the nose for the single glass of tea he had drunk.

This condition lasted a minute or two, after which he grew calm, with the resignation peculiar to the elderly.

It was then the turn of Hüseyin Yazıcı, clearly a principal actor in this affair, who had sold the tea and had not exactly divided the proceeds with his friends. As soon as he opened his mouth it was obvious that he was from Çeşmemeydanı.* That name inevitably brings to mind the world of the independent firefighters of old Istanbul. Maybe Hüseyin Yazıcı was a carryover from those legendary tough guys. Certainly he had been a tall young fellow, with a long black mustache and a black sash. He was said to be about forty-seven. Yet he was still tall, and his voice was still the sort of voice which says, "Thassit, chum!" But his long black mustache was graying and the ends of it were mixed up with his beard. Was he like that in his youth? He used to shave really close and as he passed through the neighborhood they would point him out: "Look, there goes Hüseyin." Ah, the good old days!

Hüseyin Yazıcı said, "Sir, I . . . I mean your humble servant was in Çeşmemeydanı, having a few drinks in a wine shop on Hamidiye Street. Just as I was really feeling cheerful, this Hasan turned up. It had started to get dark. 'Come on, chum, come down to the wharf,' he said. We went, and he gave me two chests full of tea. 'Take 'em and flog 'em,' he said. 'For goodness' sake,' I said, 'who am I supposed to flog at this time of night?' 'Sell 'em to anyone you like,' he said, 'and we'll divide what we get.' "

"So he said, 'We'll divide it.' "

"No, sir, that's just the way I put it. No, he didn't actually say, 'We'll divide it.' "

"Did he say it or didn't he?"

"He didn't say it."

"Very well. We'll have the record say, 'He said we'll divide it.' Then next to that we'll put . . ."

"No, he didn't say that; this is what he said . . ."

"Very well, what did he say?"

"He said, 'Sell it.' "

"Very well."

His Honor looked at the lady typist and asked, "What have you written?"

"He said we'll divide it."

"Continue."

"No, he didn't say we'll divide it, he said sell it."

The judge turned his attention back to Hüseyin: "And then?"

"Then I took the tea, sir. I carried it to Petro's wife's house in the Thursday Market and left it there."

"And Hasan here, is he involved in the tea trade?"

"No, sir, he works on the motor-barges."

"In that case, didn't you realize that the two chests of tea were not his?"

"I did, but . . . well, sir, I was a bit drunk. If I hadn't been drunk I'd never have taken it. Influence of alcohol, sir."

"The influence of alcohol covers a multitude of sins, not just theft. And then?"

"Then it was morning."

"Didn't you sober up?"

"I did, sir, but it was too late; what was done was done. I went off, found our Yirmibeş, and the two of us went together to Petro's house. We loaded up those tea chests and took them away and gave them to Asaf."

"How much money did you get?"

"One lot of a hundred lira and one of 188."

"What did you give Hüseyin?"

"I gave him 125 lira, sir."

"And Abdurrahman?"

"I slipped him fifteen lira."

"Why did you give him so little?"

"What I gave him was for porterage, sir."

"The porterage came to fifteen lira? A remarkable price! Didn't Abdur-rahman know the tea was stolen property?"

"No, sir."

"He knew what your job was; that you weren't in the tea trade. And he was getting fifteen lira for porterage. Didn't he understand anything?"

"Honest, I had no idea whether he cottoned on or not. He took his money and scampered."

"Well, what did you do with the rest of the money?"

"Me and Hasan Özer drank the rest, sir. Oh yes, and we paid five lira for a wagon."

The judge then asked whether there was any evidence that might be adduced in their favor. He went on to explain: "What I am saying is that all the evidence is against you. If there is any witness or evidence on your side, produce him or it."

At this point, Hasan rose to his feet and returned this answer to the judge's question: "Sir, Your Honor, Hüseyin didn't give me 125 lira, he gave me eighty-five."

Abdurrahman Yirmibeş stood up too. "I've nothing to say. It's nothing to do with me. He paid me my money in full, fifteen lira."

Don't ask what became of them. This was the first hearing. There being ample evidence, they were detained in custody.

As I drank my tea next morning, I found a sourness inside me that spoiled the pleasure of it. I had a vision of those three decent, mature-looking men. I have failed to tell you whether they had any previous convictions; I thought of them as having clean records. If they had been relatives of mine I couldn't have been more distressed at the way they had yielded to temptation.

Rather than write up their trial, it would be far more to my taste to see Hasan carrying men in his strong arms despite his age, or oiling the engine. Or to listen to Hüseyin telling an old firefighter's story to the young fellows in the coffeehouse: "That day we put the iron ring on the engine and it went like a bird!" Or to watch Abdurrahman Yirmibeş explaining to some young porter who had been committing a series of wharfside thefts that is was wrong to steal.

"Seylan Çayı Hırsızları"
Haber-Akşam Postası, May 6, 1942
Mahkeme Kapısı, 1956

From *The Courtroom* | The Lead from Sultan Mahmud's Tomb

Translated by Geoffrey Lewis

TWO FRIENDS who looked to be sixteen or seventeen. One had dark hair and a small mustache. Athletic build, a lively way with him, swarthy. The other rather casual, light brown hair, long face, long nose. Goodness knows where Necati and Misak had met and become friends. Both were unemployed. They spent their time wandering round the parks and looking at the photographs in the entrances of cinemas. Misak's father had a job involving pumps and water mains. They had a shop, but then they closed it. The old father worked on foot, Misak roamed the streets. Necati's father was dead, but he had a mother. He went to school but could not study. They put him out to work but he never worked properly. By now his mustache had started to sprout and he had become a strapping young man. His mother could not cope with him.

On one of those evenings before the clocks have been put forward an hour, between seven and eight when twilight was giving way to blackness, they were walking past Sultan Mahmud's Tomb. They saw a piece of lead overhanging the railing of the tomb just within their reach.

The lady judge asked, "Who first had the idea of breaking it off?"

Necati replied, "We both thought of it at the same time. We both saw it at the same time. We took one look at each other and we broke it off."

"What for?"

"To sell. We were out of work. We needed money."

After they broke the lead off they saw that it was fairly heavy. Misak hefted it. "It's five kilos," he said, "it'll fetch a bit."

They had a look round and saw it had got quite dark; there were fewer passersby. Nobody noticed what they were doing. They broke off another bit, and another, and another. They hid them in Necati's house. Next day, when Necati's mother was out, they put a saucepan on the stove. The lead melted so quickly and so oddly that Necati felt a faint melancholy.

It may be that he remembered a night when he lay ill: an old woman pouring something that sizzled from a ladle into some clear water and saying to his mother, "Someone has given the child the evil eye, my young lady daughter."[1] This depressed feeling did not last longer than a minute. They were making the lead into ingots. Three days later they called again at Sultan Mahmud's Tomb. Again the time was somewhere between seven and eight. Again all was quiet.

Necati continued his narrative. "We didn't climb onto a window or anything; the lead was where we could reach it anyway. It was very easy to get it off and take it. Next day we melted this lot down into ingots as well."

"Did you know whom you were going to sell it to?"

"I didn't know. We heard there was a friend of Misak's dad, a chap called Hüseyin Bey.* We took it to him and sold it."

"For how much?"

"Fifty kuruş a kilo."

"And how many kilos were there?"

"Thirty-five exactly. We got seventeen and a half lira."

"Didn't this Hüseyin ask you for a surety?"

"He knew Misak's dad, so he didn't ask for anything like that."

Misak had a long face and he looked as if he was vexed with his surroundings. He was a foreign subject. He did not have his residence permit on him, so his age was unknown. He took up the story. He had excellent Turkish. "He broke a bit off and I broke a bit. Then we took it and melted it in Necati's house when there wasn't anyone there. We took it to Hüseyin Bey and sold it."

"Didn't he ask you where you'd got it?"

"In the old days he had the shop next door to my dad's. He knew me. Sometimes in the old days my dad and I used to sell lead to him. That's why he didn't ask any questions."

---

1. Pouring molten lead into a bowl of water held over the head, navel, and feet of the victim of enchantment, especially against the evil eye, is an ancient remedy, by now obsolete.

"Weren't you afraid he'd mention it to your father?"

Misak did not answer. He pursed his lips and was silent.

The witness Sedat Çetintaş, an architect, gave the following information about the lead ornamentation above the railings of Sultan Mahmud's Tomb. "Let me first acquaint you with these facts about the occurrence. I work in the directorate that deals with the protection of monuments. It was evening. The office messenger came and reported the incident. I went and investigated. Five large and four small pieces of lead were missing. These are in the nature of decorative works, oval or in the shapes of suns or stars. They are antiquities, beautiful examples of nineteenth-century art. They are exquisite patterns of what in art history is known as the Empire style. At present, the great majority of these pieces are in situ. They can be dislodged from their places only with great difficulty and only by the use of tools. There are hundreds of pieces. Each of the big ones weighs seven kilos and the smaller ones four. These thieves stole twenty-three in all."

"So what is the total weight?"

"I should estimate something over one hundred kilos, Your Honor. After the police made the arrest only thirty-five kilos were returned, but their quality as antiquities had been totally destroyed. They are now so many ingots. Their value is no longer what it was."

The accused objected to the architect's testimony. They had detached the lead by hand, they said, with the greatest of ease. Furthermore, the number of pieces they had stolen was no more than five.

Of the numerous witnesses, the most compelling was the policeman, a man with blue eyes and a bad arm, who had made the arrest. His name was Tuğrul Üstün. This was his evidence:

"According to my orders, I was assigned to surveillance in this matter. Around 7 p.m., these two arrived. The policeman on point duty was fully occupied and never looked in this direction. After one glance at him, Misak began to keep watch and Necati set about detaching the lead. I ran toward them and when they saw me they started to run away. It was quite a race we had. Necati ran very fast and disappeared. I chased Misak, and in the end I caught him and delivered him to the station. At the station he told me Necati's address. I went that same evening and arrested Necati at his house. They admitted stealing the lead."

The witness Osman was the guard at Sultan Mahmud's Tomb. He didn't know who broke off the lead, but he had reported the damage.

The lady judge asked if he had made a statement at the first inquiry. He replied, "There only was one inquiry, Your Honor."

A woman was sitting next to me. While the architect Sedat Çetintaş was giving his statement, Necati tried to interrupt. Quietly, in a voice only I could hear, she said, "Just you shut up."

I looked into her eyes. They were bloodshot. She was dark-complexioned, with a serious face and a determined jaw. Seeing me scrutinizing her, she shook her head in a way that told me everything. What she had conveyed to me was, "Yes, there's no need to stare at me so. I'm Necati's mother. My poor little boy!"

Motherhood! What a blessed state!

"Sultan Mahmud Türbesinin Kurşunları"
 Haber-Akşam Postası, May 15, 1942
 Mahkeme Kapısı, 1956

From *The Courtroom* | The Wiring of the Holy Virgin's Lamp

Translated by Geoffrey Lewis

THE COURT IS FULL OF HUNDREDS of bright eyes: brown, hazel, blue, black. The pupils of a primary school have chosen the First Criminal Court for an educational visit. Those sparkling eyes attentively scan every side. To-morrow, from among these children there will emerge men and women ca-pable of distinguishing right from wrong. They are lucky that this case, although not one they will find particularly absorbing, involves a good many technical terms, just the thing to interest schoolchildren. I'm glad it's not some horrible case of murder that has come up; I should not have liked those little eyes to be distressed by seeing what grown-ups do, what they are ready and able to do. I have had my wish.

As we are going to see in this case, both lazy people—a category that in-cludes me—and hardworking people could learn a lot about electricity.

The three defendants take their places as usual, the gray-haired one in the middle, the white-haired ones on each side of him.

I had recently chanced on this same case. When Maledios Effendi and Theolios Effendi took their seats, only their pink and white heads could be seen. When Gennadios Effendi, with his greater height, was sitting in the middle, they presented an odd but pleasing sight. This is what I had noted: the white beards, the long white hair, the shining pink pates, the dark suits, the spotless white collars. The passing of the years, having whitened their hair until their present age, seemed to have stopped short of affecting their fitness and their energy. Miraculously handsome old men, ageless, looking as if they had been born under the Byzantine Empire.

The witness, Assistant Superintendent Murtaza: "I was not involved in investigating the fire, but I brought Mehmet Effendi, the *müezzin,** out of the debris of the Mehmet Effendi Mosque, which was burned in the fire. We found the poor man in front of the mosque. He must have fallen down while trying to escape and been burned."

Then came the testimony of the witness Adnan Ergeneli, electrical engineering specialist in the technical department of the Istanbul Municipality. "I did not see the incident but I submitted reports as expert witness. The porcelain insulators in the overhead installation were broken. The metal fittings of the cable were missing in places. The fuses had been wired up by some unqualified person. Nevertheless, I could not positively establish that the fire was electrical in origin, but it is very likely that the fire was due to this defective installation."

The judge asked, "Adnan Bey,* these three gentlemen you see look after the physical, that is to say, fiscal aspect, of the Patriarchate. In your opinion, can any neglect of duty be ascribed to them?"

"If it's anything to do with them, not to put the electrical installation right is a neglect of duty."

"Did this fire result from the bad state of the overhead cable or from a defect in the interior wiring?"

"As I said before, we were unable to establish that the fire was electrical in origin, but we discovered that the fire could well have been due to this defective installation. The effects of shorting would appear in the stone building of the Patriarchate, where the line starts. As there was no trace of fire in that building, the fire was not due to a defect in the overhead line. The line ran from the stone building of the Patriarchate to the wooden building that burned. So if the interior installation too was sound, we can see no possibility of the fire's being electrical in origin. But if there was a fault in the interior installation—indeed, we have established that there was, on the basis of evidence like the fuses being tampered with by unqualified hands and heavy wire has been connected in place of fuse-wire—it is quite likely that the fire broke out in the interior installation. But this is not absolutely certain."

The statement of the expert Beşir Bey was read out and questions were put to Adnan. In his statement Beşir Bey said unequivocally that the fire was caused by the faulty nature of the interior installation. The current supplying the lamp in front of the picture of the Virgin came through a bare wire.

The fire, he said, broke out here. His conclusion was that the overhead line from outside could have short-circuited at this point.

Adnan replied, "If the interior installation is not defective, the outside installation cannot be involved. If it is defective, then the cause can be the defective nature of the interior installation itself. We have not been able to establish with certainty that the cause of the fire was one or the other. There is no possibility that it was the outside installation. If a short occurs in the overhead line, there is no possibility of an outbreak of fire in the wooden building at the end of the line. There is this, however: if anything goes wrong at the place where the overhead line enters the wooden building, which after all belongs to the interior installation, sparks from that may ignite the insulation at the point of entry. Another recent incident proved that this can happen."

One witness had seen the lamp in front of the picture of the Virgin still on during the fire. Questions: "If the fire arose from this short circuit, could that lamp still be on? Could the electricity in that building still be functioning?"

"Various lines come on one cable. Each has a separate fuse. If a fuse blows on one line, only the lights on that line go out; the rest stay on. In the report presented by my colleague Fikret and myself we noted the faults we saw in the interior installation, but we did not offer any definite opinion."

"We have been told that while flames were appearing in the ceiling of the area where the fire is said to have occurred, the lamp there was still on. What do you think?"

"If the fire broke out in the building where it is said to have broken out and the ceiling was in flames, as the defendants say, then the flames must have burned the wires of the hanging lamp in that area, and consequently the lamp could not have been on."

At this point the defendant Gennadios Effendi rose and requested permission to speak. "I'm no electrical expert, but I have studied philosophy. Today we utilize electricity in all kinds of ways. But do we know what electricity is? There is no possibility of our knowing. What is it? Unknown. In my opinion, a real expert cannot say anything with absolute certainty. Indeed, this gentleman, who is an expert, shares my view. But I should like to ask him one question: on the assumption that the interior installation is perfect, can an accident occur or can't it?"

"The fact that an accident did occur indicates the installation was not done perfectly. It is beyond the bounds of possibility that a fire can break out in a perfect installation. Only some external influence, like somebody striking the wires a violent blow, could cause a fire."

Here Gennadios Effendi used a French expression. "Could it not be a *cas fortuit?*"

Adnan Bey addressed the judge. "*Cas fortuit* means an extraordinary situation. Scientifically we cannot accept any such thing. Either a fault in the installation or deliberate external action or impact. In science there is no *cas fortuit.*"

I wondered whether Gennadios Effendi was implying some spiritual fault on the part of the Patriarchate. He sat down. Fikret, the other witness, was heard. Beşir Bey, whose report was unequivocal, was confronted with the witness. All stood by their opinions.

The court decided that a warrant be sent to Ankara for taking evidence on commission from an absent witness, and the hearing was adjourned. The chairman said to the defendants, "Take care that the new date for the hearing doesn't coincide with Easter!"

The little schoolchildren's eyes were closing slowly with the heat. Their previous attentiveness had left them. This electrical installation problem had clearly been a bit too much for them.

"Meryemana Kandili Ampulünün Kordonu"
Haber-Akşam Postası, May 27, 1942
Mahkeme Kapısı, 1956

From *The Courtroom* | The Battle

Translated by Geoffrey Lewis

THE THREE OF THEM were paternal cousins. The plaintiff, Süleyman, is a tall man with a long nose and small, cryptic eyes. His face is bandaged up to the eyes. He looks as if he has come off a battlefield. In spite of the heat he is wearing a heavy topcoat, buttoned up tight, as though he is feeling chilly. He moves his lips like a ventriloquist, yet his powerful voice fills the courtroom. Even in the voice there is an air of overstatement, of exaggeration.

"I live in Süleyman's Inn at Etmeydanı.* I got back there round nine in the evening. I pushed open the door. These two were hiding behind it. One had a thick iron bar in his hand, the other had a huge rock. They rushed me and knocked me down, then they started beating me. I let out a scream. I shouted 'Murder!' They took fright and went away. I ran all the way to the police station. There they sent me to the hospital; that's where I got bandaged. I am suing these two; they damn near killed me."

While Süleyman was speaking, the defendant Yusuf was shaking his head from side to side and smiling nervously. He said, "Your Honor, this Süleyman is a relation of ours. Why would we beat him? This is how it was. The day before that, Süleyman's father, our uncle, arrived from the village. Dressed in rags, he was in a terrible state. We two cousins gave him some trousers and a jacket. The poor man was in tears. This Süleyman, his own son, didn't even look at him. When he came to my place that evening I said to him, 'Süleyman, this man is your father. Neither God nor man can approve of your behavior. Help him a bit. Look, we've given him a jacket and trousers. Give him a few coppers. Thank goodness you're not hard up. It's a sin,' I said, 'it's disgraceful.' Fat lot of good it did. He began to shout angrily. 'Not a word, Süleyman!' I said, 'Don't make me do something I'll be sorry

84

for!' I pretended I was coming for him. He's a peculiar chap at the best of times, a very odd fellow. Ask anyone from his village, sir. He doesn't talk to anybody. Nobody knows what he does for a living. He has no friends. He lives as if he's scared of something. He was very scared before I'd finished saying, 'Not a word, Süleyman!' He was in a hurry to get away and he banged his face on the door. He bled a little bit. I laughed, and he said, 'I'll get even with you!' and off he went. Seems he went to the police and told them we'd beaten him. We didn't beat him; we were just trying to give him a piece of advice."

The defendant Cafer told his story. "I was sitting in my room when I heard a funny noise. I caught Süleyman's voice. I went downstairs to see what was going on. I thought if there was a quarrel or anything I ought to separate them. I saw Süleyman running off. I said to myself, 'Another of his funny little tricks.' No one knows what work he does, what he gets up to. He's a man of mystery, sir. I said to Yusuf, 'What is it? What's his problem? Where's he running off to all the time?'

"Yusuf said, 'Forget him, Cafer Ağa.*' I was going to tell him 'Your father's hungry, destitute, hasn't got a shirt to his back. Give him a bit of help.' He ran off like a lunatic, and as he went he banged his head. Serves him right. We went to our rooms laughing. A bit later the police came for us. We went to the station and there was Süleyman, his face all bandaged up. Looked like he'd been in a battle."

The witness Rıza Coşkun was heard. "All three of them are from Keban.* They're cousins. Süleyman's father arrived from the country and these two (indicating the defendants) got him something decent to wear. But frankly speaking, that one, his own son, didn't so much as kiss his hand. So that evening I was sitting in the courtyard and I heard Süleyman and Yusuf arguing about it. I hadn't seen anything, so how could I say whether there was any hitting or fighting, because they were talking inside behind the right of the door and I was on the right of the courtyard where I couldn't see anything except the left-hand door. All I caught was Yusuf saying, 'What are you swearing for?' and Süleyman saying, 'It's not me that's swearing, it's you.' Then Cafer came down from his room. He went toward them and the quarrel stopped. Süleyman ran off and Yusuf and Cafer came over to me. They weren't holding any iron bars or stones. Then we went to the police station.

At the station he only had a tiny little scratch on his face; there was just a trickle of blood. That's all I saw and all I know."

The judge asked, "Süleyman, what did Yusuf have in his hand?"

"An iron bar, sir."

"What did he hit you with?"

"A stone, sir."

"What did Cafer have in his hand?"

"He had a stone and an iron bar, sir."

"What did he hit you with?"

"Both, sir; the stone and the iron bar."

The medical report was read out. It stated that some very light abrasions had been observed on the lower portion of his face and the left earlobe, and these had been dressed.

"Now look. The report speaks of light abrasions. If it were as you have described, you couldn't be standing in front of me now. What have you to say? Moreover, you stated that Yusuf was holding an iron bar, but he hit you with a stone. What kind of a statement is that?"

"Sir, Cafer grabbed my hands behind me and Yusuf started to hit me with the stone. Cafer was hitting me for all he was worth, with the stone and the bar. I fell on the floor and they both leapt on me. They bashed me again with the stone and the iron bar. Then they kicked me. They got on top of me and danced on me."

For Süleyman to have escaped from such a beating with slight abrasions on his cheekbone and his left earlobe would have been a miracle.

The judge: "The medical report speaks of light abrasions, the witness says they did not beat you. What am I to do? You say, 'They killed me,' but here you are, sound as a bell. What am I to do?"

The defendant Yusuf: "Sir, his fingernails are almost an inch long. He's just the sort of man to make his face bleed on purpose and drag us into court."

The judge delivered his decision: "Süleyman, however much you may claim to have been beaten with an iron bar and with stones, both the testimonies and the medical report contradict you. The slight abrasions on your face are consistent with your colliding with a door or even with scratching your own face. Because you have so greatly exaggerated the affair, I'm totally unconvinced that these men beat you. I might perhaps have believed you had you not exaggerated. So I am acquitting them. You may appeal."

Without so much as a glance at his cousins, Süleyman left the court, his topcoat wrapped tightly around him, his face as long as a kite.

"Davacıya Göre Bir Muharebe"
　　Haber-Akşam Postası, May 28, 1942
"Bir Muharebe"
　　Mahkeme Kapısı, 1956

Eftalikus's Coffeehouse

Translated by Joseph S. Jacobson

A YOUNG MAN CAME UP TO ME.

"Hello," he said.

"Oh, hello," I replied.

Then he told me he'd wanted to meet me for a long time, but he had never found the opportunity. We started to walk. From the questions he asked me it was hard to tell whether he was sincere. If his questions were sincere, it was up to him to proceed with care; if not, it was up to me. And what, yes, what if he were making fun of me? It would be a good idea to humor him, then slip away at the first chance. But if he's serious, such sincerity must be attributed to his youth and inexperience. Somehow, some day, this feeling of admiration for you, born mainly of sentiment, will be wiped away and gone. And I shouldn't trust that alleged esteem too far. It would be better for both of us if this admiration continued. That's why I'm suspicious. Wouldn't it be a sign that we both don't make any progress?

Since the young man's avowed intention is to write, the likelihood of his pretending to be sincere in order to make fun of me is strong. But what can I do? I shouldn't appear too sharp or attentive either; this, too, would be a kind of conceit. The best thing to do, the best action to take against the possibility of his making fun of me, would be to lean toward familiarity, to appear to swallow it. A very sharp person could play the role of admirer with you to the bitter end. Let him play it; he won't win anything at it! If he's truly sincere, how fortunate. It could be. After all, at that age, without having the courage to approach them, you had looked on writers whom you now don't like at all, like people from another world.

Even now, aren't there European writers you can't help admiring? If you saw Gide, how could you not look on that octogenarian with admiration? And as for an opportunity to converse, who knows what inappropriate questions you might ask?

"I never imagined that I could sit with you in a coffeehouse of this sort?"

I looked at him out of the corner of my eye. I swear he isn't scoffing. I think, if he's not kidding, should I?

"Your stories . . ."

In order to keep him from completing his sentence, which perhaps he would later regret, I have to put him on the defensive at once. Furthermore, the young man says he wants to be a critic. How he'll regret that! Let's change the direction.

"Do you write stories too?"

"I write poetry like everyone else at my age. I tried a story or two, but couldn't do it. I'm working more on criticism. I can say that there's no Turkish story published I don't know. But yours . . ."

"Look at that man across the street, he's blind from birth. Look, he's calling, 'Mahmud Bey,*' to the other side. That means he knows that he is in front of the Taksim* Movie House and a man named Mahmud Bey is across the street at the *börek** house. Who knows how many years of agonizing effort it has cost him to gain the knowledge of perceptions that come to us so easily?"

"For example, you . . . from this, could immediately write a beautiful . . ."

That could be, but I don't intend to write this story. I'm only wondering if the blind man perceives from the air around him, or from the noise, where he is, or does he count the footsteps? What's your idea? Supposing from here to the right, I take ninety-eight steps. I'll be in front of the Taksim Movie House. Was it one minute to nine when I left home? I walk slowly. Now it must be just nine o'clock. There has never been an occasion when Börekman Mahmud left his shop at nine o'clock.

It is possible that darkness in his eyes created in his head a light out of what he sensed on the outside. Then, maybe, when he was walking from Şişli,* there were differences, that we're unaware of, between the noises in Harbiye* and those in front of the Taksim Garden. Is there a change in the weather? Even in the pitch-black of his eyes, could there be a pitch-black psychological difference? Perhaps from among voices and sounds, from noises that we can't figure out, but that never change and maintain their immutability for him.

We're also not aware of the geometry of the streets. But he could have the curves, rectangles, the map of the streets, all their details drawn in his head. Perhaps the streets also have odors. Shops could have different smells. There could be holes and mounds that the soles of his feet know. Blindness resembles an outmoded literature that splits hairs.

While I am turning all this over in my head, my young friend is continually speaking words in praise of me. Maybe it is under the influence of these words that I think so long about the blind man.

Mahmud Bey took the blind man across to the nearest sidewalk. As soon as his foot touched the sidewalk, the blind man said, "Sadık Ağabey,* hello."

"Oh, hello, Monsieur Ivan, you're early this morning," replied Sadık Bey.

Ivan: "What do you mean, early? It's ten after nine."

The clock at Taksim said exactly eleven minutes after nine.

This was too much. At this point, the young friend with me asked which one of my stories I liked the best.

"I don't know," I replied. Then I asked, "Did you hear that?"

"What?"

"The blind man said it was ten after nine. A couple of minutes ago."

"He couldn't have!"

"By God, he did!"

"Impossible!" he protested.

It was something possible. Suddenly I had discovered it. When Mahmud Bey was taking the blind man across the street, he had a conversation with him that I couldn't hear because of the automobile horns. He could have asked the time then.

By now the young man and I had become good friends. We were able to gossip about some people. I listened with pleasure as he defended me against the critics who didn't like my stories. Just at this moment, we fell silent a few minutes, as if we were thinking of how the blind man knew.

Then he asked, "How do you write your stories?"

I laughed. I looked at him to see whether he was making fun of me. No, by God, he wasn't. What a good boy, this one.

"I like your 'The Futile Man' the most, then there's your 'Father Son' and 'Prayer Beads' stories . . . very nice," he said. " 'Tomb with an Arbor' also is quite good."

I was bashful and remained silent, but grinned from ear to ear.

"But you didn't answer my question," he said.

"What did you ask?"

"I asked how you write a story."

"I don't know," I managed to say.

I thought: The blind man's voice was coming from below the coffeehouse, which was set above the city wall. He and Sadık Bey were conversing in loud voices.

"I don't know," I repeated, "just blindly. Well, for example, I'm writing a story now. I've even given it a title."

"What's the title? So you give a title to the story first?"—he didn't say that.

And I didn't say, "No, I simply liked this title, that's why."

He didn't ask, "What is it?"

" 'Eftalikus's Coffeehouse.' You could even leave out the coffeehouse and it could just be 'Eftalikus.' It might even have a secondary connection with the story."

As if he had understood what I didn't say: "So that's how you write stories?"

"How?" This time I asked.

"How would I know?" he said. "I guess, first you give it a name. Then you plan it. You tie it to a conclusion."

"Not at all," I said, "I don't do it that way. Do you want the truth? I really don't know how my stories are written."

We arose to pay the check. The young man displayed a sincere haste to keep me from paying.

Two people playing backgammon for a cup of coffee beside us, grinning, watched us arguing over who would pay. Taking into account my cap and dirty raincoat, I guess the waiter made a quick decision about my condition and hesitated to take my money. And in that moment, the young friend paid for the coffee.

"You put me to shame!" I said.

We descended Eftalikus's steps.

My young friend, who is now curious as to how I write my stories, may write tomorrow that a writer who chooses subjects that never fill a fig seed isn't a good writer. I don't know if my story is all right. If not, what can I do? That's my understanding of a story, sir.

"Eftalikus'un Kahvesi"
   Varlık, XVIII/361, August 1, 1950
   Alemdağda Var Bir Yılan, 1954

The Hermit Crab

Translated by Joseph S. Jacobson

IN THE SUMMER the seashore is most beautiful when it is less crowded. We were in the month of June. There wasn't even a whiff of a wind. Above the beach, which was covered with pebbles, there were rocks and cliffs as fertile as the fields with pine trees growing here and there. Over the cliffs, yellow broom, green thistles, and pink heather grew in abundance. The sun came down like a torrent through this ferrous earth and, as if it ran into a lake, it flowed into this beautiful beach I was watching from high above. I was filled with an irresistible temptation. I slid over the footpath half-crouched. I threw my jacket, my trousers, my underwear over the pebbles, the way a sleepy man throws his things; in one minute I was in the sea.

I remember that my heart had beaten fast when I had lain on the pebbles. I closed my eyes feeling the sky inside them. I felt as though a warm body was hugging me and the fragrance of virgin lips was warming up my lust. I wasn't thinking about them, but feeling them. The breezes that blew from unknown places caressed the hair on my chest and I felt as though something was being crushed between my arms. Some time later I thought I felt lighter and had gotten rid of many of my burdens. I got dressed. Presently I was walking along the deserted shore. Everything was faraway; there were no ferries in sight. There was only a cloud of smoke over the sea. I climbed over the cliffs. Below, the water was full of shadows; it was clear and shallow. I saw a shadow out in the sea. It looked as though it were a black sail about one fathom long and as wide as my body and its shadow had fallen on the sea. The seagulls were alighting on this shadow. All of a sudden I saw the shadow plunging into the depths. Then, again, it surfaced and spread out on the sea like a shadow, a little farther. This was a skate. God knows why this fish laid its big flat body over the lukewarm waters of the sea and moved around like this! And how the seagulls thought this fish was dead and attacked it. And how this creature played games with them? Again I went down to the beach accompanied by the solitude, the bird, and the fish. I was walking amid knee-high grass. Suddenly, I saw in front of me a man standing in the sea up to his waist. His complexion was very dark. He had a handsome and strong body. Now and then little waves hit his waist and receded. I could see that he was stark naked. He was making his ablutions. His dark shaven head was turned toward the deserted shores across. He didn't hear my footsteps. He was reciting something aloud, but I couldn't make out what it was. He plunged into the sea three times and came up three times jumping up, up to his private parts. I went nearer him. As he rubbed his body he was saying, "*Euzü Billahimineşşeytanirracim, Allah . . . Allah.*"[1] Most likely he didn't know any other prayer.

The man was feeling the poison and the aftertaste of the dream he had seen the previous night settling slowly in his body like a sediment. His name was Mehmet. His father's name, too, was Mehmet; that is, he was Mehmet the son of Mehmet. When he saw me he yelled, "Keep out!"

Then covering his private parts with his hand he came to the beach. He put on a pair of long, handwoven cotton underpants. He folded the bottoms carefully and tied them in knots. After winding the waist string twice around his waist he made a knot for that too. After sitting down and drying his hands on his underpants, he lighted a cigarette.

He wondered why his parents, who lived in a hut heated with cattle manure, on the plains of Çankırı* didn't send him a letter if they were still living. His son Emin, a slip of a boy, was he taking care of the house? Was he sweeping the streets of the town? What was he doing? Satan fools us when we are in a strange land away from home. We bathe in the sea. We look at the hermit crab we find among the pebbles, with open eyes, like looking at a mystery of nature and say: "Oh God! We cannot question your divine reason, but what creatures you've created! Creatures with houses as strong as concrete on their backs. Creatures with houses made of stone. My God, such a mystery, you're so great! Creatures with stone houses. Houses without people . . . people without houses."

---

1. "I take refuge in God."

When Mehmet, who worked in a brickyard, got an answer to his letter from the village, we wrote another letter. When he slept on the stones and dreamed—with blue and green flies around his mouth—it would be like he was in the village again and white girls like white clouds climbed up his shoulders. His ears were filled with songs, ballads, and tales. Mehmet would wake up, cursing the flies settled on the particles of fish stuck to his rotten teeth under his bushy mustache. He would jump into the sea. He would paddle like a dog as he did in the river. He would have three dips in the sea. *"Euzü Billahimineşşeytanirracim!"*

Mehmet was thirty-two years old. In winter he went back to his village. His son Emin met him in town and they walked together to the village. His mother had died. His father had become all white-haired; he was ninety-two years old. Mehmet took out seven pieces of gold from his belt and gave them to his father. His father kept these seven pieces of gold for seven years. When he died seven years later, Mehmet tied four pieces of gold into the waist string of his son's underpants and sent him to Istanbul. He kept three pieces of gold. It was trying times and one had to look ahead, not back.

The day after Emin left, Mehmet was sitting down facing the hearth with a crackling fire made with three bricks of cattle manure. His wife cried every night looking at the sheepskin that Emin used to lie on. Mehmet was looking absentmindedly at the hot embers of the manure briquettes. He was as pensive as he had been when he had taken the hermit crabs in his hand. He was visualizing the creatures with stone houses whose mystery was unfathomable. He thought he had plunged into the water three times and come up three times. A teardrop came down from one of his eyes. *"Euzü Billahimineşşeytanirracim!"*

Then he felt ashamed in front of his wife who was standing sheepishly by the door and looking at him. "Woman, why are you crying?" he yelled. "Open the door, let the smell go!"

This is the smell of the Turkish village that has penetrated into every nook and cranny of the room—maybe, the smell of Emin's absence. When the door is opened it may or it may not go away.

The woman opened the door. The light of a bright winter day flowed into the room like a stream which had found its course. For a long time the husband and the wife couldn't see anything with their dazzled eyes. Then, faraway, a very white road shone on the bare hills: the road to Istanbul.

"Şeytanminaresi"
    Gündüz-Hikâyeler, VII/4–39, June 1939
    Şahmerdan, 1940

Who Cares?

Translated by Joseph S. Jacobson

THE HOUSE ON THE HILL, looked at from below, is an ideal house, one that a grocer daydreams of in his youth, where a merchant or spendthrift might live, one of those houses where a retired teacher, a novelist writing his works, or a politician in exile would want to spend his last days, but couldn't.

A road that seemingly came into being because the rocks there cracked and split apart, a road used by three or four lovers on Sundays but that sank on other days into desolate abandonment not reserved solely for roads. Few people on the island liked this road, and they used it only after dark in order to stargaze—or so it seemed to me.

One side of the road is the least-visited area on the island—pines are dense, no roads or tracks—therefore, no handkerchiefs smeared with lipstick, no old newspapers or sardine cans are found under the pines. As for the other side, although one beautiful house can be seen from a distance, there are two ugly houses. On one side the road and on three sides pine forests surround them.

It can be said that no one except for a seller of roasted chickpeas—it was not clear whether he came there to sell chickpeas or to sleep under the pines, dreaming of a country without pines and orchards—knew the people who lived in this house, which created a sense of longing to live beautiful days in it, and to smell the odor of pines and the northeast wind. The people in this house lived in seclusion. On winter days, the barber, seeing an elderly blond man running to catch the ferry on time, remarked to his customer, "That's the old dotard from the house on the hill." That was the extent of gossip about them. The old man returned with his little bundles and didn't come down the hill again for weeks.

The island people, who habitually and maliciously criticized one another, stopped gossiping for a few days if fishermen returned from the Black Sea and tried to secretly rent their houses. People who came summers to bathe and vacation wouldn't take a house if they knew it had been occupied by fishermen, because fishermen were bachelors—both bachelors and fishermen. Whether true or not, it was agreed that fishermen had lice in their shirts.

Furthermore, though it was on the tips of their tongues, native islanders told no one about those who had rented their houses to fishermen before summer. During that period, it escaped notice that the sallow old man hadn't come down the hill for weeks.

It was a beautiful, clear winter day. Fishermen had gone down to the city; none remained on the village streets. A young-faced, thin woman with gray hair wandered about the village. The owner of the coffeehouse, who had no customers, was being shaved by the barber.

"And who's that woman?" he said.

The barber, his small eyes darting like lightning, scrutinized her carefully as if to say, "For God's sake, who is she? I seem to recognize her," and regretfully replied, "I couldn't recognize her."

The woman first peered into the coffeehouse. Two local Greek fishermen were playing backgammon in one corner. The proprietor inside was getting a shave. After looking a moment, she ran to the docks. One of the fishermen saw her: "It's the woman from the house on the hill."

The others responded, "Oh!"

She found the dock master and requested help because her husband had died the night before; she needed to bury the body, and her child was hungry. He'd never received a request like that before. Here was a situation involving neither a free pass nor a price list. He couldn't think of any way to extort five or ten para.

"What can I do?" he complained. "My duty is to take care of ferryboats."

Woman: "Aren't you a Muslim?"

"Lady, thank Allah, I am a Muslim, but I'm a government employee. I can't leave this place; I'd be held responsible. Go to the head porter."

The head porter's house was right at the village center, a nice two-story building. As the woman approached, she appeared as though she wanted to say something to the flames coming from the stove. For a moment it even seemed that in a room where the stove burned, wisps of amber-yellow smoke swirled from inside a crystal bowl while a neighbor told the news.

She knocked on the door.

Around a sheet-iron stove sat two children—a boy and a girl—and between them a dark, swarthy man reading an old yellowed newspaper. He was wearing his glasses. From underneath his robe, his thick hairy calves extended like Herculean legs. One of his slippers had fallen off. An extremely ugly foot, purple and bulky, looked up at the woman.

"Come in, lady, speak up!"

The woman told her troubles as she had to the dock master.

"Last night, my husband . . ."

"Lady," he said, "do you have any money? How can I get the porters up there in this horrible weather? The swine won't come! Yet they're all hungry. They've long since spent all they made in the summer. If they don't get a share of the fish, they'll all die of hunger. I'll do something for you. I'll do it, but without money it's impossible."

"I have nothing to sell. I told you. At home, even my child is hungry."

"Can't you find money from some place?"

"Maybe, if I had money to go down to Istanbul."

"Here's eleven kuruş and ten para."

Thanking him, the woman left. She ran to the bakery. Buying one loaf of bread, she started climbing the hill. Halfway up, a little girl clung to her skirts. Within ten minutes she needed more bread.

Down the hill the woman went again. She'd thought of the government doctor, who occupied himself in winter with chemical experiments. He dissolved nitrates, turned litmus paper from blue to red, from red to blue, produced chlorine, analyzed water, generated electrical currents, and sniffed ozone.

When they told him there was a woman to see him, he was busy in his little laboratory analyzing his urine. He had added something into his urine and was looking for signs of diabetes.

First a number of gases came from the bluish urine. Then suddenly it turned tile red. The doctor said to himself, "Oh my, I've caught it. I suspected so. All that water I've been drinking! Insomnia! Allah gives a man what he deserves!"

The nurse stuck her head in the door.

"Sir, a woman wants to see you."

"I'm coming."

As if to say, I'll teach this woman not to disturb me, he grumbled, "Tell me, what's wrong. What's your problem, lady?"

The woman explained.

Doctor: "He should stay in bed until I see him."

"He isn't sick, he's already dead."

"Let's see, whether he's dead or not. How can I be certain?"

"At least make a report; have them bury him."

"I can't go up there. I'm sick too, lady. I have diabetes. I'm old, I get tired. If you find a donkey for me to ride, I'll go, otherwise I won't take a step."

Saying, "All right, I'll try to find a donkey," the woman left. As she went off, she noted with surprise that the summery weather of that morning had suddenly flown off. A biting wind had come up. Clouds were flitting along toward her house and the pine trees as if they were rushing to a big funeral. She ran home. She wrapped the body in a sheet and carried it downstairs. Snow had begun to fall. When she went outside, her clothes were turned white in a minute. She half-carried, half-dragged the corpse all the way to the summit. Crossing the top, she stopped at a level spot near the other slope. It was sheltered from the wind, almost like summer weather again.

Stillness. In the near-warmth, great silent flakes of snow fell. Only southwest winds reached this steep shore slope. The northeasterly merely touched the tips of the tallest pines.

There were cliffs just ahead. With an indefinable movement—a prayer on her lips or a shudder from the cold—she rolled the corpse off. For a moment, she heard nothing. Then, as she listened, the sound of rolling gravel reached her ears.

Three days of snow, three days of wind; and during those three days only three ferries visited the dock. The head porter sat by the stove, read two years of newspapers, and popped popcorn. The doctor, with the excuse of taking a urine analysis every day, ate only a bite of pilaf. He'd forgotten that a woman had come to see him.

The dock master, a weak, dried-up, nervous man, felt a fire inside him from time to time. Fleetingly, he remembered that a woman had requested him to have a body buried, then quickly forgot.

During this momentary recollection, he seemed to see his own corpse unburied for days.

Again it was a summery day. The barber stopped shaving his customer and, pointing outside the window with his razor, said, "The woman from the house on the hill. I wonder where she's going now?"

A pale-faced woman walked toward the dock. She stopped. Then, as if she'd changed her mind, started walking along the wharf. An old man was strolling there too. He was apparently taking advantage of the beautiful weather to relax on the islands.

The woman approached him. She wanted to tell him something. Then she changed her mind; smiling slightly, as if something funny crossed her mind, she walked toward the dock to catch the ferry which was coming around the point of the opposite island.

She was the only woman on the ferry, the only passenger without a ticket. But at the Kadıköy* dock, as many men as there were tickets got off. Neither more, nor less.

"Kim Kime"
Sarnıç, 1939

Such a Story

Translated by Joseph S. Jacobson

WHEN I LEFT THE MOVIE, the rain had started again. What was I going to do? I cursed; I swore a blue streak. I really did want to take a walk. A passing *dolmuş** driver called, "Atikali,* Atikali!"

Shall I go to Atikali at this hour of the night? I'll go. I climbed in beside the driver and off we went over hill and dale. With red, yellow, green, and other lights reflecting off the car's steamy, dripping windows, we arrived at Atikali in a wave of color.

If I walked a hundred steps from the Bomonti* stop in Şişli,* I'd be home, snug in the hollow of my two-blanket bed, thinking of my friend, Panco. For the time being, I had no one else. My mother lay ill in bed on one of the Istanbul islands. Under her bed, my black dog kept watch over her and waited for me. Panco lives on a street named Çilek. He dreams of soccer matches or playing cards. I'm in Atikali after midnight on a rainy night, on a so-called boulevard. I walk; it rains. Yes, the rain, solitude, and Atikali are certainly right. When I'm away, I miss my mother, Panco, and my dog Blackie even more.

The three of them sleep. My mother is snoring; Blackie awakens, his ears on the street; but Panco isn't dreaming, I just made it up.

In the rain, thinking of two people and one animal, I turn into Atikali's unfamiliar streets. The watchman's whistle is blowing. Someone bursts out of a house as if crazy and jumps on me.

"Man, I killed my girlfriend," he cries. "Hide me!"

I point to my overcoat pocket, wet from rain seeping through the seams and smelling of sesame from the *simit** I ate this morning. He goes into the pocket and vanishes.

"What's your name?" I call to my pocket.

"Hidayet."

"Why did you kill, Hidayet?"

"Brother, I was in love!"

"How much in love, Hidayet?"

"Like crazy, brother! Dawn broke with her! I sell sesame halvah day-times. Brother, your pocket smells sweet like *simits*. With her at dawn; with her at dusk; there's never a minute I don't think of her. Man, I was living in a dream. Every word, come what may, depended on her. People said something to me, I wondered what answer she would give. If I was going to buy something, I wondered if she would buy it. If I ate something, I would not be able to enjoy it to the full. If someone asked the way, first I would ask myself if she would help, and as long as she didn't point the way inside me, I would stare sheepishly. If I saw something nice and didn't show it to her, I got no pleasure from it, because I hadn't shown it to her."

"What was her name?"

"Pakize."

"And then, Hidayet?"

"Then, brother . . . then it got dark. I left my tray of sesame halvah at the coffeehouse and hurried to drink two glasses of wine. I don't know if that pimp of a bartender put in some opium, or what, but as soon as I drank, Pakize stood before me, alive and warm."

"Really?"

"No, man, pretending, daydreaming! I'd keep on talking."

"Quiet, somebody's coming, Hidayet."

Hidayet crouched in my pocket like a sesame grain.

The rain had stopped. It seemed as if dawn were starting to break a little.

Hidayet called from my pocket: "Shall I tell the rest, brother?"

"Don't! This much is enough."

"OK, man, I'm quiet. Whatever you want, man. But tell Panco about me, OK?"

"I'll tell him, Hidayet."

"But the rest is nicer, brother."

"I'll make up the rest, Hidayet. Come out of my pocket. My overcoat's wet and I can't carry both of you; I'm tired."

"OK, brother."

The sesame grain in my pocket turned into a flea. He hopped under the nettle tree in the Fatih* Mosque courtyard. A spark in the darkness . . . he shone like a black spark.

I sighed. I felt rested and merry. I was going to tell Panco a tall story; Hidayet had stuck a long spike into Pakize's heart. He had no other way out. Women and children who ate sesame halvah wouldn't expect such a story from Hidayet. Sesame halvah doesn't fill the stomach. Pakize had told the sesame halvah merchant, "I can't marry you." He loved her. Does love fill the stomach? That evening, Hidayet had got all decked out. He went to Taksim.* He had eighteen lira, thirty-seven kuruş in his pocket. He entered a bar, drank and drank. The drinks went to Hidayet's head. This meant that from now on when he would look at the minaret, he wouldn't be able to watch, together with Pakize, the way the minaret's crescent-topped spire rose to the sky on a cloudless moonlit night. When a poor woman asked, "Is this the way to Hırkaışerif*?" she disappeared under a yellow wool sweater in his head. And if he asked Pakize the same question saying, "Is it this road or the other? I don't know, Fatma Hanım*!" she would smile in the poor woman's face and say the same thing, wouldn't she?

Pakize, who smelled like fur, cats, like fine muslin and handkerchiefs . . . he would never be able to put his head on her knees.

Hey! Who had put this spike in his pocket? Wasn't it that bastard Abdullah? That nice guy, that freckled, dark, duck-nosed center-halfback soccer player with the Black Tiger Club, Abdullah. He must have placed the spike. Why the hell would that bastard, who left half a movie ticket, half a stadium ticket, toothbrush, monkey wrench, broken Yale lock, spermaceti candle, chewing gum, wormy cherries, soap, melon seeds, onions, and garlic, also place a spike? A big boat spike, shiny bright too, and thin as an awl. A story ready for Panco.

"What are you doing around here at midnight, friend?"

"Went to visit a friend, returning, stayed late."

"Where do you live?"

"In Şişli."

They searched me. I had sixty-seven lira, thirty kuruş in addition to my pen, a story typescript, picture of Panco, and another pen.

"Don't you have your ID card on you?"

"No!"

"What do you do?"

"I write."

"What kind of writing, are you a clerk?"

"I'm a clerk."

"For whom?"

"Kocaeli,* at the İkbal Warehouse."

How come I suddenly thought of that and abruptly said Kocaeli İkbal Warehouse?

"Come on, on your feet. Don't walk at night, you're an old man."

I'm walking along the border of Fatih Park, Panco. A man sits on the wet ground, his legs stretched out, his head leaning against the iron border fence of the park.

He was yelling, "Long live democracy, long live the nation, long live the republic!"

"Long live my friend," I said.

"Sit down beside me," he said.

I sat. Oh man! It really was comfortable. Nice and wet, cool.

"I have a wife, friend. If you saw her face, you'd run away as far as you could. I have a daughter. Allah grant her to someone like you. Are you married? If you're married, get a divorce and marry my daughter. She's blind in one eye, the other looks askew at God. She has a nose that wears out any snuff kerchief. Her mucus smells, her handkerchief smells, she smells herself. You can't stand her. Her monthly smells terrible. I have a son, nineteen years old, smells of piss. As for the house—may it not happen to you—it smells like a toilet. O great Allah! Look at these stones. Shiny clean. Look at this iron fence painted green! Hard, yes hard, but with the sweet smell of paint and rain. These lawns. These clouds, look at these passing black, yellow, red, blond, brunette clouds. Look at those lamps, which grow, open up like stars, and fill my eyes with arrows with sharp tips! Look at this apartment, washed from one end to the other! It's cold, it's rainy. Clean and odorless, I lie in light and water, among clouds, under the universe."

I leaned my head against the bars. So what if my bottom was in water? The cosmos was playing unimaginable games above my head. Vapor becomes water. Water cleans the mud and filth, makes the grass green, the trees grow. What business did I have at home? "Stay here. Don't go home. Let's lie down here. Let's sleep. Wait, first let's light a cigarette.

"Look at the flame on this match, this match that first fizzles, then says damn it, I'll burn. Is this possible, friend? Laugh, enjoy, friend. Look at the smoke coming out of our mouths! See how it flies! You're alive, sir. Sparkling wet droplets. You live like grass, crystal chandeliers, flowered glassware, my friend. Look at our smoke, our cigarette smoke, sir! What's this blue stuff? What's this stuff that kindles a person's heart with joy and pleasure? Not sleeping with a woman, drinking wine, playing cards with friends, theater, or seeing movies . . . leave all to one side, and just watch the world. Look, my dear friend! Here's a match flame for you. Here's cigarette smoke for you! Well, let's go to sleep, friend.

"Ha, before you sleep, tell Panco about me. About the man asleep leaning against the iron fence of Fatih Park and his cigarette smoke. Panco's a good boy. Lovable. Say hello to him for me."

It's a good thing I bought these shoes. Thank God my feet don't absorb water. I'm wet all over. My feet have central heating. I walked away, singing, "My cigarette smoke, no faith in the beloved, I built a kiosk of gold with silver stairs." He called after me, "Well done! Did you see? Does the world exist? Panco's friend! Faik Bey's* son."

I sat on the walls of Zeyrek.* Before me, Vefa.* Atatürk Boulevard* was deserted; genies played ball there. Wind blew clouds from tower to tower. "Long live soccer matches," I said. I wanted to decide from which side I'd get off the wall—I had taken dope only one time in my life, in Bursa. While sitting on the wall in the courtyard of the Green Mosque* writing poems about the Nilüfer Meadow,* I became confused as to from which side I would climb down. When I hailed a man passing by and asked, "Brother, from which side should I come down?" the poor man looked at me with fear, then smiling, took my hand and helped me down. Staring at the bill on my high school cap, he had said, "Don't do it again, young man. It's easy to get down. Someone will come and get you down. But, if you're confused about climbing up, you'll never recover!"

I no longer use such stuff, but, since then, when I climb a wall, I suddenly forget the way down.

Panco, it's always your fault. You got me into this. It's because of you I wander about in the middle of the night. You did this.

I looked . . . a sleeping dog below the wall on the hill in Zeyrek. I sat beside him. He opened his eyes. He rolled his eyes. Fearfully I patted his head. He closed his eyes. I gave him a lecture. I said, "Bug-eyes, my boy. I'm son of man. You're son of an animal. Millions of years ago, we were both maggots, we were worms, we were one-celled creatures. Before that, we were dust in empty space. Then, look, we came to this condition. From now on, maybe we'll remain like this. You're unfortunate and so are we. There are those sleeping at home, some sleeping in silk, some sleeping with women, and house dogs sleeping curled up by the stove. They have rubber bones and balls. Ladies throw them and they fetch. Mornings, doormen take them for a walk. There are people who take their loved ones in their arms at this hour, lost in twosome dreams. Very well, what should we do? But you're a tailless, mangy, street dog shivering on that hill; I'm Panco's friend, nothing else, a poor man soaked by rain, sleepless, exhausted, his heart on Raspberry Tree Street, his head on a dirty pillow a hundred meters from the Bomonti street-car stop. What shall I do? Let's think about living some day in a world made of friendship, with hearts beating with duty and feeling, and people and animals and trees and birds and lawns. We'll have a morality never written in a book. A morality that looks in surprise at what we do now and what we'll do in the future, what we think now and what we will think. Then we'll have a longer friendship, Bug-eyes. Then, don't worry. My friend Panco will agree. He won't talk about church morality. He'll tell his children about the extraordinary beauty of friendship."

I came across the man on the Atatürk Bridge.* His two hands clutched the railing; he was retching into the Golden Horn.* I stood beside him. Three times he stood on his toes as if ready to jump. Then he stopped. Taking out my handkerchief, I wiped his face. I wiped his mouth. With my hand, I combed back the hair from his eyes. Then he turned and looked at me with two large, friendly eyes.

"I drank too much, uncle," he said.

I didn't preach to him, didn't patronize him. "Drink, young man," I said, "drink to your heart's content."

"Thank God, uncle," he said, "you're one of us."

"You used to drink a lot?" he asked.

I stuck my lower lip hard against my upper and gave two or three light slaps at the air with my right hand. You do that, Panco, and you'll know what I mean.

"It's obvious, uncle," he said, "there's no light left in your face."

I was angry. "My light's inside, my boy," I said, "shining away. My heart is full of love, full of friendship, especially tonight. Don't look for that light in the face. It's false, it deceives."

"Is that right?" he said. As he was walking away, singing over his shoulder, "Is that what they say, plump bride, is that what they say?" I grabbed him.

"No," I said, "I'm not going to let you get away. Tell me, where did you drink?"

"Where do you suppose, uncle? Let me go for God's sake. It was just a midnight chat, I've sobered up and want to go to bed. Tomorrow, I have to hitch up the carriage early. If I can't pull the wool over his eyes, the old man will raise hell. Well, you know, uncle, there's a woman living in that damn house across the way. Jewish woman. Her husband went to Ankara. She invited me. I went, we drank together. Damned if he didn't show up at midnight. He didn't care. When he saw us together, he didn't say a word, just sat down. The woman too, didn't give a hoot: as if there was no one in the room, she served the raki to me, herself, and the guy. Without saying a word, the three of us each drank seven goblets of raki. 'With your permission, I have to go,' I said. 'Permission granted, sir!' she replied. His face pale, the husband said in perfect Turkish, 'To good fortune!' I split. I don't know what happened later in the house."

"Oh mother!" I said.

"Yeah, oh mother!" responded the young, handsome, rascal of a coachman.

The two of us, crossing the Atatürk Bridge in the opposite directions, arrived on opposite sides of the Golden Horn.

When I reached Azapkapı,* I heard him yell from Unkapanı.*

"Oh mother!"

In this way, Panco, I came to your neighborhood and the rain began again. Right in front of your house there was a broken water jug, half in pieces, half in good shape. I sat in the jug. I started to tell how I went to Atikali one midnight, how Hidayet got into my pocket, the man sleeping in Fatih Park, the street dog, and the Jewish woman's womanizing coachman.

You were asleep.

"Hey Panco, Panco!" I called.

My voice penetrated a window. It went in and found your ear. You awoke. But I no longer had the voice or strength to reach you. You fell asleep again. A car was passing by.

"Are you going to Bomonti, brother?" I asked.

"Jump in!" he said.

I jumped in.

"Öyle Bir Hikâye"
Alemdağda Var Bir Yılan, 1954

Barba Antimos

Translated by Celia Kerslake

ON THE WALL there is a depiction of a scene at the British Imperial Court, where a nobleman guilty of some offense is being pardoned by the queen. After that the most noteworthy picture is an advertisement for Optimus kerosene lamps. The lamp is hanging from a rope on the deck of a motorboat, and is being tossed by the wind. Under the lamp, fishermen are hauling in a net full of fish.

The canary is singing, and the coal tits can't keep still in their cage; they are continually jumping down off their perches and then back up again. The air above the stove is vibrating. Kanari the fisherman comes in through the door with snow on his yellowish-white mustache. The canary sings again.

Do you know Barba* Antimos?

Barba Antimos is a bricklayer who, just when he reached the age of eighty in terms of the life cycle of the human race, finds himself all alone on an island, faraway from his wife and children, as historic as the pictures on the wall and as alive as they are. He no longer has a boat, a net, or even any desire in his heart; only the Priol watch in his pocket, the red scarf around his neck, the woolen socks on his feet, and the smoke rising from his bushy, Maxim Gorky mustache.

You get the feeling that, whichever of Barba Antimos's eighty years you were to look into, you wouldn't find in it anything more than the memory of a wall that has been repaired. You can't get anything out of him. You see in him not so much a determination not to talk, or not to tell you anything, as simply a desire to be silent, to rest, to continue in the happy state of sitting by the stove in Kornil's coffeehouse, dreaming of building walls, plastering walls, painting walls for perhaps another eighty years, and retreating to his

110

one-room house among the heather, with his Villager* cigarettes in his cigarette case and his loaf of bread under his arm. The years are so unfaithful; outside the wind blows now from the southwest, now from the northeast, now from the northwest. The days of human life, on the other hand, drag on as if never changing. But they are sure to change. One day Barba Antimos will die.

"That wall was built by Barba Antimos," we shall say. "He used to sit by the stove in Kornil's coffeehouse. With eyes and hands unsullied after eighty years, he would tuck his Villager cigarette under his mustache. He would let his cheeks puff out as he smoked." But perhaps we shall roll down the hill of memories before Barba Antimos.

The canary, which is trilling away on this winter's day, when our feet are frozen, will one day sing no more. A day will come when Apostol the greengrocer will not give his donkey Marko raki to drink. And when Pandeli Effendi the milkman will not sit beneath the magnificent image of the English empress, with Kornil's cat Puços on his belly, telling the story of how he was sentenced to prison even though he had paid his tax arrears, and of all that he went through to get this sentence quashed. When I leave the coffeehouse, with its smells of fish and rubber, its ink stains and tobacco smoke, and go back home, I will grab pen and paper with a passion to live one by one Barba Antimos's eighty honest years, and I will never tire of doing that.

The old wives' remedies that had been recommended for the ulcer in his stomach didn't always do any good. Sometimes that honest expression on his face, that eighty-year-old expression of self-denial and fortitude, would be joined by a sadness and a bashful hint of complaint. The sadness that clouded his blue eyes at such times seemed to have been forced to come against its will, to have got on to friendly terms with human beings unwillingly, and to have been obliged to conform to their laws. I don't know whether it was at these times that the ulcer was giving him most pain. When he explicitly attributed that expression of complaint to his stomach, to the lesion in his stomach, the pain must have eased long before. He had not left his house for days. That was when he had really been in pain. It could be said that, when he came down the hill, the very purpose of his journey was to start grumbling about his stomach even on the way down.

"How are you, Barba Antimos?"

"I'm not well, sir. It's giving me a lot of trouble. It keeps me awake at night, and I can't eat a thing. Yesterday I managed to drink some soup. But I couldn't keep even that down."

"It'll get better, Barba Antimos."

He would purse his lips in the beautiful way that a child of four or five does. "The doctor at the Bulgarian Hospital gave me something to take, and it helped. But sometimes it helps and sometimes it doesn't. You can't rely on it."

Every wall on the island that you prop your shoulder against, sit on, stand and look at, throw stones at, tread on, or lean against has within it something of his mortar, his labor, his sweat. The walls he has built do not have mosaic patterns, nor are they imitations of log and stone. His walls are the humble walls built two thousand years ago, which conceal behind them or within them a rough-hewn philosophy, a tale of love, or perhaps a Greek god or a hero constantly fighting against injustice. Every wall his hand has touched suddenly takes you back two thousand years, as an ancient artifact does. If, three years from now, a bag of Byzantine gold is discovered in a cistern that he has built, no archaeologist will start saying that the bag must have been dumped there long afterward. If you plant a vine, an ivy, and a box tree in front of any of the simple cottages he has built, and construct a shady brushwood bower, you'll wonder why Socrates isn't there to greet you as you go in. Whenever you sit there on a summer evening at a wooden table drinking wine, you will hear Alcibiades, rattling his sword, say to Socrates, "All right, Socrates, let's accept that that's the case, that things are as you say. But what I can't understand is this: Why is it that man is born and grows up, and lives beyond the age of eighty, as you have done, as if he is never going to die? Why is it that, having become a veritable mine of wisdom, reason, and ideas, and having reached a state where it seems he will make all mysteries clear, just at this his happiest time he passes away and is gone?"

If you are not of the caliber to think what answer Socrates would have given, you'll keep quiet. You'll just turn to look up at the stars through the hanging bunches of grapes, and then, just as effortlessly, turn back from the stars to your wine glass. The walls that Antimos has built, the cisterns he has carved out, and the houses he has constructed have not disfigured any part of the island; on the contrary, they have made it more beautiful. But while we have found, in this rough-and-ready manifestation of the classical spirit, a path leading from Byzantium toward the simplicity and poetry of the ancient Greek world, and are advancing along it, and while, thanks to Barba Antimos, we wander around our island house in the company of Homer, the age we live in has decked itself out in ugly modern villas.

Barba Antimos was one of those people who have an indomitable spirit. He only just earned enough to make ends meet. As long as he had the strength left in him he went on making a good job of everything he turned his hand to. But when eventually this stomach ulcer came he could no longer put away a loaf of bread and 250 grams of halvah. Without this sustenance his muscles, which were like the gnarled branches of a tree, suddenly went flabby. He was left with only his clear blue eyes, his Maxim Gorky mustache, yellowed by all the tobacco smoke it had absorbed, and his mortar-colored hair, which he had let grow long. Now no one remembers that it was through the handiwork of Barba Antimos that a certain corner of his house was made beautiful. Never mind remembering, no one had ever noticed that it was through his hands that a wall had become beautiful, or mortar had become firm, or lime had been made so that it would not easily discolor.

I don't know whether he himself was aware that these hands of his made everything beautiful. Surely if he were not aware of it he would not have been so modest. He would have said, as Hristo Kalfa* did, "That's a wall that I built. It can't be knocked down just like that by ripping out one or two stones." But he didn't.

Now he comes down once every two days from the cottage that he built with his own hands up on the hill, and in which he lives with Diyojen. I come across him in the mornings, drinking milk in the dairy belonging to his old friend and compatriot Pandeli Usta.* After drinking his milk he smiles, and a mountain breeze blows into his cheeks. His blue eyes become themselves as pure and clean as something to drink, like milk. Barba Antimos doesn't breathe a word about what is troubling him. Let us, nevertheless, reveal it.

The walls he has been building for a full forty years must surely feel the greatest of his great, bitter, unspeakable secrets. Some evenings when I lean against them I feel them violently trembling.

"Barba Antimos"
> *Varlık,* XX/388, October 1, 1952
> *Son Kuşlar,* 1952

Sleeping in the Forest

Translated by Nilüfer Mizanoğlu Reddy

ON SUMMER NIGHTS when I sat on a Tring Galata[1] bench under a big umbrella pine to watch the lights of the shrimp- and crabcatchers' rowboats off Kaşıkadası* shores, I would recall my childhood days: The table set under a large mulberry tree, my father sitting at the head of that table surrounded by friends, their raki glasses, and the black mulberries falling into the plates. The lamb tethered to the sloe tree, the dragonflies with shiny purple and green wings swarming over the town's lake and the reeds around it, my swarthy and affectionate friend for whose sake I would willingly sacrifice my wristwatch, the lambs, my father's novels that he kept under lock and key, the birds and ants and chickens—where are you all?

For exactly two years I had been running away from people. I didn't know whether I was happy or sad. I was only pretending to love. My tongue felt rusty; my sleep was disturbed. But now, I can't believe that my sickness that was cured by the lights of the fishermen ever existed at all. I don't need the bromides or the tonics any more. I have turned into a person who is a cross between a doctor and a poet and I say: "Every evening at this hour after dinner, mix the carbide from the lamps of the shrimpers with lots of sea water and drink it. The whole world will change its color. You will sleep as you did in your childhood, like a plant, like a living creature that grows taller every day without even noticing it."

When I was ill my feelings and my thoughts had an ineffable quality that seemed like a dark poem. I could easily find the reasons why I didn't love people. I was full of hatred and rancor. Every single beauty dragged me be-

1. A foreign company that advertised its name on benches and billboards in Istanbul in the early part of the twentieth century.

115

yond normal pleasures and when my lips touched other lips, I felt the approaching steps of stagnation and death. Did people die like this? If so, what is called the last breath was such a horrifying thing. I would go and embrace another person with the fervor of a man who had no power of combativeness left. Every now and then, I erupted like a volcano in order to become an entirely new person.

The fishermen had gone to the other side of the island. I got up from the bench and went home by a dark road. As soon as I was in bed, I fell asleep.

I had a long and sound sleep. When I awoke, the sun was up and had entered my room. I heard the chirping of a bird. I felt as though I was seeing and enjoying the tree in front of the window for the first time in my life. I watched the shiny silvery leaves to my heart's content. I looked at the children with lithe legs, who were carrying fish in basins through the deserted streets of the village. I gave some money to the stunted children with skinny legs. I lit my cigarette with the matches of the elderly servant of a seaside mansion. I went down to the shore. I started walking toward the beach.

I saw a very fair girl. She had freckles on her nose. She was quite plump, almost fat, curvaceous. Her face was the face of a four- or five-year-old: it was undefined, small, and limpid. Her lower lip was fuller than her upper lip. I used to see girls like this all the time; I was always filled with a melancholy feeling and my nerves would burst with an irresistible desire. I wanted to do something, but couldn't—I ended up gulping and shaken. However, all those feelings belong to the past: this girl's beauty and its effect on me now seem quite ordinary.

Now, I could hold out my hand and touch this creature lying in the shimmering water. In the past, I thought that touching the girl lightly would make me lose some of my desire. But now, I know that touching doesn't lessen the desires; on the contrary, it increases them. I went into a cabana and undressed. I lay next to the young girl. I looked at her. She wore blue earrings.

After I had lunch, I went to the fields. I became a referee for the kids who were playing soccer on the grass. I ran among them, but when we had arguments about a penalty, just to be impartial, I didn't look at their faces. Some children were very good looking.

I so much liked the fifteen- or sixteen-year-old healthy girl I saw on the beach yesterday morning that I went to find a friend who could make women laugh and could become friendly with them in four or five minutes. I said to him, "Hey, pal, can we talk to this girl?"

The moon had transformed the sea into a tasty liquid. First, like most people, I wanted to be able to walk on water. Then, I wanted to lean over and drink, listening to the sounds around, like a wild but harmless animal; then, with its lust, I wanted to pet this young girl under the bushes.

My friend had managed to do what I asked him to do in ten minutes. I could only see her two little shiny blue earrings. How strange!

"What kind of desire does moonlight give you?"

Without waiting for her answer, I said, "It makes me want to cry!" I really wanted to cry, "Young lady, I am an incurable romantic."

"It makes me want to sleep under a mosquito net."

My friend had found things to say about love and marriage.

The young girl said, "In our tradition, the girl buys the boy. Most girls without money can't find husbands. Our young men don't know anything about love. They say such a thing doesn't exist anywhere in the world."

"As for us, the men buy the girls."

"That's worse!" she said.

"Does this show that there's no love, or that mutual interest creates love?"

My friend said this in French. I didn't fully understand the meaning of the phrase, but it suggested that one expected affection in exchange for the money paid.

Like a grown-up, the young girl said, "I want to sleep. Nothing, no arm of a young man, could prevent me from sleeping for another hour. I am not in love with anybody. Dancing once in a while pleases me, but only with my relatives. I am not sentimental in the moonlight, or on a dark night. I am a young girl and I want to sleep."

"Then, good night!"

I also wanted to sleep. I went to sleep in my moonlit room, prepared to have a dream with the girl who wore the blue earrings, and later in my dream I saw these things:

In the moonlight, I am again a wild animal with big ears and four long legs. I stand stiff as a ramrod. Stretching my long neck, I drink water from a lake—being on the watch and alert lest a more ferocious animal should attack me while I drink. Then, I listen, and run with the speed of a rabbit into the forest and the bushes through the strawberry and the fig trees. The southern wind brings to my nostrils the smell of a nearby female. The air is charged with electricity and my fur is shiny. Under a pine tree I copulate with a female, who is sweaty from running.

I suddenly woke up. I looked at the clock in the anteroom. It was 11:30 p.m. I ran outside. Presently I was climbing a steep pathway. There were no trees around and there was plenty of light; everything seemed gilded. Down below was the small town. The huts and the palaces were indistinguishable. After climbing a little more, a pine forest became visible. The crickets were chirping nonstop. Otherwise, I might have thought I was still dreaming, and the minutest crackling sound would wake me up and, like a frightened sleepwalker, I would grope my way around for many minutes. I crossed the pine forest from one end to the other. I found myself on the terrace of a small outdoor café. All of a sudden I saw the sparks of cigarettes under a trellis. I walked quietly and sat down.

Soon I could hear a French song in which the words "travel" and "village" were often repeated. Also feet shuffling along on the dance platform.

At an hour when everybody else was sleeping, the young sleepless ones were dancing in a hidden, deserted outdoor café in the moonlight. This is happiness! I feel so serene! I have always been opposed to dance halls, bars and even balls. They irritate me. It seems to me that there is only one purpose in such places—to seduce women. The rest—the band, the lights, the drinks, and the dances—are the vulgar means to that end. But here I don't think like that. Here, I say, a woman is a woman. She won't be seduced. She is the seducer. This is the proper way, the better way. It's been this way all along! What am I thinking about? What is the meaning of being seduced, or seducing? Here, in the moonlight, in a quiet, deserted outdoor café, "seduced" and "seducing" have no meaning. I think, this is a different world. But, a minute later, I change my mind and think that perhaps in this outdoor café the moonlight has no influence on these people who are turning round on the dance floor. They are as they would be in a dance hall. The rules of that world are valid here, too. The people, who are not dancing but sitting on the sides with their cigarettes flickering, secretly control everybody. Maybe they are the parents. Therefore, here too, seducing and being seduced matter.

Nevertheless, here, from a distance, I see a world the way I'd like it to be—a world without gossip and without lies. Moonlight makes the hut and the palace look the same and has the same effect on people. Every hut person is also a palace person. In fact, this includes me, too.

I heard the crackling of a branch nearby. I trembled. I turned back: at a distance of about ten steps, there was an apparition standing against a tree. That apparition was looking in my direction. I took a few steps: it ran away; I ran after it and a little later, breathing heavily, we both fell under a pine tree.

Who was she? Was she beautiful or ugly, did she wear blue earrings? I don't know. The only thing I remember is that her skin was ice-cold from perspiration. But this is something all people who perspire have in common. She was definitely very young. One can tell the mouth of a young person from its smell; it is the smell of a bird, of feathers.

We had a noiseless, quiet fight. Her face was covered with sweat. I'll always see her white, sweaty forehead which was a little low. I didn't see her eyes since I was kissing them constantly. We'll never see each other again because kissing the eyes doesn't bring good luck. Well, well! But something in me was saying, too bad, too bad! I sniffed her breath. Her mouth was open inside my mouth. She neither kissed nor bit; her mouth was open as if she was stunned and bewildered. A little later I kept mumbling, "*Mon enfant, ma soeur.*"

Finally my feet got untangled from hers and my hands released her waist. I crouched in a corner, like a timid child. I pulled my knees toward my nose like a sleeping child, and watched her.

She had gotten up. She had her back turned toward me. She made some bending and stretching movements. Her hair was tousled and the back of her neck looked lovely! She turned and looked and made a sweeping, effusive gesture with her hand as if she was saying, "Thank you!" or "Greetings!" I closed my eyes and slept. I felt as though I was on the plains lying in a meter of snow. I felt numb and cold. In a book I had read in my childhood, a rider traveling on a snow-covered plain sees a pole. He tethers his horse to this pole, covers himself with his sheepskin coat and goes to sleep.

In the morning he wakes up to a bright sun. He finds himself in the courtyard of a church. He looks for his horse. The horse neighs from the bell tower of the church. I also feel that the snow is melting slowly and I am coming way down to the courtyard of the church. As a child I often wondered about how that rider had brought his horse down. I still wonder. Then I feel as if I am not asleep. For a minute I hear the wind and the gramophone, then I fall asleep again.

I used to hate the mornings more than anything else in the world. I hated them as much as a Parisian does. For years I haven't seen the sunrise. For years I haven't seen how life renews itself. I didn't even want to. I used to go out after everything had taken its daily course. At night I used to walk around the streets in a certain quarter of Istanbul. I was surprised and saddened to see that at around 10:00 p.m. all the shops were closed and the windows darkened. This gave me a feeling of despair. But, this morning I got up as early as a Muslim tradesman who opens his shop in the bazaar before sunrise and strokes his beard with the money he receives from his first customer. I have the joy, the laziness, the softness, and the sensuality of a southerner. I want to lie down in the sun like a native of Marseilles, Piraeus, Naples, or Alexandria. Once I was in Naples on a January day. I saw a boy with an extraordinarily beautiful face, sleeping, curled up in front of a building that protected him from the north wind. Later, I walked across a square and there, too, I saw a group of people lying around, with a lazy sensuality, under the morning sun. In Piraeus I watched shoeshine boys, immigrants from Turkey who spoke with Anatolian accents, sleeping by panniers of red grapes. I've never been to Egypt, but there, too, the children of the south wake up early on hot days, but later feel drowsy and fall asleep because of the lust and the torpor that come from their blood and from the sun. I thought about the people of the rainy northern cities who are always restless and run around to make more and more money while the people of the south remain poor, wretched, lazy, and sensuous, but good and artistic. In all profits made in the north and in that type of civilization, I saw injustice committed against the children of the south. The gambler in Naples and the porter who sleeps on the steps of Yeni Cami* in Istanbul are miserable but good in their sensuality and laziness. And the northerner is rich and bad. No, the northerner is good and drunk with the rain, the bar and the booze. Oh, God!

Do sensuality and laziness have roles to play in human happiness? Could a genuine and balanced civilization come into existence from the differences in spirit and character between the people of the north and the people of the south? I wondered if working hard to make a lot of money was really bad. The forest was shimmering with the light of the leaves. I felt as if I was immersed in an ocean. The wind was blowing. I heard a sound of breathing. Did the trees in the forest continue sleeping despite all this wind?

I place the palms of my two hands behind my head. First of all I think of a cup of well-steeped, hot, dark tea, a slice of toast, a piece of white cheese with holes, a glass of water, and a bunch of grapes. Then, I think about people, life, all kinds of fruits, and the world. I think of inhaling and exhaling, of sensuality. The joy of sleeping here in the forest is beautiful! It is good to love people and to love life. We can only love people. But how can one person love all people? There are two ways: one way is by being a great man. How wonderful this is! But who knows how difficult it is to be a great man and how much torture one has to go through? There is also another way to love people: by being an adventurer. This is to love life more than people. The difference between an adventurer and a great man is that the former knows more about life and loves it while it is the other way around with the latter. I understand the difference between Don Quixote and Cervantes.

Setting my eyes on the prickly bosom of the forest and the azure sky beyond, I think about the difference between loving people as a great man and loving life as an adventurer.

I am inspired by the ambition of being somebody who loves people immensely and wants to do a great deal for them. I feel the tensing of my body and my nerves. However, I feel neither a great desire nor a disappointment due to my lack of desire. Since my mental condition isn't disposed to disenchantment, I am immediately filled with the spirit of an adventurer: to run at full gallop to a new adventure. Then, I think of my sleep that would be ruined again along with my family happiness, stuff like the centrally heated rooms, a living room with modern furniture, which has a radio that talks, and the movies that stifle all the dreams and destroy the adventures of the people in the city. No! Perhaps this, too, is impossible. If so, it is quite possible to love people as a human speck, humbly to the extent that one can, but . . .

This morning, as a human speck with a futile love, I love all the people, all the children, all the birds, all the fruits, all the wretched, and the hungry. No time to be sad. I jump to my feet. I run out to meet the first ferry. I wait.

A lot of strangers disembark from the ferry. I can't find a single face of a friend. I have so much to tell. Since nobody I know comes off the ferry, I return to the embrace of the paper and the pencil.

"Ormanda Uyku"
  Gündüz-Hikâyeler, VII/35, February 15, 1939
  Sarnıç, 1939

A Man Created by Loneliness

Translated by Joseph S. Jacobson

WHEN HE RAISED THE FUR COLLAR on his trench coat, I looked to see if he was cold. His face was as pale as wax.

"You're cold," I said.

He raised his eyebrows. There was no blood on the carbuncle scar on his cheek. I stopped, took his face in my palms, rubbed it.

"How did you get this way?" I asked.

He laughed, spat into the darkness, and jerked his head from side to side.

"I get this way occasionally!" he said.

"Let's go inside somewhere," I urged.

"Let's go in, but let's not drink any more," he replied.

"Let's drink," I countered.

"You'll die, man!"

"Yes, I'll die."

We stared at the glasses in our hands. How placid, quiet, and dark his face was. It was still pale, but alive.

"Your face is worn out," he remarked.

"Worn out," I replied.

He ate pistachio nuts, drank beer. I ate pistachio nuts, drank beer. I heard a ringing in my ears. I felt as though I was fainting. He was looking at me intently.

"You've aged a lot," he said.

"I've aged."

He looked at my hair, my eyes. He laughed.

"Stop it," I said, "Come on, don't stare!"

He must have warmed up, he took off his fur-collared trench coat.

I said to myself: His trench coat has a fur collar, his trench coat has a fur collar. A voice inside me said: So what? So what, I'm going to have one like it made for me.

"Won't I see you again?" I queried.

He got angry.

"That's for me to know!"

Two days later I had asked twenty people: " 'That's for me to know.' What does it mean?" Not one could give me a definite answer.

Not two days had passed. I was back at the beer hall. I didn't notice the people around me. I didn't see him either. Does one see the air? I was musing.

"Come on, get up, let's go," he said.

"Where to?"

"The soccer match."

"Match? Is there a game at this late hour?"

"After all, they have night soccer in Europe!" he said.

I didn't say: Well, they don't have night soccer here. We left, went down the hill, and stopped some place. He changed clothes. Below, near a stairway, he joined men playing soccer in the half-light. I heard voices. I heard whistles. I heard swearing. I looked around. There were thousands of people.

At one point he came up to me.

"Are you playing?" I asked.

"Are you blind?" he asked.

"In that case, what am I doing?"

"You're playing too."

"I am playing too? What am I playing?"

He laughed. I saw his teeth. One was broken on one side.

"You," he said, "are playing spectator."

"Oh yeah, right," I replied.

I was playing spectator. I started to stamp my feet, clap my hands. I was cold. I pulled up my collar. I was going to have a collar made like his. I felt the coolness of the fur on my cheeks.

I no longer moved. The spectators disappeared. Soccer players disappeared. Later, he came back.

"The match is over," he said.

"Good," I replied. "Who won?"

"The other side!"

"Come on, they didn't!"

"Who did you want to win?" he asked.

"Our guys."

"Who's our guys?"

"You."

"Us?" he asked. "You wanted us to win?"

"Right, naturally!"

"Why?" he asked.

"After all, I didn't know anyone on the other side."

"Know anybody on our side?"

"There's you!"

"Stupid!" he said. "I had nothing to do with it."

"I saw you."

"What position did I play?"

"Fullback!"

"You really did see," he said.

"Somebody tripped you."

"He did trip me."

"You're limping."

"I am limping," he said. "What's it to you?"

"Nothing. It's nothing to me."

I was dismayed.

Something snapped inside me. I called, "Panco, Panco!"

I received no answer.

Someone called my name in the dark: "İshak, İshak!"

I didn't answer. The voice wasn't his voice. But then, thinking I might get some news of my friend, I said, "Well what's up?"

The voice repeated, "İshak, İshak."

"Come on, what's up? Here I am!"

"I recognized your footsteps coming toward me!" he said. There were three youths beside him. One short, with an Armenian face. Another wore a fisherman's jacket. He had a vacant expression. The third was very tall. They were speaking a tongue the words of which I had heard thousands of times without understanding their meaning.

I followed them up a hill. We reached an avenue. It was asphalt-paved, lighted. The ground was wet. The rain had stopped.

It must have rained, I said to myself.

I had lost them. I found them at the ticket office of a movie theater. He was waiting at the door. One of them was buying tickets. The tall one and the one wearing a fisherman's jacket had nasty grins on their faces. He was dark, calm, and placid. Without looking at me, he seemed to be interested.

I tried not to be noticed. I too bought a ticket. They seated themselves in the front section. I stood at one side. I saw him moving from left to right in the darkness. He was moving to left and right with the man in front of him. For a while he settled down in his seat. His hand rested on his cheek. Then he watched intently. He straightened up again, and started to bite his fingernails. Nearby, a man in a raincoat, about forty years old, yelled, "Don't bite your fingernails!"

He smiled. The lights came on. His three friends had disappeared. The man in front who had told him not to bite his fingernails came up and sat down.

They spoke awhile. I didn't hear. My old friend with the fur-collared trench coat, took a scarf from his sleeve and wrapped it around his neck. I saw his black hair. He turned and looked, without recognizing me, as if looking at rocks or at a wall.

I opened my mouth to say, "It's me, come on, it's me, your friend; me, İshak!"

The stultifying air in the theater filled my lungs like water. I fell silent. They got up. They went through lighted shops. I gazed after them sadly. It seemed as if I'd been left alone. Talking to him, I entered a restaurant. The owner was a woman with a mole on her cheek. She still looked like a young girl of my childhood. She greeted me with a smile. Suddenly I went twenty years back.

When I was very sick and my temperature approached forty degrees centigrade, my hands swelled. They became gigantic. This mostly happened when I was a child.

"My hands are swelling," I would say.

My grandmother, or my mother, held my hands in her cool ones. "It's nothing, my child, it's nothing! Look, your hands are in mine," they would say. I stayed quiet for a minute or two. Still my hands kept swelling.

My hands kept swelling. My God, the way they swelled! When I went outside, the swelling quickly subsided in the cold. I was on the street, one against thousands. I was one against tens of thousands.

Panco, Panco! I screamed inside myself.

I looked at a clock. It was a quarter to eleven. There were very few people on the avenues, movies not yet out. Drunks didn't bump into me; I was weaving my way among them like a snake. They all resembled Panco. Everyone was going to the soccer match. I ran after the youth who had turned up the collar of his trench coat. I thought of grabbing his collar. I was going to say: Let's go to the game.

No, no, I'll take you to that German restaurant. They make a terrific potato salad. You'll eat *Spätzle*[1] too?

How about going to that beer hall in the arcade again, and what if I sat at that table? If only people came, men and women in couples. I'm all by myself. All by myself among millions. The pain gradually increases. A pain like sour melon or poison. The thing you find after losing it. Can you figure that out? Can you figure that out?

What we can't find without losing, you just don't know! Who looked from the window? Why did he look? Go ahead and shut your eyes, close them. Are your hands swelling? No, they are not. Not swelling, not swelling, hooray! But they hurt! No, they don't hurt, don't lie. Like there's something weighing on your heart, right? False. You read it some place for sure. Or someone told you. Or it remained in your head like that. There's nothing weighing down your heart. Solitude. Solitude's beautiful. It's not beautiful. Sour melons. And what are sour melons.

Some man ordered piping hot *börek** brought to him. If the man in the trench coat were here now, he would eat them. I don't know how he ate. His trench-coat collar was fur. He had a small carbuncle scar on his cheek. He had a dull, dark complexion, as if no blood flowed under his skin. He had black hair and eyes. What difference will that make, one way or another? Even if they weren't black, and he wasn't dull, dark skinned, I would still love his faded and angry color as if blood were not flowing underneath. If I found it in someone else, I wouldn't like it.

I looked at the stars. So where are the stars? Stars in a beer hall? I looked at the stars. I dashed into a movie theater. The other day, he was rushing along the avenue. It was a quarter to five. He was late for the showing. He hurried into that movie theater. I stood and watched him. I couldn't go in.

---

1. *Spätzle:* a vermicelli and cheese dish popular in German-speaking countries.

He was being stubborn. He didn't talk. Didn't say a word. Then I broke into a sweat as if I had entered a place swirling with heat. Then snow kept coming down on me. Snow fell, patter patter. Big flakes of snow. I think of pistols. Knives, knives. I don't like knives. Pistols. A small hole somewhere in my brain, a strange hole with a black ring around it. Blood trickles from it. The brain had quickly clogged the hole. Oozing out of it was something like pus.

What does he care; what does he care about this? This hole in my skull. Should I tell him about it? I should. How else can one be saved from loneliness? To die alone? No, in humanity, two dead people in a million. Three dead. Four dead. Five dead. Stop counting the dead. This is the fifth beer. Never mind this beer hall either. Or what's outside the window. After all, he isn't going to come.

Oh yeah! We were at the movies, really: The man who came out of the flying saucer took the little boy's flashlight. He went into the street, the boy after him. Two watchmen guarded the flying saucer. The robot in front of the flying saucer sat bolt upright.

He hadn't taken off his fur-collared trench coat. The fur was still cool. He pressed it against his cheek with the carbuncle scar. The fur's lips caressed his cheek. He was startled. He remembered me. He shrugged. On the table was a plaster of Paris figurine of a sailor. I had won it at a fair in a far-off European city. I used to put money under it.

"Did the sailor give you your money?"

"Yes he did, he did. Good for the sailor."

"Thanks to the sailor."

Summer days, when he stretched out beside me, I fell into a comfortable sleep. I used to see nothing in my dreams. Nothing. Is there anything as beautiful as nothing? If there is, give me a bit. At this hour, nothing is as beautiful as death.

The man who came from the other star jumped from a taxi. The whole army behind him. They had orders to fire. They fired. The soldiers surrounded him.

I used to go crazy when he came late. Unfamiliar footsteps on the stairs would drive me mad. Then suddenly, his footsteps. I used to leave the door open. He would come as though he was coming from another planet. I used to greet him.

He must go. He must leave here. The movie is over. I must walk through the streets dragging along myself and my destiny. I must go way into neighborhoods. I must see the houses. I must see the softly lighted windows after midnight. I sit on debris and look over this house at No. 2, sit on rubble until the night watchman shows up. There are flowerpots on the upper balconies. Upstairs ruined. Downstairs ruined. The middle section perfect. In which ruin does he live? Must not light a light. Slowly I move down a corridor.

"Stop thief! Stop thief!"

Must run in the street. Must run. Watchmen, whistles behind me. No, no one heard. I open the door to a small room. There, in a dilapidated bed, one of his feet out. Then, both his feet outside. I tuck his feet under the quilt. He takes a deep breath, turns toward me. I look. The carbuncle scar is on the other side. There is a sweet pinkness on his strange, furious, pale face. His eyebrows are wet. His lips dry.

The candle is about to go out. Mary flickers. Who's in this small bed? I lean over and look. She has enormous eyes. She has angry skin. She doesn't yell.

"Quiet, quiet!" I say.

I cover the little girl's mouth with my palm. She struggles.

"If you don't make a noise, I'll take away my hand," I say.

She opens and closes her black eyes. I take my hand from her mouth. Then I go and sit on the other bed. He still sleeps. I look around. His trench coat with the fur collar is there. I put it on. I walk about the room hunch-backed, my wrists sticking out of the sleeves. The little girl looks at me. She holds her hand over her mouth and laughs. I get off the debris and take to the streets. Now there are only drunks, pimps, and others in the avenues. They're all charming people. All dragging themselves and their destinies. Each one all alone. They are alone even when sleeping with a woman. If I could only find a place still open and drink another beer. No. They're all closed.

He still sleeps. His eyebrows are wet. I stick my face close to his breath. I take one of the two pillows from under his head and put it at his feet. I curl up and lie there. My hands are swelling, swelling, swelling, swelling.

"Yalnızlığın Yarattığı İnsan"
Alemdağda Var Bir Yılan, 1954

Four Stories of a Shore

Translated by Joseph S. Jacobson

1. The Onion Boat

A BOAT LOADED WITH ONIONS came to the island one day and anchored. The greedy profiteering tradesmen of the island lumbered about the dock where the big boat was anchored, sorry they couldn't unload all of the goods. I was more interested in the boat than the tradesmen, and more so in a particular boatman—a young, robust village boy. The moment he stepped on the soil of this rich island with his misshapen or deformed bare feet, his mien appeared that of a wild animal. He prowled about with hungry and vacant looks. His face, which had a remarkable nervous, puckered expression in the presence of women, would lose its energy and nerve upon turning to the white pants and blue shirts of young men of his age, his eyes losing their vivid colors, turning quiescent and sad.

Maybe he was envious. He was caught by surprise and it slipped his mind that he brought onions from his distant village to this island annually. He seemed without memory of the previous year. Yet when I asked him one day, he replied, "We come to this island every year." How fast the world was changing for him! Two days later when we met, he looked at me vacantly again. Then, without in any way showing his indifference, he left. However, I was determined to work on him. He would lie face down on the bow of the boat. He would keep on staring with an expression that revealed not even the slightest wonder.

One day, I saw him undressing on the shore where fair-skinned, plump women bathed. He didn't dive into the water like athletic youths. Like a plank let down from over the rail, he toppled in, formless and directionless.

When he reached the surface, there was a grin on his face. Having also undressed, I swam to him. Pointing at the women, he licked his fingers. Then, he took off like a tiny sailboat. He was swimming so masterfully he caught every eye. When the young, tanned girls and plump, fair-skinned women became aware of a young sportsman swimming among them, slipping around their legs like a snake, they chattered coquettishly and squealed. Some even made stylish remarks. He kept grinning all the time.

He was astonished to see that outside the water the same women passed by him without taking notice, not even bothering to look his way. Evenings, after the lights were on, when he slipped among them like a snake as he had done in the sea, he was astonished to see that the same women, frowning and looking menacing, rebuffed him, using blasphemous language he didn't quite understand. This went on for three days. In the sea, the same fun and flirting went on, the women seeming impervious to this young sport's improprieties; but evenings, when the lights were on, they wouldn't recognize the boy in rags. Days went by—he was unable to fathom the mystery. He gave up.

One day, I saw him sitting by the side of the boat. He'd given up swimming. Fishing line in hand, he now busied himself fishing, no longer turning to look at passersby with vacant and curious eyes. The fish so entranced him that his face puckered anxiously when they got off the hook, but then he grinned when they flopped at the end of his line.

We'd now become friends and chatted together. Pointing at the women again, he licked his fingers and uttered short, staccato, empty sentences. When fishermen or boatmen were around, he wouldn't talk to me. He knew he shouldn't be talking to this man in white pants and blue shirt. On the other hand, he didn't realize that neither could I be talking to him when I was in the company of people wearing white pants, blue shirts, and sport shoes. This, too, remained a mystery for him.

The island's greedy, profiteering tradesmen, at odds with one another for four or five months, finally made peace, agreed among themselves and shared the onions. One morning, I found the onion boat about to put to sea. The sail had been pulled to the yardarm. The dinghy was ready. Stones had been loaded as ballast to replace the onions. The boat was ready to sail. Near noon, the onion boat ballooned its sails with the northeast wind. I expected a farewell wave from the village boy, but he gave none. The onion boat slowly sailed away. Without waiting for it to turn into a speck on the sea, I left.

2. The Cats

My friendship with cats began this way:

One evening, I was wandering along the dock alone. It was crowded. Girls walked arm in arm with their boyfriends; noisy youths without girls on their arms passed by, singing and making remarks at girls without boyfriends.

I had seen this cat at the edge of the dock, its eyes on the moonlit sea. But because I was looking more at people than the cat, I wasn't curious to know what a thin feline might think looking at the moonlit water. A soccer-playing youth kicked the helpless cat for a goal. I saw the cat fly toward the sea, fall three paces away and bounce up in one quick motion. I paused in astonishment. The cat was at my feet. Who wouldn't be interested in such a creature, which bounced off the sea like a rubber ball, and landed at one's feet? Amazed at this extraordinary reaction and agility, the boy intended to kick it a second time, but the cat was rubbing its head against my feet with a warm, intimate motion. The young sport's eyes met mine; he smiled, changed his mind, and rejoined his friends.

I stroked the animal rubbing against my feet. Now at ease, the cat withdrew to the edge of the dock and again gazed at the sea. Then he went to the shore, exposed at ebb tide. From there, with the speed of a tiger, he sprang into the water, emerging with a fish in his jaws. Eyes on me, grumbling, he ate it. If I reached my hand to take the fish from his jaws, I felt he might suddenly remember his half-forgotten primordial wildness and rely on his reflexes such as at the moment he bounced from the sea, possibly biting a piece off me as fiercely as he ate the fish. I left him in peace at his banquet and withdrew.

The island already had lots of cats. In addition, the summer vacationers brought their more beautiful, sleek ones in baskets, some in bags. Then on lawns and roof tiles, biting and fighting, they would make love with one another. When a house filled with seven or eight kittens, they were left in the street. I saw tiny kittens uttering bitter cries while big tomcats smothered them in the deserted streets. Later, those that survived hunger or escaped the teeth of big tomcats grew to full size. Sometimes I used to see them lined up in rows on the docks, waiting all night long for fish. Some mornings, after nights when there had been high waves, I would find dead cats at the edge of the water, which had risen with the tide but had then subsided. There were white ones, black ones, and tabby ones, with their bellies swollen and their agility melted away in the waves of the sea. Having turned purple yet remaining wild, they would softly hit their heads and backs against the dock that they couldn't climb. I would be quite distressed; had this happened before midnight, perhaps they could have been saved. All that remain on the island now are indolent butchers' cats and the fluffy ones. My feral cats have disappeared one by one, or maybe they have abandoned their agility and wildness, withdrawing their claws from every kind of adventure.

3. The Children

I soon found new friends.

Evenings, island boys would gather around me; I would give them cigarettes. We smoke, hiding from the entire world. They tell me about the birds and how they make birdlime from honey to catch them. I learn what birds perch on which branches. I discover that bream fish live in the rushes, red mullet don't come to hook, the king of fishermen could pull in a twelve-kilo fish with a nine-gauge line. A boy fisher with round cheeks and black eyes, who is chubby, warm and clean as steam, guileless as he is plump and as sensitive as he is guileless, and who has salty skin, told me the story of a dragon who ripped up the nets, destroyed the fishing weirs, and snatched old fishermen at the shores of the deserted, steep-cliffed island across from us. He told no one but me since his other friends make fun of him. He told the dragon story to no one but me, for I was the only one who didn't call him Drummer because he played drums by striking two fingers against his cheek. I quietly listen to the dragon's description, believing it as much as he does. Its eyes shine like two huge spotlights; it has long tough hairs on its back, like bear fur. Its mouth is as big as a well.

4. And the Dead One

The other day I left home early, and came across the small fisherman. He was pale. He'd grown up in sun and sea head to toe. He enjoyed the sea as much as the fish and seaweed. But who knows, maybe the harshness of this northeast wind and overcast skies had made his complexion sallow. Nothing else could have made that face turn pale. Seeing me, he smiled. He was carrying the gurnard fish in a large copper dish—and he left it by the church. "There is a body," he said, "a fisherman's corpse, there at the end of the dock. Go and see what the dragon has done!"

I went and saw it. The body was on green pebbles. The police hadn't arrived yet. I hadn't yet seen the face of the man. His feet and torso resembled a mannequin's or a scarecrow's. Now, I am going to describe his face:

The teeth were sound; his chin jutting from drooping cheeks moved as if laughing at wind-driven foam. Dead-white flesh on his chin appeared ready to slough off. A five- or ten-day fisherman's stubble on that white flesh of his seemed to come and go like tiny flies, collecting then dispersing. The most fearsome sight, however, were the eye sockets—the bottoms were still pinkish. One eye was missing, the other swung out on a stark-white thread, still gazing at distant waves, and from time to time into the deep. Onlookers turned pale and commented:

"I can never eat again. Awful!"

"I wonder who he is? Dreadful!"

"Not very old either. Truly terrible!"

"There is a gold ring on his finger."

They stopped talking, then resumed. Only one woman had the courage to go up to the corpse; she looked and smiled. I recognized her. She turned to me.

"I don't see anything as frightening as they say."

"Is that so?" I said. "Don't you see?"

The woman, who had buried her loved ones, was elderly and sound. She took my arm as if she had found a confidant.

"If there is an omnipresent being, then it's frightening," she said. "But I don't believe in that. That omnipresent being has taken all I had!"

Then she fell silent, teary-eyed, and shed two teardrops on the body of the unknown fisherman.

I left the woman. My feet took me again toward the body, around which it had become very crowded. Police had arrived and were wandering through the crowd. For an instant, I fancied that the dead one was among us.

On our backs, beneath our clothes, in our eyes, weren't we each carrying around a future corpse? Were this a creature who could see and observe his own corpse for a while, then this corpse might have arisen and looked at his body, turned a little pale, as had everyone else, and told those around him:

"I won't be able to eat today."

"Bir Kıyının Dört Hikâyesi"
    Varlık, III/62, February 1, 1936
    Semaver, 1936

Master Yani

Translated by Joseph S. Jacobson

WHEN I MET MASTER YANİ, he was fifteen. At that time he wasn't Master Yani yet. He was a dark-eyed, dusky-legged, black-haired, swarthy boy.

I? I was a grown man. Why should I lie: I was unemployed, an idler. I was alone in the world. I had my mother, that's all. Other than her, I had no one. Now, Master Yani is twenty and I'm pushing fifty. But Master Yani is my only friend. And you would be amazed at how he can spread oil paint on walls. In my eyes though, he remains that fifteen-year-old swarthy boy. When he isn't painting, he goes to the movies; he goes to soccer matches; he plays *pişpirik**
at the coffeehouse.

If it occurs to him, he comes and finds me wherever I am. If it doesn't, he doesn't even look for me.

"Why would I look for you, Grandpa!" he says.

We have an out-of-the-way beer hall. I go there and sit. I keep thinking: What have I done for this world? What have I seen? Why did I come? Why am I going? What have I done?

When it snows outside, even though it's hot inside, I freeze in this beer hall. Six o'clock and still no one is here. The waiter has gone into the other hall. The clock on the wall makes one nervous, forces a person to drink. Am I expecting Master Yani? If I expect him, he won't come. If I don't expect him, will he come? There's hope. When I don't expect him, there's hope.

He comes and takes a seat right across from me. What do I say to him? What does he say to me? I don't remember a thing. Later on, I invent what he said. The beer hall has regular customers. There's one who comes and sits by the window. He has a bottle of mineral water opened. He has a double and a single shot of raki poured into it. He has them bring a plate of fruit, has them grill kidneys, and sometimes he has an omelet.

Master Yani comes. There are deep frown lines between his eyebrows. The girl's father is giving him a five-thousand-lira dowry. Evidently the girl's quite pretty. He knew her before and this time he sees her at a tea party. The girl's mother says, "Why don't you dance, Yani!" Master Yani: "I don't know how to dance or anything. If I did know, I wouldn't anyway." The mother was plainly willing. Master Yani: "Talk it over with my father."

So Master Yani won't be coming to the beer hall to drink my two beers: "It's best not to be seen at places like beer halls for a while," he says, "there's five thousand lira hanging on the deal."

Oh, for the good old days, Yani! I said the other night, you were a skinny, dusky little kid. Now you've become a big man, and I've become a grandpa. The beer hall's the old beer hall. Tables the old tables. The world's another world. You're another man. But I'm still me, Master Yani! And I always see you the same, Master Yani! Black hair, dark eyes, a boy bright as a button.

I remember going to the movies with you. Sitting next to me, you went crazy. You clapped your hands, slapped my shoulder.

"Wow!" you said, "did you see that? Look at the detective! Did you see what he did? With one blow . . ."

That movie theater, too, is gone. It was full of mirrors. In rainy weather it smelled of clothing and people. When we mixed with the boys in the first-class section my heart filled with passion. Every face was beautiful, every boy friendly. Every hand was callused, small, dirty, and warm.

The days passed. My health declined. I could no longer drink the way I used to. You became a big man; big enough to get a five-thousand-lira dowry. Do you at least love the girl, Master Yani?

"Women, Grandpa? I sure love 'em."

"True, Master Yani, women are there to be loved; but because I've remained a boy at heart, I love boys more than I love women."

"Don't you love me?"

"You? Do you have to ask, Master Yani? You? I love you a lot."

"But I'm no longer a boy."

"In my eyes you're a boy."

"If you take me for a boy, I'll be angry, offended. I'll never speak to you again."

"Won't you invite me to the wedding, Master Yani?"

"To *that,* I'd invite you."

For a time we remained silent. Then, I don't know how he thought of it, but he said to me, "When you go to the theater, take me along some evening."

"Gladly. Whenever you want."

We agreed on Monday night. I went to the theater window early and bought the tickets. I went there. Master Yani came all dressed up. He came, but the tickets were for the next evening. There was no performance Monday nights.

"Master Yani," I said, "there's no show Monday evenings; I got the tickets for tomorrow night."

"No harm done, give me my ticket," he said.

We drank four beers each and parted. The next evening I went to the theater at eight-thirty. He wasn't there yet. When the chime sounded for the curtain to rise, someone else came and sat beside me.

Master Yani had sold his ticket and not come to the theater.

Master Yani had played a childish trick on me for the last time. I liked it. I felt strange—a sensation of loneliness. Yet, I always used to go alone and enjoyed watching plays by myself. I used to choose nights when there were few people. I would go up to the balcony. I'll probably never see a performance again as bad as the one that night.

Oh, for the good old days, Master Yani! What happened Master Yani? If you didn't come, you didn't come. So what? When I run into you in the street, you're still that young boy sitting next to me in that theater with the mirrors. But after all, something like an iron hand clutches my heart. But forget it? Don't believe it! Never mind! Don't worry, Master Yani. When you see me, smile. Don't give it a thought! What's the theater anyway? There's friendship in this world, damn it! That sure hasn't died!

"Yani Usta"
Varlık, XX/404, March 1, 1954
Alemdağda Var Bir Yılan, 1954

The Armenian Fisherman and the Lame Seagull

Translated by Talat S. Halman

DIALOGUES BETWEEN THE LAME SEAGULL and the fisherman have been witnessed. I'll bet my life that it was the seagull that started the conversations. It's impossible that the fisherman addressed the seagull first.

Tattletales have reported the conversation as follows:

Seagull: ". . ."

Fisherman: "You gonna shut up, you lame thing? At this hour of the morning . . ."

Seagull: ". . ."

Fisherman: "Patience ain't gonna kill you, you know! We haven't even got to the seamark yet."

Seagull: ". . ."

Fisherman: "For heaven's sake, hold your tongue! Look, if you keep quiet, we're gonna get there sooner."

Seagull: ". . ."

Fisherman: "You keep chattering so much, I guess you're starved."

Seagull: ". . ."

Fisherman: "Now wait: I'm gonna cut up a mackerel for you."

Seagull: ". . ."

Fisherman: "Damn it, with all this gabble, you're making my head swell!"

He flung toward the seagull the head of a mackerel and its bony tail which was quivering. Then he grabbed the oars. In a short while, the Hayırsız Islands* appeared ahead of us, looming larger in the fog. The gull was now quiet. They no longer talked. It was then that the fisherman turned to me: "Whenever I go out to sea, he spots my boat at once and follows me. And the way he brings me luck—it's somethin'."

139

"Why do you call him lame, Varbet?"

"He is lame, that's why."

"What happened to his leg?"

He didn't answer. We kept quiet. The wind carried to me the smell of land. We were surrounded by the stench of watermelons turning sour. The fisherman remained silent as though he regretted having talked this much. One could say that a fisherman is a man who talks to himself, but this description may be incorrect: he doesn't even talk much to himself. I've never run into a talkative fisherman. If a man is talkative, he is no fisherman. If he is a fisherman, he is not garrulous.

The way he looked around, it was as if we were having the following conversation:

"See the tip of Kınalı Island*?"

"I see it."

"On top, there's a white strip of land. Do you see that too?"

"No."

Fish like tranquility and prefer people who are taciturn like themselves.

My head is reeling again. Would I ever go fishing again? The voice of the sea: what an enormous, deaf, deep sound that is! The human body is so tiny in the boat. Oh, land! There are winds on land. How sweet it is to stand on firm ground and gaze into the open sea. But to listen to the deaf sounds like the breathing of a huge mouth while you are in a boat in the middle of the sea, under the furtive glances of a lame gull, frightens you and makes you shudder. Oh, if only we could go back! As soon as I set foot on land, I am going to sacrifice a sheep. Sacrifice? My God, that's so horrible, so barbarous! How can they slaughter animals while women and children look on? What a primitive custom!

"The sea is pretty rough! And you're about to pass out! Let's go back, huh?"

"Yeah, please let's go back."

When we arrived at the coffeehouse in Kumkapı,* I felt warm blood swelling up all over my face. What marvelous relief! The fisherman gave me sharp glances:

"Would I ever go fishing with you again!" he said. "Man, you're a nervous wreck."

He pretended he had been cross with me for many days. Well, he was cross with everyone anyway. He must have been in mourning. He had a black ribbon on his lapel. People who knew him were saying: "Someone related to Varbet is probably dead. No one could ask the old bastard. He'd explode!"

Once again I had the urge to go fishing, to have the same psychological experience. It was a terrific pleasure to fear and to plunge into dreams. I had to relive that.

I ran into him. He was busy polishing the guts with his fingernails that were like amber from cigarettes.

I said: "Going fishing, Pop?"

He didn't answer.

To the owner of the coffeehouse I said: "Bring Varbet a cup of coffee."

"I had my coffee. No more for me."

"Going fishing, Varbet?"

"That's right. So what?"

"Why don't you take me along?"

Varbet, like other people, has his needs and debts. It wouldn't be beneath his dignity to get a bit of money from a gentleman.

"But," he said, "I ain't gonna go back even if you die in that boat."

"That day, I got sick a little."

"You're gonna be sick again. Never mind. Anyhow, you're so high-strung that you ain't gonna relax on land, either. Listen, nothin's gonna happen out there on the sea. Besides, what if you die? When death comes, what difference does it make if you're on land or sea?"

"Where's the lame gull?"

"He died."

"What? How?"

"I don't know how. One mornin' when I got to the seamark, his tiny body was floatin' right on the seamark—dead."

"Do you think he came and died on the seamark so that you could find him there?"

He didn't reply. It suddenly occurred to me that perhaps he put that black ribbon on his lapel because his gull was dead.

"Varbet, could it be that you put the black ribbon on for the seagull?"

He looked me straight in the eye:

"Good for you!" he said. "Today, your brain is working like it does on land. No fear at all!"

"Ermeni Balıkçı ve Topal Martı"
Mahalle Kahvesi, 1950

From the Novella
"*The Source of Livelihood*"—*A Fishing Boat*

Translated by Nilüfer Mizanoğlu Reddy

ONE OF THE DOORS of Mr. Dimitro's barbershop opened onto the seashore; the other door opened onto the alleyway in front of the dairy and the bakery.

Pandeli, the Bulgarian milkman, had converted at least half the rowboats on the seashore into restaurants. The shortest way to his simmering pots filled with pilaf and navy beans is through Dimitro's barbershop. That's why his doors are usually open to all passersby. On busy days people pass through the barbershop as nonchalantly as through a street.

Dimitro is a man capable of saying things unpleasant enough to prevent people from passing through his shop. If that didn't work, he would leave the door to the seashore open and close the door opening to the street in front of the dairy.

But those who went through his shop got shaved by Dimitro once a week. That was the price they would pay for passing through. No man with stubble could escape Dimitro's razor if he wanted to pass through the shop. Dimitro would immediately notice the beard, whether it was a week or a month old: it had to be shaved according to the status of its owner. Dimitro, a man of sixty, with white hair, white mustache, and blue eyes, had the knack of hitting people at their softest spot. For instance, he would say to the young man who played footsie with Evgenia, "Ah, you can go through Dimitro's passage but you cannot give up Evgenia!" The young man who is taunted in such a fashion has to keep his affair secret for some time.

Dimitro has to make the dirtiest insinuations for his bread money—and has to learn the gossip about the most secret goings-on for his raki, which on rare evenings helps his blue eyes to cast a blue luster on the glass.

On winter days the village would be deserted; the cats would line up in a row at the pier; the old Greek women, the sick, and the hungry would wait together with the cats for the fishermen to come home. The northeast wind would blow, striking its dragon's head from wall to wall and from tree to tree. On those violet-colored days, both doors of Dimitro's shop are closed, the windows are steamed up and covered with newspapers; inside the shop it is white and cloudy like a glass of raki mixed with water. Ashes covering the water pitcher, dust on the cologne bottles, cigarette smoke, Dimitro's five-day-old stubble, and his neatly combed white hair completed this picture of mistiness. Looking through the window one could barely make out Dimitro's figure. With his glasses on he is reading the local Greek paper, presumably with fine enunciation. Listen more carefully and you'll notice that he is reading in a booming voice.

When somebody knocks at the door, he would sense slow movements as though something stirred inside a white liquid. A key opens the door with a creaking sound. The customer glides in. One kick by the northeast wind and the door is shut. Dimitro opens the door, the customer enters, and the wind slams the door shut so swiftly that the person entering can't help thinking: "Where was I? Where am I now?"

On early December days when the northeast wind shoves people around and the rain hits their faces in a blinding fury and their necks in a stinging manner, inside Dimitro's shop it is warm and quiet and it smells of soap and cologne. On winter days it is impossible not to be happy there for just a moment or two.

It was a Friday; Dimitro was busy reading his papers. One of his customers had left him some Athens papers as well. There was a knock on the door. Dimitro pushed his glasses up on his forehead and wiped the steam off the window. Carefully he inspected the short man standing there. He didn't want to open the door; he wanted to get back to a statement by Venizelos* he was reading in the paper. Then he thought that the person who had knocked on the door might be a Turk with whom he had recently become friends. He opened the door with a sympathy acquired from reading Venizelos's article entitled "Two Brotherly Nations."

"Is that you, Kondos?" he said.

The northeast wind slammed the door behind Kondos. (Kondos means a short man in Greek.[1]) The face of the man who had come in for a shave had the look of a street boy. It was as though he was about to say, "C'mon, let's skip out! Let's go to Şehzadebaşı.* We'll slip into a movie theater. For heaven's sake, dumbbell, c'mon, what are you waiting for?" It was as if he would like to lure the whole population of the island, have them walk across the sea, and have them enter the movie theaters in Şehzadebaşı without paying a penny.

The man told Dimitro, "Give my old hide a close shave."

But Dimitro could immediately tell from the man's demeanor and his merely one-week-long stubble that he had come either to give him some news or to ask his advice about something. Had Kondos become so affluent as to have a shave once a week? Or, was he about to borrow money again? Turning all his pockets inside out and bellowing an atrocious oath he would say, "How could these pockets hold money? Look, Master Dimitro, they've all got holes!"

Barber Dimitro knew that Kondos didn't come to him when he had money, but one had to be careful not to arouse his ire; that man could be a pain in the neck. Without even heating the water and making a lather, Dimitro gave him a clean shave in two minutes. After the shave, Kondos lost that street-boy expression and some of the lines on his face were strong, deep, and even meaningful. One could see right away that the street-boy expression came only from his eyes. As Dimitro was wetting his hair, Kondos started saying, "Master Dimitro, I want my daughter to work for you. What do you say?"

"Ali Rıza, are you going to make her a barber?"

"God willing, I want her to be."

"What has happened to the Turks?" Dimitro thought to himself. "My God . . . even Turks like Kondos! Unbelievable!"

"How is it possible?" he said, "Isn't it a sin, Ali Rıza, in your Muslim religion?"

Ali Rıza got angry. "Hey you, barber, are you gonna teach me my religion?"

It was the custom of the island: every poor boy served as an apprentice to

1. Dimitro uses Kondos as a nickname for Ali Rıza, a Muslim Turk. In the present text, the translator employs Kondos and Ali Rıza interchangeably in many passages.

the grocer, dairyman, bread seller, baker, butcher, or the barber. Nobody hired an apprentice from anywhere else so all the children of the island could find jobs. The only exceptions were those who stole, or smart alecks. Like that boy who stole the olive oil from Karamanlı* last year and the one who snatched the church candles and whisked them away to Istanbul the year before last.

But those were the exceptions, otherwise all the others would find a place somewhere. These kids, greasy all over, barefoot, with bent backs, climbed the steep streets and carried everything in baskets on their backs—in the summer they carried water jugs, ice that dripped onto their shirts, and cans of olive oil. They swept in front of the stores. They would save their two-lira-a-week pay for months and toward the end of summer each one had a blue shirt on his back—and on his feet a pair of large shoes given him by a gentleman. Now with their immaculate white trousers they could join the children of well-to-do families. But it was also at that time that the kerosene can from Karamanlı's store, the peaches and melons of the greengrocer, the loaves from the bakery, and the cookies from the pastry shop would start disappearing. Because of this, the apprentices who spent their weekly pay right away were the most appreciated ones. Karamanlı, the grocer, used to say, "Money corrupts people; when people are well fed their bad traits show up." He knew this from personal experience. There might be some truth in this, but this truth is interpreted differently by each person. Quite often Karamanlı had sold two cents worth of ice for a quarter, but this could not be called stealing—it was being shrewd.

As for the boy who stole the candles from the church: six months later he, too—after putting a school cap on his head and linen trousers on his legs—had realized that there were beautiful things in the world. The candles of the monastery were piled up in a corner. They burn in vain. To go to Istanbul by ferry one had to have money. Then somewhere lights are turned off; on a [movie] screen children would play games, men would strangle each other, and girls with silvery legs would kiss. There were so many other things in Istanbul. But the candles of the monastery burned uselessly for the horrible, yellow, and worthless dead bodies in the church.

Of course, no child ever thinks like this; we grown-ups think this way.

Why does a child steal? We can suggest twenty different hypotheses, but we still don't know why a child steals.

Barber Dimitro was very tolerant of the children who stole. Perhaps because he had never trained an apprentice himself.

He wanted to reject Ali Rıza's daughter. Then he again remembered Venizelos's article. He still wanted to turn her down. But, according to the village customs, turning a child down who had never stolen would be considered an insult, or at least, a sign of selfishness. The scissors he used to trim Ali Rıza's mustache made clip clip sounds that became more audible.

Only master barbers are capable of balancing their thinking and the clipping sounds of their scissors. When the unskilled barber thinks, the scissors in his hand become frozen or make discordant sounds. The master barber is the one who can control both his head and his hand. The harmony of the scissors should not be disturbed by the rapid flow of thoughts and by his mood. It can be said that another barber who is in tune with this harmony can understand something from this clip clip of the scissors as though it were Morse code.

Although Ali Rıza was no barber and didn't know the Morse code of the barbers, somehow he could sense what Dimitro was thinking about. Yet, at this point, he couldn't figure out whether Dimitro had arrived at the mastery of his trade or was still a novice.

Ali Rıza surmised that within three years the people of the island would flock into his dark-complexioned daughter's barbershop. They would bring two apprentices from Istanbul. Under the gas lamp there would be a table piled with foreign magazines and Turkish newspapers. People who needed a shave would wait in front of the curtained windows; in the women's section, separated by a screen, big, mysterious gadgets would be hanging from the ceiling and hair curlers would be heated in a copper brazier.

In the evenings Ali Rıza would be able to spend one lira from the day's take in the cash box as he wished. He would buy a gallon of wine, newspapers that smelled of fresh ink, and a hookah with a long tube wound with golden thread. Maybe he was going to be the first Turkish father with a daughter who was a barber. He was already thinking of himself as an open-minded, freethinking man.

Dimitro said, "OK, Kondos, let her come."

"Will she be able to learn the trade quickly, master?"

"It won't even take a year. Girls are adept at this job."

"Is that so?"

"Yes, yes."

"When shall I send her, Dimitrakimu?"

"Eh, whenever you want, Kondossi."

Ali Rıza ran out in a hurry forgetting to pay. Dimitro thought he'd deduct it from the girl's pay."

As soon as Ali Rıza left the barbershop, he noticed that it was getting dark and the northeast wind had become harsher.

He thought he couldn't go fishing that night and he felt unhappy. He started looking for an evening newspaper. Every place seemed to be closed. The big waves were crashing against the rocks of the pier. He walked along the pier facing the wind. He was still dreaming the same dream: the image of the barbershop set up by the open-minded father for his daughter.

He came to the church square by a passage just big enough for a man to slip through. He walked toward an electric streetlight in front of the church. Under the lamp there were two comfortable rustic benches that either belonged to the church's entrance or to its custodian; they were sometimes occupied either by an engaged couple, who liked to flaunt their love in broad daylight, or by two pious old Greek women. The only times the benches were free were on such windy days when everybody was home at the dinner table. Ali Rıza sat on a bench and lit a cigarette. His daughter had wanted to be a dressmaker. How could he say to her, "I'll make you a barber, Melek!"? While he finished smoking his cigarette, he thought about how he would behave when he got home. It was a delicate situation! He went back to the marketplace. He knocked on the door of a shop that had light coming through its wooden shutters.

"Hey Yanko, give me a glass of wine," he said.

The man called Yanko made a sign with his two fingers indicating money.

Ali Rıza shouted, "I've got it, I've got it!"

Yanko was still sitting and smiling. Ali Rıza searched all his pockets and managed to find some coins only after going through them the second time.

He gave them to the wine-seller. Yanko filled a beer glass with a tea-colored wine that seemed lukewarm. Ali Rıza drank it in one gulp. He moved his eyes around the shop as if he was looking for something. The wine-seller offered him a fish tail on a piece of bread as if to say that he had understood what Ali Rıza was looking for. The money he received must have been sufficient for another glass of wine, because this time Yanko filled the glass without making the money sign. Standing up, Ali Rıza swallowed that glass, too, in one gulp. He bit into the fish tail and ate it bones and all. Then, with a pleading expression with his street-boy eyes, he said, "Yanko, fill it up! I swear I'll pay tomorrow."

Yanko filled the glass again and this time he offered just a fish head. Like a real drunkard, Ali Rıza sipped the wine slowly, taking it in as if he were sucking it.

This shop wasn't exposed to the northeast wind because part of a nearby building protected it. But the spray from the sea had reached Ali Rıza's feet. His body was ice cold where a whiff of air had penetrated through his trousers; the upper part of his body was as warm as the centrally heated room of a big shot on a winter day.

As soon as Ali Rıza finished his last drop, he balanced the glass on his head for a long time; this gave him the appearance of an acrobat. Two of the customers standing at small tables were eyeing him. Ali Rıza had such a ludicrous posture that one of them couldn't help saying, "Fill it up, Yanko, a glass from me for Kondos."

Yanko hesitated. Ali Rıza could be a nuisance when he drank: he swore, he broke glasses—he did all sorts of scandalous things. And it always ended with him getting a sound beating. On this windy day, beating him up could be a problem. What if by accident he landed in the sea? It could happen!

"Hey, what are you waiting for, you jerk of a sexton, fill it up, the gentleman's ordering!"

The cursing impressed Yanko in the desired manner, but he didn't fill the glass. Ali Rıza didn't want to drink too much. He, too, knew that when he drank too much he would be a nuisance; he would become quarrelsome and his speech would be slurred, whereas three glasses of wine usually gave him the eloquence of a Young Turk.*

"Count my last glass as the one the gentleman ordered. I don't owe you anything," he said. Then he moved as if he was about to leave and turned: "It's better to be in debt to a dog than it is to you, you son of a bitch!" he said.

A Greek curse was thrown after him like a bottle. The wooden shutters were closed. Presently Ali Rıza was walking toward the church square again and thinking about the speech he was going to give his daughter as soon as he entered his house.

"Melek, my daughter! Thank God, you're a reasonable girl. Listen to me carefully. Today I'm here, tomorrow I'll be gone. All my thoughts are about you and about Hikmet. Where is he, hasn't he come back? Did he go with Captain Rıza? Good . . . he'll bring money tonight. Of course he must have gotten his share. He'll be here when the last ferry gets here.

"Well, let's talk about our own affairs: as I was saying, in this world of ours that is full of deception, you reap what you sow. If you amount to something I'll be very happy. We, too, will have a roof over our heads. Look, Melek, we're poor people. We have to work with our daughters, with our females to get to where the others are. Otherwise we'll end up badly. After all there's sickness, there's old age. Thank God, I'm as strong as an ox now. I'm a jack-of-all-trades, we won't starve, but (here he made a sweeping movement with his hand pointing to the damp basement with its stained walls, piled up with odd-looking, old, and useless furniture) how long are we going to live in this dump where even a dog won't stay? In fact, how long can we stand this without jumping off the pier into the sea? We don't even know this, do we, Melek?" Suddenly, he felt he had to get to the point.

"I want to make you a barber. I spoke with Dimitro. You can go there and work anytime you want to. In one year you'll learn the trade. It isn't a bad trade, is it? Once you learn it, there's no problem. Leave the rest to me. I'll obtain the capital."

Melek didn't protest. She was already feeling the independence of a shop owner and the warmth of the place on a winter evening. A shop of her own: black-bearded customers, bright-eyed young men with reddish, golden necks, the hissing of the gas lamp, the northeast wind outside the windows, the foamy sea, and the steam on the shop windows.

A ladder, made by her father, hung on one of the walls of the basement. Melek took it down and put it up against a man-sized hole that would have seemed very mysterious and startling to someone who entered it for the first time. Melek, with her boyish legs, climbed the ladder and entered the hole that was her room.

Though the young girl was crawling on her knees, she still had to lower her head. A soft light coming through a tiny window permeated the room, and a birdcage was barely discernible in that dim light. Melek lay face down on a mattress casually thrown on the floor. When she was very unhappy, or when she decided to think about good or bad things, she couldn't stand the smallest light. She loved to think in pitch-black solitude without even feeling her own body. Melek was fourteen years old. Her face had the beauty of a native or a mixed race from an island somewhere in a sea. But her true beauty was in her body. Almost all her limbs were too large for her age—a characteristic of people developing and growing stronger. Her feet were big and her fingers were long and rather thick. Her shoulders were even wider than the shoulders of boys her age. She was flat-chested. But despite everything that promised her a strong and beautiful future, her face was sallow like the face of a sickly person. Her lips were colorless. Yet, her eyes were large, lively, darting, clever, and bright.

As Melek lay face down, she felt her body had stopped belonging to her. Now only her mind was working; the rest of her was inert like a piece of rock. But with her mind and with a different body and different feet created by her mind, she would attain all sorts of beautiful things. She imagined herself with carnations in her hair and wearing a wrinkled coat with a rose attached to its lapel. And she wore a comb in her hair with the carnations.

Melek suddenly got up from where she was lying. She thought if she didn't move her body she might forget how to move. She went to the window. Outside, a semi-dark, narrow, small-town road joined the city lights at a juncture where there were two adjacent houses, and it came to an end at that point. The world beyond that, with its fishermen's cafés, rocking rowboats by the pier, and the porters running to the last ferry, wasn't any worse than home. There were at least the ferries that came and left. Perhaps, Melahat was there seeing off the cadets from the Naval Academy. Young men in navy blue uniforms with gold buttons beckoned to Melahat, and Melahat flirted with them.

Melek wondered if she should go to the pier. She yelled downstairs, "Papa, what time is it?"

"Must be past ten."

Melek said, "It's late," to herself; she again threw herself on the mattress, put her hand under the pillow and fell asleep.

After his daughter went upstairs, Ali Rıza got busy preparing his hookah as he hummed a song. The basement door was open. When Ali Rıza looked toward the door, he could see two feet in front of it; someone is bending over and looking inside. But the face of the person bent over and looking in was not recognizable, even if he might know them. Then the man who looked down would be gone and Ali Rıza would mumble, "Who was that?" He would be irritated and he would go and shut the door.

Melek's father had picked up a good gilded sofa that did not go with the rest of the furniture in the room; he had put it in the middle and settled on it. The hookah was ready; it was already repaired in three or four places, but the smoke was still escaping all over because it wasn't properly circulating. He got up from the sofa he was cozily settled on. He looked for something among the weird odds and ends in the room. He found a spool of thread. He wrapped the smoking parts of the tube with rags and wound them with the thread.

When he was settled on the sofa again with his legs rolled under him, he suddenly remembered that this evening he didn't have a newspaper. He got up and pulled a paper from a pile of old newspapers and sat down again. He opened the paper. He was reading and daydreaming at the same time.

Once he had been the stationmaster in the Doğançay* train station. It was a place of gigantic rocks, flowing streams, and little Circassian villages squeezed between two mountains. There were Circassian girls who stuck their white Georgian faces to the windows of the stationmaster's warm room and looked in with their dark eyes. Ali Rıza would always remember that when he was the stationmaster in Doğançay he always read the papers sitting cozily like this. At that time he was not in the habit of smoking the hookah. He used to roll his cigarettes putting yellow—almost pumpkin colored—Hendek tobacco in the finest Seferoğlu papers. The room was warm. A cast iron stove consumed endless piles of split logs. At the train's arrival time, Circassian girls came to the station to sell fruit; they stuck their snow-like white faces to the window of the stationmaster's room to see the clock. The stationmaster wanted to hold and squeeze their noses.

At night the howling of the jackals echoed in the mountains and, on the nearby highway, riders passed by mounted on black horses that went clip clop. Sometimes pops from Browning rifles coming from Circassian weddings pierced the star-studded, bright Doğançay nights until the late hours.

The train used to arrive, its stack pouring a yellow smoke into the night. It roared like a huge dragon. It left with monstrous sounds, spitting tiny sparks, and rushed through the Geyve* gorge as though it might get stuck there if it didn't move fast.

The hookah and the newspaper always let Ali Rıza abandon himself to the pleasure of remembering the most important job he had held as a young man. He always had the same old dream. But at the end of this beautiful old dream he also couldn't help remembering a very recent event that had annoyed him. An incident that might have seemed ordinary a little while ago would be remembered as silly and senseless, like the speech he had made to his daughter that evening.

He was overcome with a sense of shame. "It's disgraceful," he said, "What did I tell the girl? But I'm right! No, what right do I have? Why am I right? Those were such empty words. Should I have put it like this, he thought to himself? I should have said: 'Daughter! We—I mean, I am in no position to work as a porter or a fisherman anymore. I have aches all over. I feel miserable. I look so shabby! I don't give a damn myself, but I'm embarrassed because of you. They'll say, "Look at Melek's father." If you want we can buy a little store. I can take it a little easier. In a few years we can buy a little house—three or four rooms. We can live in two rooms and rent the other rooms in the summer. You may find an honest boy, a shopkeeper, and get married. I would be able to see my grandchildren.' If I had talked like this it would have been better and I would have been able to express what was really on my mind.

"Ah, being half drunk makes you a liar, a hypocrite, and puts the wrong words in your mouth. I should either never smoke this damn thing, or I should pass out. Isn't one pack of tobacco in three days enough for me? Right now even this is too much!"

It was late at night. The distant sounds of the fishermen had stopped; now and then only the sound of the sea was barely audible.

Ali Rıza wondered: "What time is it? Why is Naci late? He must have come back from the city. He must be in a café. Aren't the cafés closed? Ah,

Sultana's café is open till the wee hours. Maybe there's a party on a boat. They must be getting drunk. That rascal!" He continued: "How about Hikmet, where's he? Is he with Naci, too? Probably. I guess Naci won't let him go. But he should come home and sleep. Day in, day out he slaves for those SOB fishermen. Well, there are some decent fellows among them! That old man who gave him the dark blue serge trousers; the young man who gave him the mountain climbing boots imported from Romania—he's a good guy, too!"

Ali Rıza had found Hikmet in the street one night during the Armistice [presumably 1918] when he was patrolling the streets as a militiaman. Hikmet was not a day older than seven. He was like a refugee boy, skinny and weak with blond hair and freckles on his white nose. Ali Rıza had brought him home. His Bosnian wife (Melek's mother) was still living then. She was the woman he married when he was the stationmaster in a place near Edirne after he had left Doğançay.

The Bosnian wife had made such a big fuss! "You're not even capable of taking care of your own children and you pick up children from the street, but does it end there? If only he were good looking," she yelled.

According to her, good looks should be something like this: curly, oily hair with the nits gleaming. In the evenings by the light of a gas lamp, that Bosnian woman used to pick the nits from the hair of their now-deceased daughter—with such pleasure, too! In the big cold room of their house in Horhor, Ali Rıza felt squeamish watching the little girl and his Bosnian wife, who was at it for hours drooling with pleasure. Because of this, often he had taken over the night watch duties of his friends to make sure the Horhor neighborhood wouldn't get burned down. Many nights when there was a fire Ali Rıza had run home to find his wife and his daughter picking each other's nits. And how many evenings had he eaten those disgusting dishes made with raw meat? And how about that Serbian dish made with fava beans, meat, cucumber pickle, and cinnamon?

After the death of Ali Rıza's Bosnian wife and after he had left his official job, Hikmet, who was fourteen years old then, had taken care of the family. He sold newspapers, he read from the Almanac, and recited quatrains to passersby at the head of the bridge.

Ali Rıza had fallen ill after the Armistice. Then Hikmet, whom he had found in a dark street of Galata* and brought home, took care of him. Behind the lattice of the window, sitting on the settee with his bare, thin, purple legs, Ali Rıza watched with strange feelings how Hikmet ran to find a doctor and felt pity not for himself but for the boy's emaciated body.

Then he was suffering from migraines. His temperature was never below forty degrees centigrade. He still has no idea what his disease was called.

Since he recovered from that illness he sometimes carries the feeling of emptiness in his head—feeling bottomless and vast. If this feeling of emptiness lasted all day it would be devastating. Usually, it lasted for an hour. Ali Rıza couldn't think about anything, or remember anything; he would walk around with his face yellow as wax and his eyes blurred.

His affliction disappeared when he roamed around the hills of the island. Then he would find himself in front of Yanko's shop, his blood lending color to his skin and his usual cheerfulness restored.

Indeed, Hikmet has been working hard since then. He clung to Ali Rıza and Naci as if they were his father and his brother. But he didn't get along well with Melek; they quarreled a lot. He wasn't afraid of Ali Rıza and he didn't pay much attention to Naci because he was six years his junior. But he heeded everything Melek said and, oddly enough, he was intimidated by her.

Ali Rıza fell into a deep sleep.

The day Hikmet settled into his job as the second motorman of the fishing boat called *The Source of Livelihood,* Captain Rıza bought him yellow coveralls; Melek, whose weekly salary had gone up to four lira at Dimitro's, gave him a pair of sturdy army boots and a close shave; and Ali Rıza furnished his head with a secondhand cap whose insignia was still shiny.

On this spring day, Hikmet walked awkwardly, wearing for the first time in his life the outfit he had long desired. The coveralls were too large for his skinny body. His hair, cut in a hurry, made his naturally handsome head look as if it had been plucked. Lowering his chin a little and pinching his neck, he walked with a bizarre, threatening swagger. Because of that, people who passed by laughed behind his back.

But he was proud. He felt at ease because for the first time in his life he mingled with people without any part of his naked flesh showing. At last he was a man: a motorman.

He held a cigarette between his fingers; his pencil with a shiny metal clip was in the pocket of his coveralls; also his handkerchief and his two bucks. The world is vast and beautiful. The stars shine at night. In the daytime a golden yellow sun rises. The seas are calm and the motorboat is noisy. Melek is his younger sister. The owner of the motorboat is a drunkard, but he too deserves to be loved. We all know that even the worst person has something good in him. We are destined to find that good part and obliged to make something out of it.

When Captain Rıza came too near Hikmet, the young man experienced a bitter sensation that he had never felt before. This feeling cannot be defined, or talked about, but can be likened to something: Can you put your head into a press? Does that press crush you slowly? Do you feel that your spirit is also pressed with your head? Nobody has put Hikmet's head into a press, but Captain Rıza's slow, sneaky, and surly approach was very much like that.

One night the motorman had beaten Captain Rıza to a pulp and had left; the new motorman made more serious insinuations against Hikmet than that press business.

Hikmet endured it. What the hell could he do? He learned the motorman's job in a year. Then, one evening, it was his turn to give a good thrashing to the motorman. Then he became the motorman for Captain Rıza, working by his side without looking into his eyes; although Captain Rıza was as compassionate as a father he had not been able to kill the devil in his soul. For a helper Hikmet found, somewhere, a bowlegged, black-faced, filthy-haired, and hideous but good-natured boy who was worth the whole world. Captain Rıza was really making a lot of money. He was almost the only person who provided the transportation between the little island and the city. Nobody but Hikmet could negotiate the big, violent storms of the Marmara* with such a rotten boat. If Hikmet didn't help, Captain Rıza couldn't send his son to the boarding school, provide his wife's and his daughter's finery, drink raki, and go to town every so often to have a fling. Hikmet received five lira a week from the captain. The captain made sixty lira profit a week. Hikmet guessed that the captain's monthly household expenses were more than three hundred lira, but the captain thought nothing of five hundred lira a month.

Hikmet gave one lira from his weekly pay to the boy who was his helper. Fortunately, Captain Rıza had taken the responsibility of feeding the boy with the leftovers from his house. The boy slept in the hold; he always woke up singing songs. His eyes were always sleepy and there were purple rings under them. Hikmet sometimes pulled the helper's ear and said, "You bastard, I'm suspicious of you! Do you dream all night?" But the poor little one was yet to have any dreams. He didn't know anything about anything. Actually, he was old enough to have such dreams, but with the leftovers from Captain Rıza's table he couldn't have them for a couple of years. He had a weak constitution. His kidneys didn't function well. Dampness didn't help his condition. The purple rings under his eyes were due to the lifelessness of his soul, though he worked hard.

The Source of Livelihood remained idle for some time after she carried furniture for the summer people, the ice and the other items for the grocer, and the parcels of people who returned in the fall. Then when the bonito came from the Black Sea in great numbers, *The Source of Livelihood,* with rowboats tied to its stern, sailed to the place where the fish were teeming. It was then that the beautiful nights started for Hikmet.

In half an hour the lights seemed far away. Now, right here where a gentle wind from the northeast licked his face, Hikmet could think of someone lying on a daybed covered by tattered kilims in a tiny, unheated room, its windows painted with morning glories, and he could also catch the cold, glistening, and snakelike creatures in nets from the bubbling surface of the sleepless sea that swarmed with fish and sea monsters.

"Hisaa . . . throw the nets in!"

"My, my, look at the fish, Captain, look!"

"Hey, turn, turn!"

"Hey, you, what are you waiting for?"

"Get your rowboat out of here."

"Ah, you mean thief!"

"Hey, Captain, whose goods are you saving from whom?"

"I'll poke your eyes, damn you!"

"Poke yourself!"

The noise they make when they throw the sea creatures into the boat's hold with the speed of lightning is such a wonderful noise. Hikmet imagines himself sitting in a movie theater. It sounds like people are thumping their feet because it is after 9:00 p.m. and one has to restrain oneself not to yell, "C'mon, let's start, c'mon!"

"Nine hundred pairs, six hundred and fifty pairs, twelve hundred pairs . . . can't the boat take more? C'mon, load them. Don't be a chicken! Let's go down with the fish, it's OK. Damn it! Let the fish sink us. Hey, you bums, your share, take as much as you want! C'mon! What are you waiting for, fill up your boat."

"Ah, the monsters are worthless . . . worthless. Italy isn't buying."

"There's going to be a war next year."

"Let's see if there will be any fish next year."

"A pair, not even worth ten kuruş?"

"Enough, enough! The boat is going to sink."

"No fear; this is *The Source of Livelihood*, it won't sink."

"Did it ever sink?"

"Last spring it almost did. Remember, when the sea was so wild during the storms in May."

"It's three thousand already. Enough! I can't even take one more fish. I'm steering."

"Hey, steering to where? You can't go anywhere. What about our agreement? Ah, the boatmen of our country, where are you? Look at this gutless bum!"

Hikmet yelled at the helper who was oiling the engine: "Tahsin, my boy, give it some fuel oil, we're splitting."

They split. Then, as the lights of the island became bigger and bigger and the seas underneath grew more and more distant, they arrived at the pier where the crowds had gathered. Customs officers, policemen, old women, children: everybody was waiting for them. It was morning already and everybody was holding a big bonito in his hand.

"We'll be late, c'mon let's go to town!"

By twilight, the sound of the sea has stopped and everything has gone to sleep. The fish are exhausted and the sea is worn out. Children in faraway houses wake up to the sound of the motorboat, but fall asleep again. As the town starts waking up in the midst of a fog, fishermen arrive at the places where people and fish intermingle and there they find out that bonito isn't worth anything. They sold a thousand pairs of fish to the Greek ship *Avriyonos*. Then the boatmen and the captains set out to throw two thousand pairs into the sea cursing religion, faith, women, and the whole universe.

The bonitos floating on the sea are like the carcasses of land animals, holding the city garbage between their tiny, pointed teeth. Small rowboats are just taking their catch to the market amid the shouts of, "Take them, you'll get plenty of dough!"

The boatmen who pull their oars fast have bitter doubts: They clench their teeth, their faces look tired. They are sleepless and miserable. However, men's eyes occasionally twinkle with the naughtiness of a raki revelry or of a Galata night. In half an hour, they, too, bring their catch to the Golden Horn* and unload it. Because of the bonito carcasses floating all over the place small ferries have a hard time coming up to the pier.

The patrol boats go around the shore of the whole town and try to catch the rowboat men who dump fish into the mouth of the inlet. The big barges rock to and fro with their enormous bulk.

The people in the city become sick and tired of the winter mornings with their ceaseless rain and the mud. However, drinking raki has to go on. Whether there is fish or not, whether it is sold or not, there is always hope. Anyway, it is impossible that there should be no fish. The sailboats with foreign flags are all lined up; they will buy this delectable creature that is all flesh, and luscious like Turkish delight; they will pickle it in barrels and eat it with gusto—if not this year definitely the next.

"Hey, long live bonito!"

"To all of us, fellows!"

"Captain, for God's sake, one more drink."

"No, no . . . you'll be soused! It's enough!"

"OK Captain! To your health!"

The other man nods, "Cheers!" The sailor with the combed mustache gets crazy. Hasan who drinks a lot of raki becomes brazen. The mad captain opens his cuplike, bloody eyes and yells, "C'mon, let's scram! We're rotting here."

The foulmouthed, hardened little whores wait in quiet bars with the lights turned on as the evening descends. Oud player Sotiraki with his plectrum, zitherist Himmet with his thimble, and singer Melahat with her white neck are at the fishermen's disposal.

"Hey, long live bonito!"

"To hell with bonito!"

"Shut up! You'll be cursed with the plague!"

Hikmet has already been paid and he is on his way to the village. Two live fish wiggle beneath the bow. Hikmet is going to pickle them; in the summer evenings he will eat that caviar-like fish together with a big onion smashed with his fist and he will drink raki from a teacup in front of Sultana's café.

"Hey, Hikmet! Long live bonito!"

"Let's all live together, my sonny boy!"

"To your health!"

This is how the boatmen in the stern return from the city.

Captain Yakup telephoned to say that two Italian ships are waiting. The fish is twenty-five kuruş for two.

It is still daytime. The motorboats and the rowboats are all over the place. A gentle south wind is blowing. The fish are lucrative. The sea is calm.

"Let's find the monster."

"C'mon, rowboat men, start looking!"

"Hey, Tahir, throw the line!"

"Pull the line up; there are no fish there!"

The land has turned copper and the sky iron; for days every corner of the sea is searched, but there are no fish. Italian ships are waiting.

Then the northwest wind blows; the sea becomes turbulent, wretched, and wrathful, spitting and swearing like a captain with a trembling white mustache. The mast of the motorboat moans. The water is ice cold. The hands of the fishermen are red as beets.

The fish come out and make the whole town tremble. The fishermen corner the bonito that were chasing the mackerel. The motorboats are full to the brim. After loading the Italian ships, the Greek ships, too, are loaded with fish. All the bartenders in the harbor have already started polishing their glasses. The small pitchers are all lined up, and the aniseeds in the raki bottle are twinkling. Everywhere it smells of fish. In poor neighborhoods bonito is sold as lamb. The fisherman lives from day to day. Those who keep their earnings in their pockets for the future are a rare breed.

Hikmet loves the fishy smells of *The Source of Livelihood* during the fishing season. Sailors' mouths reek of raki. But the bosses go around with cognac bottles in their pockets. The big boss puts soda in his cognac and drinks it with candied almonds on the side. Let him drink! Of course, he has a right, after all he owns everything; but why doesn't he see fit to drink raki? The sailors resent this. The boss says to himself, "If I drank raki, could I be a boss?" That's true.

Melek was happy with her boss. Although Dimitro was abrasive and gossipy, he could suddenly be as compassionate as a mother. Some days he seemed to have drunk a mysterious potion. On those days he would soften up not with the love of a proper father, but with a motherly compassion and with a crushing feeling experienced by lovers. Even if this wasn't becoming to a man, Dimitro behaved in a way that made Melek feel free and instinctively close to him. His white mustache and his blue eyes quivered with a powerless love whose source was a mystery.

However, Dimitro was a proud man. Even if he didn't consciously think that his helplessness might be noticed, he had some gut feeling about it, which immediately made him put on the mask of a teacher. He would grab the scissors from Melek's hand and show her how to hold them properly and tell her, in his studied Greek diction and his vocabulary of the evening newspaper *Apoyevmatini,* never to hold the razor up straight. Sometimes he would restrain himself. He wore his instructor's mask for many days. And then, sometimes, with the mellowed emotions of his old age, he would watch Melek's movements, lazily, sitting on a chair, with melancholy as if he was contemplating a summer evening.

Melek had gradually learned about Dimitro's life. Sometimes, on rainy days, when there were no customers, they sat around and Dimitro talked, his mind wandering off every now and then.

Dimitro's father had been an official of the Patriarchate. He knew classical Greek and wrote poetry. He stood tall in his dark official suit; he was a handsome man with a military bearing. He was also associated with the Court. During Easter he was the one who presented the gauze-wrapped cakes and eggs sent by the Patriarchate to his majesty.

He was an elegant man. He wrote the Turkish petitions, the transactions, and all the business of the Patriarchate in precise and elegant Turkish; he was the one who met the Court officials, top government men, and functionaries as the representative of the Patriarchate.

When he spent the golden coins given to him by the Court in gilded pouches, even the members of Prince Mavrokordatos's family envied him. He used to commute to the Patriarchate in a carriage driven by white horses. His name came after the name of the Patriarch. They lived in Galata in a solid stone building with iron-barred windows. The interior of the house was large, mysterious, and enchanting. Now, when Dimitro closes his eyes he can almost see the candle in front of the pictures of Virgin Mary, the light of the fireplace reflected in the velvet curtains, the gloomy darkness of the room, his father's armchair mounted on springs placed in front of the fire-place, the bearskin rug on the floor, the hunting rifles on the walls, and the hunting dog who licked him inside out in the barren, silent, and lonely days of his childhood.

The chandelier gave a light that neither tired the eyes nor lit the room properly. The dog kept yawning. His father, looming tall like a ghost in his nightshirt, would walk to and fro in front of a bookcase with a ladder; stand-ing he would read a page from a book, then he would sit down, then pick up another book and read it for a while by the fireplace, with one of his elbows on the mantle piece. Then he would work until late into the night at a table covered with thousands of papers and folders.

First, the Patriarch who supported Dimitro's father died. Then Sultan Hamid* was imprisoned. After that Dimitro's father died because of the abominable things the new Patriarch did to him, according to Dimitro's mother. The houses were sold. This upright and quiet man somehow had tremendous debts. When Dimitro was fourteen they moved to a house in Tarlabaşı,* their landlord was a barber.

Now Dimitro is sixty. Soon St. Dimitro's festival will come and in a few days Dimitro will be sixty-one.

His trade had kept him from starving and he had managed to provide for his aged mother to live until the day she died without experiencing poverty. He got married after his mother died, but he did not have any children. However, in his youth, Dimitro had had quite a few (some major, some minor) affairs. Perhaps because of his blood ties, he had fallen madly in love with the daughter of a wealthy Greek. It was predictable that this affair would not end well. The owner of the famous Aslanlı Alley and Aslanlı Of-fice Building couldn't give his daughter to a barber. But the whole Greek community buzzed with this story. Since Dimitro was a graceful youngster with blue eyes that conformed to Victor Hugo's poem "Un enfant aux yeux bleus, un enfant grec," of the then fairly cosmopolitan Greek community, Mademoiselle Fotika fell in love with him when he came to their house every now and then to shave her papa.

Both the girl and the young man were desperate. The Kerem-Aslı tale[2] of the poor Turks circulating in poor Greek neighborhoods seemed to have been written for Dimitro and Fotika. The Beyoğlu* of those days was astir; songs were composed in the cabarets; arguments took place in the Skating Palace. Greek liberals and Greek aristocrats had fights. But, eventually, when the aristocrats found out about Dimitro's father's and grandfather's ancestry, all the factions were united. They tried to persuade the girl's father to no avail. The man gathered his belongings and flew off to Paris. He was soon forgotten.

Meanwhile, Dimitro had become famous; his shop was teeming with customers. He, with his barbers and apprentices, worked with pride in a big establishment situated between Beyoğlu and Tarlabaşı. He made a lot of money. His fortune made everyone forget about his love affair. Others gradually forgot the love he had forgotten himself. Then the barbers were laid off. The apprentices grew up. Dimitro was again all alone without customers, barbers, and apprentices; he then seduced the most flirtatious girl of the Tarlabaşı quarter and married her. His whole interest was to have a child. Ah, it would be great to have a child—a daughter! He didn't want to have a son. Contrary to the wishes of all oriental men, he was dying to have a daughter. But they didn't have a child. The girl he married was willing to give him a child in whatever way she could, but it was better that this was done without Dimitro's knowledge. However, she wasn't able to, and they divorced.

Beyoğlu circles did not forget the famous barber Dimitro. The smell of scandal was everywhere once more. Rumors spread as far as Greece. Dimitro closed his shop. Soon he was traveling in Lesbos, Rhodes, and Alexandria. He roamed all over.

When he got back to Istanbul it was still under British occupation. On this subject Dimitro was always taciturn and during the period of the

---

2. Traditional Turkish tale of star-crossed lovers.

Armistice he never wanted to talk about his patriotic fervor. Perhaps, because of this nationalism he felt a little guilty, and from then on started saying, "I am Dimitro, the famous barber!" But the barber Dimitro had long been forgotten.

In Istanbul he married again, but again there was no child. Then he adopted the daughter of a very poor Jewish family who had moved to the island. Now the girl was about twenty years old. She had become a playful and flirtatious Greek girl. Dimitro kept looking at her and thought, "Maybe her ancestors weren't Jewish." Yet, he sometimes thought that people weren't born as Jews, Muslims, or Christians. He puzzled over it. "How come?" he said. But when the subject came up he didn't say "How come?" Instead he said this: "When I was born, if my mother had left me in the synagogue in Balat, now I would be a perfect Jew. And you Mişon, if your mother had left you in the Süleymaniye Mosque* when you were born, by now you would have become a *müezzin.**"

After Dimitro's wife died he took care of the little Jewish girl. In the evenings, in the old house on the shore when the northeast wind beat the windows, Dimitro used to comb the curly blond hair of the girl, give her supper, put her to bed and sing her Greek lullabies until she slept.

When the girl grew up she took a job in the big city. She learned French and learned how to type, and became a young lady of some distinction. She had a fondness for fine things that Dimitro couldn't meet her desire for, nor could he afford the dresses she wanted. Nevertheless, one day his adopted daughter started wearing smart clothes; in fact, they were more than that, they were very elegant.

It was after this event that Dimitro started to learn who did what and with whom on the island and prepared himself ahead of time to have an answer to the slightest insinuation directed at him. The girl came home at night, but Dimitro didn't comb her hair anymore.

He would remember his youth, his old shop in Beyoğlu and utter the words: *"Ekinos Kosmos"* (such is the world). Then he would add as if somebody had died: *"Pseftikos Kosmos"* (the world is a liar)!

Every year on New Year's Eve Dimitro was in the habit of giving a party for himself and, sometimes, for his close friends. That year he had invited Melek and her father to his house. The whole family came and rang the bell of Dimitro's wooden house on the shore shortly before 8:00 p.m.

That night among Dimitro's guests there were two proprietors. One of them was a rotund man about fifty, who seemed never to have had a painful thought even for one day in his life; he had a cheerful face, red cheeks, full lips, and graying hair. He spoke with the singsong rhythms of the people who live on the Black Sea and told funny stories.

The other guest was a sad-looking man with a bony face. His accent had the faint traces of his Anatolian background. He had an athletic but slim body that suited his face.

That evening Ali Rıza was dressed to the nines. He looked very elegant, without a touch of exaggeration. Although he had worked for days in order to acquire this attire, in the end his outfit gave the impression of belonging only to himself.

Hikmet looked grimy in his coveralls. Naci was so dirty and his fingernails were so black that even Ali Rıza couldn't help looking askance at him.

Dimitro's daughter was terribly elegant in a low-cut dress. With his eyes transfixed, the thin proprietor was composing ditties in his head for her transparent dress material, which he could not name—"The daughter of the giaour all done up in tulle."

Dimitro looked even more soigné than all the others. Wearing a lavaliere necktie, he was dressed in the fashion of the 1800s, like a character in the novels of Alphonse Daudet, or Alexandre Dumas *fils*.

They were drinking beer, eating pickled bonito and *tarama salata**; they talked about fishing, haircutting, rowboats, and the city of Trabzon.*

At the beginning Melek felt a strange kind of resentment. Even that skinny, silent, pale-faced Hikmet, who had been looking at her with doleful eyes for many years had lost all his mysterious demeanor in this house; her father, that drunkard and artless man became a pitiful and lonely creature as he talked to the captains of fishing boats. The captain who drank and laughed and talked about his money, his exploits, and his life without a care in the world, lost the businesslike manner he had when he gave orders to his men, or jumped into the boats with his agile legs.

The feeling of estrangement Melek felt at the outset became even more pronounced; she was all alone among her closest friends. She was beginning to wonder if she was really the child of this man who was faking the postures and the manners of a big shot, and who was speaking pretentiously as he talked with the captains there.

Who were these people? What was she doing there? Was this barber, who looked like a painter, going to keep looking at her as if she were a lesbian?

Ali Rıza said, "Let her drink a glass of beer. What does it matter?"

The thin young captain said, "C'mon, young lady, let's have a glass." Hikmet filled Melek's glass.

Half an hour later Melek had stopped feeling out of place. If she was cavorting with such people anything could happen. Dimitro had told her that everybody in the world was having fun that night. When dark destiny had flung Melek into this funless and quiet village that night and when the whole world was having fun, she said, "Let's have fun."

The thin young boss asked Dimitro's daughter Marikula to dance as the gramophone was playing fox-trots. When they left the party, Melek, like all the women in town, told her father, "Ah, we had so much fun!"

Ali Rıza was thinking about the business the captain proposed to him. "It was both fun and business! I think that this year we'll be able to get the mirrors and the appliances for your shop," he said.

He was the one who couldn't get this New Year's party out of his mind. The silverware, the pinkish china, cut-glass carafes, the chandelier on the ceiling, and the bearskin on the floor made Ali Rıza feel the sweet pleasures of owning a house. Occasionally he had moved the furniture of summer people from the pier to the empty rooms, but he had never realized that a couple of hours later these strange pieces of furniture that were thrown into the empty rooms would create such a bewildering and soul-pleasing comfort and order.

He had never imagined that the sea and the uninhabited island in that sea would be so beautiful when one contemplated them while sitting in an armchair with metal coil springs.

The fat captain, Rafet, had helped Ali Rıza quite a lot, but this barely covered his gallon of wine and the hookah tobacco in the evenings. Eventually the captain became an unbearable man. For every favor he did he would look into Ali Rıza's eyes and always expect all sorts of sacrifices from him.

If he had done this in a proper manner, such as saying, "Effendi! God willing, let me marry your daughter," it would have been OK. Then he would have answered him, "Let me sleep on it." After drinking three glasses of wine, Ali Rıza would start imagining Trabzon. He would visualize wearing father-in-law nightshirts and handmade slippers over his bare feet while roaming through the rooms of the house on the Trabzon coast. The windows of the house opened to the dark face of the Black Sea. When anchovies piled up on the shores in waves, the house would be redolent with the smells of rice cooking with anchovies. He would quietly take from the cupboard a carafe of cut glass (like the ones Dimitro had), he would hold his cap with his left hand and, with his glass in his right hand, he would swallow his drink in one gulp; then sitting around a long, wide table crowded with the relatives of his son-in-law, he would laugh with them; because he knew how to imitate that singsong male accent of the Black Sea so well, he would dip his spoon into the pilaf pot without others being taken aback.

After sitting on the bench belonging to the churchwarden and dreaming like this, he would run home and say, "Melek, my child, God bless you," and things like that.

But Captain Rafet has no such notions in his head. He makes his future father-in-law wash his boat; he takes off his shoes and gives them to him to take to the shoeshine boy, Mişon, and in the evenings he makes him clean the salted sardines saying, "Hey man, you make good appetizers!" After that he would hurl mouthfuls of insults at him: "Ah, you'll never amount to anything. You haven't got a single hair that isn't gray but you're still no good for anything."

They finally had a big fight one day. That morning Ali Rıza had cleaned the cesspool of the famous businessman Mahmut Bey.*

If there's no sewer system in the big city, how could this little place have one? Since this was the case, the cesspools quite often overflowed. Although it was virtually necessary to have the cesspools for bright green lettuce and blood red tomatoes to grow in the barren soil of the island, it was difficult to find a man to clean them.

There was no one but Ali Rıza who could do this job. However, when he worked at this job he used all the curses he knew, seeing the horrid transformation of delectable red mullets, lobsters, and sweets that went through the intestines of Mahmut Bey's family in the summer, which made him feel nauseous day after day.

All those who had their cesspools cleaned knew that it was Ali Rıza's right to swear that much; they would leave him alone, closing all the rear windows of the house; not even the gardener went to the garden and the birds made a half-circle in the air and flew away. He was left all by himself to think and to utter his thousand curses against Mahmut Bey's family.

The real problem was Ali Rıza's drinking many glasses of wine and his excessive irritability after he cleaned such a cesspool. Every word uttered made him feel touchy and every phrase gave his usually soft and darting eyes a spiteful glint that seemed to come out of the blue. In short, each time Ali Rıza had this job, he even cursed himself and became unbearable even to himself.

One day Captain Rafet asked him, "Hey, do you clean cesspools, too?" He answered, "I take care of the cesspools and also your kind."

Even the strongest and bravest sailor rarely dared to take on Captain Rafet, because in the evenings there were four people around him who drank raki at his expense.

Captain Rafet wanted to settle accounts with Ali Rıza alone. They grappled with each other. The captain was a very strong man. Ali Rıza set his teeth in the captain's shin at the first attack, but then felt out of breath. This incident took place on the beach. The captain's four men were just watching without interfering. Then the captain grabbed Ali Rıza and threw him into the sea. The sea there only came up to Ali Rıza's waist. He walked out and attacked the captain again with his endless curses. Then the four men carried him inside the big *gazino** and put him down by the stove. One of them took out a whip from his pocket and the other one stuck a handkerchief into Ali Rıza's mouth. They gave him a good whipping, saying, "See what happens when you challenge our boss!"

As soon as Ali Rıza had freed himself from their hands he went to the police station. Captain Rafet was called. As the sworn testimonies were about to be signed, Captain Rafet showed Ali Rıza two ten-lira bills. Ali Rıza was beside himself with joy and said, "I'm not suing." But this time the police chief put his foot down. Finally, the incident was closed with Ali Rıza's testimony: "I just happened to fall into the sea and hit my back against the rock."

Ali Rıza ran home with his big bottle of wine. He had already changed one of the bills and filled his handkerchief with loose change. "Melek, take it! Here's the money for the appliances for the store," he said.

Melek had started working for Dimitro only two and a half months ago: She still didn't know how to hold the scissors properly. She laughed secretly.

She knew that her father would manage to go through the twenty lira from the first of February to the end.

Indeed, it happened exactly like that.

Ali Rıza couldn't resist the beauty of the April morning. He untied the mooring rope of the decrepit rowboat that Hikmet had bought for twenty lira. He jumped into the rowboat. He pulled the oars quickly a few times and then he let the rowboat float on its own. From the stern he picked up the toolbox that he called Nasrettin Hoca's* tomb; the box had a lock on one side and it was so fragile that if it were held tight with two hands it would shatter. He started preparing a garfish line by wrapping a piece of red silk around the end of the fishhook. He repaired the line in a few places. Now the line was ready to use. The rowboat had drifted near Kaşıkadası.* He rowed a little more; now he was right in front of the small island.

He had gone there to prepare bait because he was going to take customers perch fishing that evening. The shallow water around Kaşıkadası are full of purple-boned garfish as thick as a man's wrist and about fifty centimeters long. When he had left the village, Hikmet was busy working in the motorboat and Melek was with Dimitro. The whole village was fast asleep. He hadn't wanted to wake anybody to take them out for garfish, but this was something that couldn't be done alone. One had to row so the other could handle the fishing line. Ali Rıza had a solution for this: he rowed slowly with the fishing line held between his rotten teeth, which were more sensitive than his fingers and could feel the fish caught by the hook. Then he abandoned the oars and with his free hands and with thousands of curses brought the garfish, hopping and skipping over the sun-drenched sea, onto the gunwale. He put the small garfish in a bucket to be fried for supper and threw the others, to be used as bait, under the planks of the rowboat where there was always a few centimeters of water. As the fish kept moving and wiggling there, Ali Rıza stomped his bare feet against the plank imitating their motions and said, "Shut up, damn you! Go to hell!"

He put the fishing line between his teeth and pulled the oars again. But he was getting tired. He pulled the rowboat into a small cove of Kaşıkadası. On this cove there was a deserted white building.

Ali Rıza hauled his boat onto the pebbles of the beach. Then he immediately sat cross-legged in the bow of the rowboat. For a long time he thought about some important matters. (We call them "important," but this is only a preconceived notion we decide by ourselves: even if it's true it means nothing. How can we know whether a person is thinking about serious or absurd things?)

Now he was talking to himself: "Damn it, what am I waiting for? I'll bring the kids and settle here as a watchman. Nobody would mind." He made this pronouncement not in his head but aloud. Before he got up he thought a little more: "Huh, who would mind my business?"

He pushed the rowboat with all his might and jumped into it with the bounce of a rubber ball. Once he was in the rowboat he pulled the oars forcefully and brought it to the island's coal-loading pier. He lowered the anchor and tied the seat of the rowboat to the metal ring. He started walking toward the house. The basement looked altogether different in daylight. It had the smell of spoiled food and human misery. The walls bore the squashed imprints of the ghosts of killed mosquitoes and crushed bedbugs. At night half of these would be nearly invisible. Everywhere there were signs of dampness. Now he could see each piece of furniture—one by one. God forbid, nothing was missing! A broken table, a saw, a quilt, a brazier, a pitcher, a large wine bottle, the well-known hookah tube, a lead pipe, a useless half-torn fishnet, about ten sardine cans . . . he picked them up quickly with agile motions. Then he picked up a straw mat from the corner that was covered with the remnants of a woman's yellow skirt. Except for the table, he put all the stuff he collected inside the straw mat and rolled it like a cylinder. He tied both ends with a heavy rope. After he had put the load on his back, he stopped suddenly and shook the straw mat off his shoulder: "God damn it, I forgot the lamp." There was, indeed, on the rickety table a beautiful big lamp that was so out of place in this basement, and stood out even more now that the place was more orderly. Ali Rıza said, "Damn it, I'm like a blind man, I couldn't see!"

He held the lamp with one hand and the straw mat with other and stopped again. Without putting them down, he kicked the table and cursed: "You damn shitty table!"

This was his habit. When he was leaving his house, or whenever he felt like it, he cursed the things around him—and when he met somebody in the street who deserved to be cussed at, he would go on swearing: "Just like the table, just like the straw mat, just like the fishnet you're shit too."

He half closed the basement door with his foot and was walking away quickly, but before he had walked a hundred meters, he bumped into a bandy-legged fisherman carrying a tray who said, "Hey! Didn't you say you didn't even have a straw mat in the world?"

"You're shit like the table."

"What do you mean?"

Ali Rıza walked away without feeling that he had to answer. He was annoyed at the fisherman's rude remark since he had burned the old straw mats. There was a story behind it.

One evening (was it last year?) he was drunk and somebody said, "Ali Rıza, there's going to be a war!"

His answer was, "Let it be! I haven't even a straw mat in this world that would burn. I'm sixty, I don't have to serve in the army. Let the whole world burn."

After he reached home the dirty old straw mat got tangled under his feet. Right there, in the middle of the windy night when the night watchmen blew their whistles, Ali Rıza burned the old straw mat by pouring a few drops of kerosene on it right in front of his basement, and threatened the whole neighborhood with fire. And when the fire was blazing highest, he jumped over it repeatedly just like the infidels do on their *Irımsız** holiday.

When the priest from the church across the way was about to light his usual last cigarette before he went to bed, he saw this ritual and he stopped and crossed himself several times and made heavy, deep "churchlike" sounds; he dashed to find refuge in the bosom of his wife who had always made him wonder why and how he had sacrificed his despotism for her.

Ali Rıza finally reached Kaşıkadası with his shabby belongings. He dug up all the furniture—a table, three chairs, and a tattered rug—he had left with Hrant, the old watchman of the pigsties. In a corner of the sties Hrant had also left a spring landscape painted by an Armenian painter; it was wrapped with newspapers and tied with string. Ali Rıza dusted it off and sat down and looked at it; he liked it. There were red and pink plum and peach trees in bloom by a stream. There was a red bird flying in an azure sky.

On one side, the sun was rising and, on the other side, there was a castle scene that had no relevance or connection; way in front was a heavy-browed Armenian shepherd with a flute.

Ali Rıza said, "Not bad at all. Good for him! The man was a good painter!" In the corner of the painting the signature, H. Nalbantyan, was barely legible. The downstairs room of the two-room stone building was covered with corks, nails, and fishing gear. Ali Rıza looked them over hoping to find something useful, but everything was moldy, rotten, and too far gone. He dumped them all into the sea. For hours he cleaned all the furniture with water he carried from the nearby sea. He arranged the furniture and hung the painting directly across from the window. Then he stood outside the door and looked with pleasure at the room he had arranged as though he was contemplating an oil painting. He smiled with joy. He yelled to himself, "Hey, you can light a cigarette now, you deserve it."

The evening was closing in. Flocks of seagulls were returning to the rocks. Cormorants, perched on the rocks, watched the poetic and melancholy sunset. A solitary heron, mighty and proud, stood on one leg as though contemplating his kingdom.

Ali Rıza threw a stone toward the heron. The bird took flight and with difficulty flew up to another rock; crestfallen, he stayed there. Ali Rıza shouted, "Son of a bitch! I'm the king of this place now!"

Ali Rıza jumped into his rowboat like a rubber ball again. He brought his daughter and son into his kingdom. He yelled at Hikmet from a distance: "Untie the bundles, jump into a rowboat and come here to Kaşıkadası. We moved. Otherwise, I'll send the boy to get you. Will you finish your job in half an hour?"

Bewildered, Hikmet said, "Yes, I will." Then he turned to the helper, Tahsin, and added, "My stepfather is crazy!" But a little later he, too, went to Kaşıkadası.

That night the children, for the first time in their lives, slept a cool, dreamy sleep in a clean, sea-smelling room with a spring landscape on the wall.

Hikmet was the exception; almost all night he stayed awake. He felt as though a warm rain was trickling down inside his body and he couldn't sleep. He remembered his childhood days. He closed his eyes; a purple light coming from the only window fell on his face. In a state of strange wakefulness he remembered things and told himself as if he were telling a friend:

Mücahit was sitting in the bow of the rowboat; two kids were at the oars.

I was sitting crouched down and I couldn't see the water. But I could see a very bright and transparent sky that was moving like a river.

Odyssea was singing a Greek song. İdris, bare from the waist up, was listening to Odyssea. From time to time there was a quick flicker of moonlight reflected in his blue eyes. Next to me sat a boy whose name I didn't know. He had a face like a miniature and his body, too, was tiny. He was tiny all over—his hands, his ears, his eyes. We called him Sultan's Dwarf.

We were going to Kaşıkadası. We all had the feeling that we were Robinson Crusoes; the ship had sunk and we were on a raft. We were going to a deserted island; we were going to build a hut and raise goats.

We didn't talk and share the private feeling that each of us was a Robinson Crusoe lest we ruin these beautiful dreams. There were seven of us and each was a Robinson. With only a few words, we reminded ourselves that we lived on an inhabited island; near this island was Kaşıkadası that looked like a spoon laid with its bottom up in the moonlight. Kaşıkadası had belonged to a man who had no heirs, so when he died the government took over the property, and even though there was nobody there at present, tomorrow it might belong to five or ten people and their houses, even bathing places might be built there; then this dream boat we built along with our hut, our raft, and our fantasies and savages would be crushed against the rocks. After that none of us would go to Kaşıkadası in search of adventure. We would make fun of İdris, because he would no longer strip his upper body, wear the clothes of the savages, and resort to a thousand ruses to accommodate his dreams to ours.

When I stuck my head out of the bottom of the rowboat, I noticed that we were coming close to a cove with gleaming pebbles. All of us were looking at a white building (this very building where I am sleeping tonight) with amazement. A building on an uninhabited island! Fantastic! We were still silent.

Odyssea had stopped his Greek song suddenly. The little one had fallen off like a dwarfish rubber ball. Those pulling the oars had acquired the magnificent grace of people who work hard and sweat. İdris was as proud as an emperor. The boys who rowed looked like galley slaves and Mücahit, with his whip, resembled a cruel slave master. When we landed on the shore, İdris immediately gathered us together and said this:

"This building was built in the time of the Portuguese. Portuguese pirates discovered this island first. They left the youngest among them on the island because he had rebelled against the pirate chieftain. Then they went away. Let's walk quietly, maybe the Portuguese is still alive. There's a savage tribe on the island, let's be careful!"

Since Odyssea was going to be the savage one and İdris the Portuguese sailor, these two soon disappeared among the tall reeds of the island. The Jackal followed them, making howling sounds. I remained with the Sultan's Dwarf. The other three boys walked to the deserted white building where I am sleeping now.

Kaşıkadası is full of cisterns. It was very dangerous to run on the island, especially at night. We walked carefully over the hills, where the tall reeds waved, so as not to fall into the cisterns that were full of black water, leeches, and frogs.

When we were on top of the hill, the Sultan's Dwarf and I looked around. Over there in the window of the white house there was a faint light. Beyond that, the pigsties, which were built when the island was a farm, were barely visible. This was the house of the young Portuguese sailor left behind on the island. It was very dangerous to go there. The sailor had trained the wild animals like dogs and cats and he let them out at night. On the other side of the sties there was a gardener's hut. The chief of the savages lived there. A little later a light appeared in the window of this hut, too. We walked slowly toward that light. We knocked on the door. Odyssea opened the door. He was alone with the dog. He wore a wreath made out of grass on his head. With his bare feet, suntanned chest, blue eyes, delicate face, and striped shirt he looked much more like the Portuguese sailor than İdris. He was as wild as a pirate boy, and he was also very handsome. So much so that I immediately had the desire to become a bandit on his side. I was a fierce bandit and he was our chief.

Outside, the Heybeli* beach could be seen across a beautiful open space; it looked like a big ship, which was sailing away with all its lights on.

Odyssea started singing again. İdris and the other boys listened to this song until it ended, then, first the little ones would find us and take us captive and, after that, we would lay siege to the mansion of the Portuguese. He would surrender. Then Odyssea would sing Greek songs again; İdris would talk about this or that and we would go back.

On the way back we argued a lot. İdris didn't talk to those who spoiled the game. Odyssea didn't sing. The little Sultan's Dwarf was cross and didn't perform his innumerable clowning acts in the bottom of the rowboat.

The three of us, İdris, Odyssea, and myself, were the real islanders. The rest could not cope with comradeship and adventure as well as we did. The truth of the matter was that their parents would find out about their wanderings and prevent them from going out with us. Because of this, sometimes our team consisted of only three people. But even then we jumped into the rowboat and went across. We spent some nights there. The Jackal slept by the open door of this building and the rest of us slept inside on the torn fishnets, the corks, the nails, and our dreams. We never spoke about real things. We always talked about savages and pirates. I barely understood Greek. Odyssea spoke Turkish well. İdris could say funny things in broken Greek.

Odyssea was the son of a gardener. He was the best swimmer, fisherman, singer, and rower; his laughter was the best. But he was a strange boy; all of a sudden he would feel sad. He felt saddest when he sensed that enough attention wasn't paid to him. The most commonplace words would hurt his feelings and he would be cross at the whole world. Then the simplest word of sympathy drove him to behave with heroism. The thing he was afraid of most was fighting. He would suddenly become pale, he would stutter and his face would look devastated. He was not afraid of anything like monsters, or the Portuguese sailor, or the savages that the children feared. But when he faced a real person, he instantly changed and he was always humbling himself in a fight. I used to get nervous for his sake when I saw him beaten up by such lowly boys. It was rather strange that Odyssea who took so many risks in games and in the sea was not the same when he faced real people.

İdris seemed to like Odyssea because he was useful to him. Sometimes he would give the impression of doing a job he was incapable of doing, but then would change his mind hinting that it was a lowly job and would give it to Odyssea.

One day we were once more on the island. We couldn't find the Jackal anywhere. We decided to spend the night there. İdris told Odyssea, "Wait at the threshold until dawn in case something happens. You can sleep during the day and we can watch. Maybe savages will attack. You never know!"

Odyssea wasn't stupid, but sometimes he gladly accepted appearing stupid if it led to bravery and goodness. I slept and woke up off and on and found Odyssea awake. Before dawn I went to him and held his hand. Suddenly he put his warm head on my chest and said, "If my father wasn't a gardener, I would have amounted to something like you; I would have gone to school, and if I knew how to read, I would read and not fall asleep."

I turned his face to the left. The light was coming from that side. His eyes were red and full of tears. He let go of my hand and walked toward the pomegranate tree.

I said, "I don't even have a father. I learned how to read without even owning any books. And this year I am dropping out of school and I'll never go back. Even though I know how to read I won't read anything. C'mon Odyssea, you too sleep a little, I can't sleep anymore."

He lay down under the pomegranate tree. I lighted a cigarette, maybe for the second or third time in my life. He was already asleep.

Again there was moonlight. I don't know if I mentioned before that we always went to Kaşıkadası when the moon was full. For the first time in my life, I watched a person sleeping.

I now remember it and find it a little funny. The sleep of those young people who are pure and healthy is a precious thing. Those who contemplate them enter the good, beautiful, and peaceful world of the sleeper; to enter the dream world of the sleeper when one is wide awake is thrilling. It was as if I, too, was sleeping the way he slept, although I was wide awake. I entered the mystery of all the braveries, friendships, comradeships, tall reeds, the sea, the fish, the rowboat, the fat woman in the gardener's hut (Odyssea's mother), the gardener with the bushy mustache whose breath smelled of wine and tobacco (Odyssea's father), the rickety but clean furniture in their hut, his tall, dark sister with long legs and windblown skirts, the berries of the arbutus trees, and the pines. My desires swelled in me like a fountain.

I bent and kissed the cheek of this friend who slept with an open mouth and half-closed eyes. Perhaps, for the first and the last time in my life, I kissed a human being over and over with a longing that was purified in an unknown place inside myself.

To tear myself away from there, I ran up to the hut of the Portuguese. But childishness made me act cautiously as though the Portuguese was still there. I walked silently without making any noise. I looked inside the hut from its window, which I could barely reach. The hut was filled with moonlight that came from another window; in the corner a girl was sitting with the head of a young man on her lap. She was caressing the young man's hair and with his lips the young man was searching and finding the other hand that didn't caress his hair. I watched for some time with amazement. Then I ran down the slope, slipping and sliding. I dashed to the building where İdris slept and woke him up. I told him everything. İdris asked about Odyssea.

"Idiot" he said. "Is he still waiting?"

"Don't torment the child! He's a good boy!"

"He's the best boy in the whole world, don't I know it? I do it on purpose because I love him. Just to test him. He would give his life for me, right? What's he doing?"

"A while ago I woke up and told him to sleep. He's sleeping now."

"Was he awake until now? What an idiot!"

We walked to where Odyssea was sleeping. İdris looked at him carefully for some time and bent and caressed his hair as though, he, too, had had the same dream of good children. He said, "Let him sleep, c'mon, let's go and see what's up."

The same scene and the same movements continued in the hut up there. The young man lying on the girl's lap was still searching for the girl's hand with his lips. When the young man turned his face in our direction, we drew back from the window. The girl's head was bent toward the young man; without moving, she looked at him longingly. When the young man turned his face in our direction, İdris and I crouched under the window. There, I looked at İdris's face. His face had lost those familiar, smiling, sweet, and fun-loving lines and seemed to have become darkened.

"He's my age!" he said.

"What? Who?"

"The boy who's lying on the girl's lap."

Standing up there he gazed for a while without any fear. I was afraid. We returned. İdris was preoccupied. He kept repeating, "He's my age!"

I didn't answer him. In fact, the man on the girl's lap wasn't İdris's age; he was quite a grown man.

In winter we kept our dreams along with the rain, snow, cold, and fog. Some of us were at school, some were apprentices in shops, some were in the cabbage patch covered with mist, and some, like İdris, were in their fathers' rowboats with their sails full-blown against the north and the south winds.

Every child emerged from winter into summer looking different. Many of them would be plumper, whiter, and splendidly grown. I had the notion, then, that children grew only in winter.

By the time that winter was over we had completely lost touch with each other. I found Odyssea grown taller and with a face that had acquired murky and sly meanings. He was still singing, but his voice wasn't the same pure and clear voice. That voice, which used to create such warmth in me, now seemed like the shrill voice of the sly, stingy, deceitful, gossipy, and fear-filled people of a strange country; wine drinking, hunger, sleeplessness, and wrathful nights had given that shrillness to their worn-out larynxes.

That face, which had belonged to a comrade, a friend, that I was ready to be a slave to, had thrown away all the meanings I had attributed to it, like a superfluous skin—the skin of a snake. I was surprised when I saw the same kind of expression on Odyssea's face as the expression on his uncle Yorgo's face when he was selling a week-old lobster.

Before, when I looked at the faces of these two people I used to say, "How is it that these two people's features are so similar, but one makes me feel warm inside and the other shows me the real world—cold and ugly?" I had vaguely felt that there was a strong relationship between a face and morals. I won't say that a beautiful person is the most honest. I won't deny the mind-boggling mystery of immorality behind a beautiful face. I only want to say that the expressions and even the colors that morality furnishes for the face can exist only when both the face and the morals are good; they are charming only at a certain instant and in a certain place. If morals don't go bad they stay pure and attractive to the friend who may even want to emulate them. But when the bad and real world is discovered the way Odyssea discovered it and assimilated it into his new life, things weren't the same anymore. For instance, Odyssea's wrinkling his nose as if he was sniffing something and opening his mouth when he listened to what was told seemed charming at that time. Didn't I imitate these manners when I was listening to the others? But today these mannerisms, the very same ones, unite him with his uncle Yorgo, and Yorgo's deceitfulness, jealousy, and lack of civility.

When I met him a second and a third time, I was full of remorse. "What did I do?" I kept repeating, "Why did I kiss this boy? How could I love this face?" I had a terrible feeling of embarrassment.

İdris, too, had grown up a lot. He had a straight neck like the neck of the young man we had seen last year in the pigsties in Kaşıkadası. With his raven hair he appeared to have been spruced up by the hand of a barber. He hadn't shaved his first mustache, which was pencil-thin and fashionable.

Despite all outward lack of charm, İdris's face possessed the good features of those days of dreams and adventure. Even more so. But he wouldn't let anybody say a word about Kaşıkadası. He told stories about young girls all the time:

Eftihiya had colorful legs that were ready to be burned like the yellow tapers in a church. Her teeth were white as baby corn and her hands deserved to be kissed with a constantly searching and finding mouth.

İdris met Eftihiya during the fall when the brambles had red flowers and the berries of the arbutus tree were ripe. They picked the berries together and Eftihiya ate all the ripe and big ones. She became drunk like the women of the island who say, "Arbutus berries make you drunk!" She put a ripe berry in her mouth and told İdris, "You eat the other half!" They lay by the bramble bushes smelling the honeyed scent of red flowers.

Eftihiya's face was the ordinary face of a Greek girl: lively and naughty, that's all; she was neither homely nor beautiful. But when the swimming season started, in her navy blue bathing suit, with her shiny straight legs and her tiny breasts, Eftihiya was so beautiful! In the summer her beauty could knock a man down in one second and make him bury his hands in the earth, pluck the grass with his teeth, and smell the earth. She was an excellent swimmer. When the families of the sporty young men in white trousers rented the houses in the village, Eftihiya abandoned İdris (who wore a coarse gray suit with a pair of trousers baggy at the knees) without much fuss.

Odyssea had become friendly with the children of the new summer vacationers. With the money he saved in winter he bought a pair of white trousers, a short-sleeved purple silk shirt, and a sailor's cap, which he acquired from a young man after much pleading. At a distance he really gave the impression of a strong, handsome young man. But when one came close to him, he looked a little strange, as if he was too dressed up in his Sunday best. One could immediately tell that he was one of natives of the village. He only said "Hello" to me and to İdris and spent his time with the children of the vacationers. He introduced the girls of the island to them. Occasionally he even carried letters. He played cards with the strangers in open-air *gazinos*, and since he usually won fair and square, he always had money in his pocket.

That whole summer we went to Kaşıkadası only once. We did this with Odyssea's gang. They were four Greek boys. Odyssea, speaking Greek, was telling the things we did last year and the years before that, with a smirk on his face as though the things we did were not wonderful, but idiotic. I also understood from the bittersweet expression on İdris's face that he, too, considered them silly, but at least he didn't enjoy telling them to the others.

Odyssea's friends were bursting with laughter. With their Greek tangos they ruined the silence and the Robinsonesque aura of the island; they enraged the Portuguese sailor to tears. And I kept thinking, how could I have kissed Odyssea, and I tore the skin off my lips and threw it away.

Hikmet was dazed with the lovely memories of his childhood as he lay in bed with his eyes closed; they made him feel shrunken, made his feet cold, and he pulled his legs toward his nose and pulled the quilt over his head. He thought he was asleep. What he thought about or wanted to think about seemed as though it was written in sleep and in a dream and there were pieces of paper strewn all over. He had always felt like writing on pieces of paper and, if there was no paper, he wrote things in his head as he lay in bed. At that time they were sending him to a Greek school. He felt he was suffocating. He pulled the quilt away from his head and stretched his legs out.

It was still dark inside the room. He couldn't see anything. Only Naci's deep breathing and Ali Rıza's dry cough filled the room. If these sounds weren't there, he would be like people who woke up from a dream and didn't know where they were.

All of a sudden he saw a light coming through a window higher than a man's height. When he had first awakened, this window too was all dark, but now it looked as though a blue sponge had been passed over it.

He saw a dark blue ray of light, which had a dubious brightness. This illumination helped him to go to sleep. He thought about the room where Melek slept. He felt drowsy again and he slept.

Medarı Maişet Motoru, 1944

 *Poems*

TRANSLATED BY TALAT S. HALMAN

The Friend

One of these evenings, I shall sit like Selim the Third
    at the city's mirrored *gazino,** staring right into the mirrors,
With raki before me . . . dusk outside, a current, rowboats, passersby . . .
Some guy who cups his hands around his eyes and looks from the bar's
                                     entrance
Is going to say: "This bastard is in love!"
A big boat
Will pull out of the current
A girl with disheveled hair, ink-stained lips, vagabondish like me,
And will prop her up between me and my booze.

I shall say:
Not tonight, but some other night, I shall whisk you away to a big city
Where the ground must have blown up by now
Demolishing everything I used to know:
Stock markets and palaces with their enormous façades,
    perhaps even the courthouses and dungeons . . .
They have become fairy tales now:
Their heroism and compassion and virtues . . .
Calls to prayer, requiems, battles, battalions, heroes . . .
No booze in my head, no handcuffs on my wrists,
Some early evening, from Sotiraki's *gazino,*
From between my booze and myself, I shall whisk you away
To a country
Where golden evenings and blond children climb over
Where birds chirp and all sorts of fruit is eaten,
A country without boundaries or fences,
Without fairies or jinns,
Without chicken coops or houses,
That is to say, without numbers.

As soon as we get off at the station,
Subways could take you some place and me somewhere else.

Doesn't matter!

But when I'm left all alone again
On such chestnut-colored evenings in November,
You, with your crumpled coat, disheveled hair, ink-stained mouth,
And sisterly face,
You will prop your feet on a chair
To ask me a couple of things:
"What did you do today? Did you work?"
If you like, you can then get up and take a walk
Without me . . .
You know best.

Sundays

On Sundays
I drink beer
With radishes and pistachios.
A young boy
Serves me
For a pittance,
But all I want
Is to be his father.

Apple and Fig

Our first cover:
FIG.

Our original sin:
APPLE.

Note:
I am no sinner.

Letter I

If I whistle a tune at the helm of the ship
And sing on the rain-drenched deck
All that is a pretext to approach you,
Not to forget you, dear love.
It's only after you're gone that men
Will realize the lies they were taught.
Only after you're gone
We understand how empty all things are.
Cups are full only when you are with me
Wines are blessed only with you
Cigarettes fume only with you
Fireplaces crackle only with you
Meals are meals only with you.

Letter II

I'd rather keep mum unless you are the topic.
Kınalı Island,* the ferry, the sea, the dolphin
Are pretexts to talk about you.
Why wasn't it the sky until now?
Why did it get to be this way?
Why was I fond of books?
Both of us breathe together in this city;
Or else what good is this strange city?
It's known to me that you were born here;
Otherwise would I ever love the minarets
And the Süleymaniye Mosque*
Although you are a heathen?

Not To Be Able To Write

There was fog over the sea,
Over the hills and our house.
Leaves were misty in the garden,
Water trickled through the iron bars,
At the touch of a hand.
Trees were hazy . . .

The woman's eyes were warm,
Her hands burned,
Her feet were ice-cold.
Fog over the sea.
Enraged because I couldn't write,
I kept biting my fingernails.
The woman kept stretching,
Her feet were ice-cold.

Fog
In my head
And over the sea.

Morning,
A May morning,
Nothing came into my head.
Had I taken the ferry
I would have heard the ticket punching.
Punching
And rumba dancing.

A man is reading a newspaper.
A woman is knitting.
There is fog over the sea.

Morning,
A morning in May.
The ticketman is punching the tickets.
"Tea, coffee, anyone?
We got tea and coffee.
Gentlemen, tea or coffee?"

. . .

You are a friend dear to me like life
As night when I lie down on the grass
Gazing at the stars
Ants crawl all over your arm
Or on your forehead
My days to come are in your hands
My friendship is in your eyes
I shout your name to the mountains
Trees are happy because you are in Istanbul
The wind blows because you are in the world
People are good because you're alive
And bugs are all green
All black too
And ants are cute
Flowers all fragrant
To whom can I reveal but you
The blue of the sea
The icebox of the ice-cream vendor
The voice of the pine trees
To whom could I disclose but you
The rose garden
Who'd weep hearing the story of the wafers
Who's tagged happiness onto a cup of coffee
Who loves that minaret, the Yüksekkaldırım,* the Gypsies?

My dreamy kid
People pass by right before me
I know them all
But who are they
Why are they rushing to the city
Why are their faces so relaxed?
I am not so relaxed even when I am happy.

Naples

Naples, white city,
Gondolas go through Venice,
Statues are erected in Rome,
All in your honor.

It's in your honor
That the handsome fisherman of Naples
Moves his lips
Over the girl's breasts
That have turned the color of dates
No, turned into dates.
Hey, Naples, it's in your honor,
Naples . . . White city.

Girl from İmroz*

In rainy weather
Her lips are filthy all week long
On Sundays Eleni is a show-off.

Compote

At one end of the road I saw
Fig trees
At the other end mulberry trees.

By the desolate road I saw
Hushed, bulletless
Bandits.

Sicilian Forests

Sicilian forests
Are mysterious like the sky
And vengeful too.
In the straw hut,
In that ramshackle hut
Lit by a gas lamp,
The kid who eats corn bread
Loves you
And the girl who's colorful like corn bread just out of the oven,
Blue and warm like goat's milk just taken out.
This heart
That I hitch onto the waves of the Adriatic
To the sails of ships loves you.
I say to you: "Come!"
I'm waiting for you.
If you don't come
Remember, Sicilian forests
Are mysterious like the sky
And vengeful, too!

Back When

Some days at dusk I would sit
And write stories
Like mad!
As I was writing my stories
The people in my mind
Would sail out to sea for fishing.

Women
Fire up their kerosene lamps with the blue beams to heat up the coffeepots.
—At night, in the dark, on a bald mountain—
A miller,
Face down, would plunge into his long sleep.

Peasants used to come
To the marketplace to sell yogurt
Out of their copper buckets.
I was holding a child's naked feet in my hand.
In the street snow was knee-deep.
At the head of a bridge
I would stab anyone of my choice.
From the suspension bridges of major cities
I would jump into the sea
And hear how I rend the water,
I would see
How my fall splashes water over the bridge.

Glossary of Turkish Names and Terms

THIS GLOSSARY CONTAINS Turkish words, proper names, and a number of other special terms that are cited one or more times in the short stories and poems. They appear in their original forms and conform to standard modern Turkish spelling. None has been anglicized, translated, adapted, or altered in the text. A few other descriptions or definitions have been provided in the form of footnotes throughout the text.

For the reader's convenience, an asterisk has been placed next to each name or word listed in the glossary the first time it appears in a story.

Words like "imam" "kilim," "halvah," "pasha," "effendi," and "pilaf," which may be found in standard English dictionaries in anglicized form or in their Turkish spelling, do not appear here. Names of major cities (Istanbul, Ankara, Edirne, and Bursa) have likewise been excluded. Numerous place names, particularly those of small villages and minor streets, have been left unidentified.

Adapazarı: Provincial city of northwestern Anatolia, approximately 125 kilometers from Istanbul.

ağa (occasionally anglicized as *agha*): Versatile term meaning a big landowner in the rural areas; a local feudal lord; mister (provincial term); elder brother or paternal uncle; or master.

ağabey: Older brother.

Anaçıpay: A very small town in the province of Istanbul.

Arifiye: District in the province of Sakarya.

Atatürk Boulevard: Major street between Unkapanı and Aksaray in Istanbul.

Atatürk Bridge: A bridge over the Golden Horn.

Atikali: District on the European side of Istanbul.

Ayastefanos: Former name of an Istanbul district commonly and officially known as Yeşilköy.

Azapkapı: Istanbul district.

baba: Literally, "father," frequently used in addressing an elderly man; occasionally used in reference to an elder of a religious order or sect.

Babıali (Hill): Historically, the Sublime Porte, the central office of the Ottoman Empire in Istanbul; literally, "high door"; also the name of a hill in Istanbul, which has a concentration of publishers.

Babıali Avenue: Istanbul's Fleet Street, publishers row.

Bağdadi Baba: A dervish famous for his poems on Topkapı Palace. From his poems it is understood that he was from Baghdad; at the end of the eighteenth century he lived in Istanbul for a short time.

Bakırköy: A Europeanized section of Istanbul on the northeastern coast of the Sea of Marmara.

barba: A form of address for a Greek-Turkish fisherman.

bey: "Gentleman" or simply "Mr." (used after the first name).

Beyoğlu: A Europeanized section of Istanbul; a center of commerce and the principal entertainment district.

Bolu: Provincial city in northwestern Anatolia, approximately 250 kilometers from Istanbul, famous for its fine food and able cooks.

Bomonti: Section on the European side of Istanbul; one of the first industrial parts of the city.

börek: Flaky pastry with thin layers of cheese or other fillings like chopped meat or spinach.

Burgaz: The third-largest island in an archipelago of nine (the so-called Princes' Islands) in the Sea of Marmara, near Istanbul. Sait Faik's principal residence, now the Sait Faik Museum, is located here.

Çanakkale: City in northwestern Anatolia; also the name of the strait known as the Dardanelles.

Çankırı: Administrative district and provincial city near Ankara.

çapari: A fishing line with ten or more hooks.

çavuş: Sergeant or guard; occasionally used as a form of addressing a foreman, fisherman, or gardener (used after the first name).

Çeşmemeydanı: Literally, "fountain piazza," a plaza in Istanbul.

Doğançay: Town of the Anatolian province of Sakarya.

dolmuş: A taxi or motorboat that usually begins its run only when it is filled with passengers; jitney.

Edirnekapı: A section of Istanbul around Edirnekapısı, one of the principal gates of the Istanbul city walls.

Etmeydanı: Historically, the name of a square in Istanbul's Aksaray district where the Janissaries had barracks.

Fatih: Literally, "conqueror," a section of Istanbul named after Sultan Mehmed II (reigned 1451–1481) where the Fatih Mosque is located.

Fatiha: The opening chapter of the Koran.

Feast of St. John: See *Irımsız.*

Fındık: Literally, "hazelnut," often used to refer to a short person.

fitil: A card game.

Galata: District on the European side of Istanbul; also the name of a major bridge at the mouth of the Golden Horn.

Gallipoli: A section of Çanakkale near the Dardanelles; also the name of the peninsula on the western side of the Dardanelles.

gazino: Place of entertainment offering beverages and refreshments, usually outdoors, where, in Sait Faik's time, one could often listen to music and sometimes dance; from the Italian *casino.*

Geyve: A provincial town near Doğançay.

Golden Horn: An inlet on the European side of Istanbul near the mouth of the Bosphorus.

Green Mosque (Yeşil Cami): A mosque built between 1412 and 1421 in Bursa.

hanım: Lady, woman, or wife; or simply "Miss," "Mrs." or "Ms." (used after the first name).

Harbiye: A Europeanized section of Istanbul.

Hayırsız Islands: A group of islands in the Sea of Marmara; literally, "useless islands."

Heybeli Island: The second-largest island in the archipelago of nine near Istanbul.

Hırkaışerif: A section of Istanbul and the name of a mosque on the European side.

Irımsız: Popular Greek celebration of the Feast of the Nativity of St. John the Baptist (June 24) which includes remnants of pre-Christian sun worship connected with the solstice. On the eve of the feast day children light fires in the streets after sunset and jump over them for good luck.

İmroz: Provincial town in the province of Çanakkale.

İzmit: City and bay at the eastern end of the Sea of Marmara.

İznik (ancient Nicaea): Provincial town and lake in the province of Bursa.

Kadıköy (also spelled *Kadiköy*): A large section of Istanbul on the Asian side.

Kâğıthane: The name of a district and a river valley in Istanbul at the tip of the Golden Horn.

kalfa: Master or qualified workman; overseer of workers.

Kalpazanlar: A rocky section of the shoreline of Burgaz Island.

Karamanlı: Someone from Karaman, a provincial city in central Anatolia.

Karamürsel: District of Kocaeli, an administrative province near Istanbul.

Kaşıkadası: One of the smallest of the Princes' Islands in the Sea of Marmara. It is uninhabited.

Keban: A section of the eastern Anatolian province of Elazığ.

Kınalı Island: An island near Istanbul.

Kocaeli: Province of northwestern Anatolia, near Istanbul.

Kumkapı: A neighborhood in Istanbul.

lokanta: Restaurant.

Mahmutpaşa: Istanbul district with a heavy concentration of wholesale textile firms and apparel shops and peddlers.

Marmara: Inland sea linked to the Black Sea and the Aegean.

maşallah: Literally, "What God wills," a formulaic Arabic phrase used when expressing admiration, in order to make clear that no envy is involved (which could attract the evil eye).

Mevlanakapısı: One of the gates of the Istanbul city walls.

mevlit: The night of the birth of the prophet Muhammad; the chanting of Süleyman Çelebi's "Poem of the Nativity" forty days after a death or on the anniversary of a death.

müezzin: One who calls Muslims to prayer.

Nasrettin Hoca: A widely popular humorist and satirist in the Middle East, North Africa, and Central Asia. It is speculated that he lived in Anatolia in the thirteenth century.

Nilüfer Meadow: A meadow in Bursa, a province in northwestern Turkey.

pişpirik: A card game.

reis: Head, chief, chairman, president; also captain of a small merchant vessel, skipper, able-bodied seaman.

Sapanca: Hilly section of Sakarya, a province near Istanbul; also the name of a lake in that area.

Silivrikapısı: One of the gates of the land walls stretching from the Sea of Marmara to the Golden Horn in Istanbul.

simit: A bread roll in the shape of a large ring, covered with sesame seeds.

Sultan Hamid (Abdülhamid II): Ottoman Sultan (reigned 1876–1909).

Süleymaniye Mosque: Monumental mosque in Istanbul built by the great architect Sinan for Sultan Süleyman the Magnificent in the mid-sixteenth century.

Şehzadebaşı: Istanbul district.

Şişli: Administrative district on the European side of Istanbul.

Taksim: A major public square on the European side of Istanbul.

tarama salata: Appetizer made from fish roe.

Tarlabaşı: A section of Beyoğlu in Istanbul.

Tophane: A section of Istanbul on the European side.

Topkapı: The palace of the Ottoman sultans in Istanbul; a museum since the mid-1920s; also the name of the district where the palace/museum is located. The name was also given to one of the gates of the city walls, which stretch from Sarayburnu to Yedikule. Because one of the largest cannons was installed there, it was called Topkapı, which literally means "Gate of the Cannon."

Trabzon: Provincial city in the northeastern part of Turkey, known to Westerners as Trebizond.

Tünel: An underground funicular railway in Istanbul, built in 1875, linking Karaköy and Beyoğlu; also the name of a district at the Beyoğlu end of the railway.

Unkapanı: Istanbul district near the Golden Horn.

usta: Master; craftsman; foreman.

Vefa: Istanbul district.

Venizelos: Eleutherios Venizelos(1864–1936), Greek statesman and prime minister.

Villager cigarettes: The cheapest brand of cigarettes produced by the Turkish state tobacco monopoly.

Yassıada: An island in the Sea of Marmara off the coast of Istanbul.

Yedikule: Literally, "seven towers," the name of a section of Istanbul and a fortress adjoining the land walls near the Sea of Marmara.

Yeni Cami: Literally, "new mosque," a major mosque built at the end of sixteenth century near the mouth of the Golden Horn.

Young Turk: Member of the Unionists (Ottoman Society of Union and Progress), the dominant political force in the empire from the revolution of 1908 until the end of World War I.

Yüksekkaldırım: Winding stairway from Galata to Beyoğlu in Istanbul.

Zeyrek: Istanbul neighborhood, as well as the Turkish name for the Byzantine Church of the Pantocrator later converted into a mosque.

Biographical Notes

TALAT S. HALMAN is professor and chairman, Department of Turkish Literature, Bilkent University (Ankara). From the early 1950s to the late 1990s, he was on the faculties of Columbia University, Princeton University, the University of Pennsylvania, and New York University, where he also served as chairman of the Department of Near Eastern Languages and Literatures. His books in English include *Contemporary Turkish Literature, Modern Turkish Drama, Süleyman the Magnificent Poet, Living Poets of Turkey, Yunus Emre and His Mystical Poetry,* and two collections of his original poems, *Shadows of Love* and *A Last Lullaby.* In 1983, he served as editor of *A Dot on the Map: Selected Stories and Poems by Sait Faik.*

JOSEPH S. JACOBSON was for many years a professor of Turkish language and literature at the University of Utah, where he had earned a Ph.D. after retiring from the U.S. Army with the rank of colonel. Dr. Jacobson lived in Istanbul and Ankara in the 1950s and served as an assistant U.S. Army attaché. He has translated into English the memoirs and selected short stories of modern Turkey's foremost satirist, Aziz Nesin, as well as a novella by him. He is also the translator of numerous volumes featuring short stories by the Turkish-Canadian writer İlyas Halil. With his wife, Viola Jacobson, he serves as publisher of Southmoor Studios, a publishing house in Holladay, Utah.

CELIA KERSLAKE took her B.A. in Oriental Studies (Turkish and Arabic) at Cambridge University. For her Oxford D.Phil. she made a critical edition and translation of a sixteenth-century Ottoman historical text. She was lecturer in Turkish at the University of Edinburgh from 1980 to 1988, and since 1988 has been University Lecturer in Turkish at Oxford and a fellow of St. Antony's College. She is the translator of a novel by Aysel Özakın, *The Prizegiving.* Her academic publications have focused mainly on Turkish language and linguistics. With Aslı Göksel, she edited *Studies on Turkish and Turkic Languages.* She is currently writing, with Aslı Göksel, *Turkish: A Comprehensive Grammar.*

197

GEOFFREY LEWIS, a fellow of the British Academy and founder and former director of the Bicultural Humanities Program at Robert College of Istanbul, is professor emeritus of Turkish at Oxford University. He has been a visiting professor at Princeton University and the University of California at Los Angeles. Lewis served as president of the British Society for Middle East Studies from 1981 to 1983. For his service to Turkish studies, Lewis has received the Order of Merit of the Turkish Republic (1998); Queen Elizabeth appointed him Companion of the Most Distinguished Order of St. Michael and St. George in the 1999 New Year's Honours List. Among his published works are *Teach Yourself Turkish, Turkish Grammar, Modern Turkey, The Book of Dede Korkut*, and *The Turkish Language Reform: A Catastrophic Success.*

NERMİN MENEMENCİOĞLU (STREATER) was a prominent translator of Turkish literature. Her major work was the *Penguin Book of Turkish Verse*. An alumna of the American College for Girls in Istanbul, she held a graduate degree from Columbia University.

SÜHA OĞUZERTEM graduated from Bosphorus University in Istanbul with a B.A. in English language and literature in 1986. He received his M.A. (1990) and Ph.D. (1994) degrees in comparative literature at Indiana University. He taught Turkish and comparative literature at Indiana University and Ohio State University. He has been teaching at the Department of Turkish Literature at Bilkent University since 1998. Oğuzertem's areas of interest include modern Turkish literature, comparative literature, literary theory, and criticism. He has published critical essays in Turkish and English on such writers as Halikarnas Balıkçısı, Ahmet Hamdi Tanpınar, Abdülhak Şinasi Hisar, and Sait Faik in numerous journals, including *Defter, kitap-lık, Toplum ve Bilim, The Turkish Studies Association Bulletin,* and *Varlık.*

NİLÜFER MİZANOĞLU REDDY, educated in Turkey and the United States, is the translator and editor of *Short Stories by Turkish Women Writers*. Her translations of Turkish poems and short stories have appeared in U.S. journals and anthologies. She contributes articles and critical essays to Turkish literary magazines.

JAYNE L. WARNER is currently director of research at the Institute for Aegean Prehistory in New York. She holds a B.A. in classics, an M.A. in ancient history and, from Bryn Mawr College, a Ph.D. in Near Eastern and Anatolian archaeology. Since the early 1970s her work has focused on Turkey. Her publications include *Elmalı-*

Karataş II: The Early Bronze Age Village of Karataş. Warner has served as assistant editor for the American School of Classical Studies at Athens and executive director of the Poetry Society of America (New York). She has also served as director of the American Turkish Society (New York) and director of the office of the Board of Trustees of Robert College of Istanbul. She was the editor of *Cultural Horizons: A Festschrift in Honor of Talat S. Halman.*